NUCLEAR WEAPONS AND
INTERNATIONAL LAW

Nuclear Weapons and International Law

Edited by

ISTVAN POGANY,
Faculty of Law,
University of Exeter

St. Martin's Press   New York

Printed in Great Britain
First published in the United States of America
in 1987

Library of Congress Cataloging-in-Publication Data

Nuclear weapons and international law.
   Includes index.
   Contents: Foreword / Sir Anthony Parsons —
Nuclear weapons and international law / Malcolm Shaw —
The legality of nuclear weapons / Nicholas Grief —
[etc.]
   1.   Nuclear weapons (International law)
   2.   Nuclear disarmament.   I.   Pogany, Istvan
JX5133.A7N82 1987   341.7′34   86-31342

ISBN 0-312-57986-1

Contents

Foreword
Sir Anthony Parsons

There has probably been more public agitation about the threat of nuclear warfare during the past six or seven years than there was over the previous two decades; this in spite of the fact that superpowers came closer to armed confrontation in 1962 (the Cuban missile crisis) and 1973 (the closing days of the October war between Israel and Egypt) than at any time before or since. There are many reasons for the present recrudescence of anxiety: the abrupt end of the era of détente following the Soviet invasion of Afghanistan at the end of 1979; the extravagant rhetoric of the first term of the Reagan administration; the controversial deployment of cruise and Pershing missiles in Europe; the array of Soviet SS 20 missiles facing NATO; the launching of the Star Wars programme – all these developments have helped to stimulate public debate in those countries where public debate can be carried on without governmental constraint.

I vividly recall, during my last days as British Permanent Representative to the United Nations in New York, the emotional atmosphere which surrounded the unsuccessful Second Special Session of the General Assembly on Disarmament in the summer of 1982, both inside and beyond the United Nations building. There was a widespread feeling that the nuclear arms race had become uncontrolled and uncontrollable, that there was little or no hope that the superpowers would agree to put a clamp on the upward escalation in numbers and sophistication of their devastating nuclear armouries, let alone make a start towards reducing them. The very phrase 'arms control and disarmament' rang increasingly hollow. And it has to be admitted that very little has happened during the past four years to soften this bleak landscape. The only reassuring feature is the fact that the United States and the Soviet Union, however inflammatory the rhetoric may have been on both sides, have exercised great prudence in situations which could have drawn them into confrontation: notable examples are Grenada and the

Lebanon in 1983 and, perhaps most strikingly of all, the war between Iran and Iraq which has now been fought for six years in an area where the interests of both superpowers are deeply engaged.

It has been for me both an education and a relief to turn away from the high emotionalism and the strident political partisanship of the public debate on nuclear weapons to the objectivity of the essays in this book, all of which bear on the different aspects of the problem in terms of international law. It is in my view particularly important at this moment in the world's history to reinforce regard for international law as a factor in governmental decision-making processes. The 1980s have seen the growth of two distinct tendencies which have converged to weaken it. Influential political circles in powerful western countries have started to decry international law as being vague, deficient and unenforceable and have been disposed, instead of trying to strengthen it, to fall back on the vigilante's dictum that 'a man has to do what a man has to do'.

Simultaneously many newly independent states look with disfavour on the corpus of international law which has been built up over the centuries, taking the view that they need not automatically accept a series of rules and regulations which were formulated without their participation in an alien cultural environment. With the slaughter and devastation caused by so-called 'local' wars over the past 40 years of 'world peace', and with the capability of the nuclear powers to destroy all life on our planet, it is surely more important than ever to establish norms of international behaviour and to do more than pay lip-service to them. Any step in this direction, such as this collection of essays, is to be warmly encouraged.

Sir Anthony Parsons
formerly UK Permanent Representative to the United Nations.

Preface

The catalyst for this collection of essays was a challenging paper on 'The Legality of Nuclear Weapons' which my colleague, Nicholas Grief, presented at a Law Faculty Staff Seminar at the University of Exeter, in February 1985. The extensive and lively discussion which his paper stimulated amongst all those present convinced us of the enormous interest which exists in the legal aspects of nuclear weapons and of the fact that the available literature had not yet satisfied this demand. Unprecedentedly, for a Staff Seminar, the meeting attracted the active participation of secretaries and students, reflecting the unique and powerful fascination which nuclear weapons exert on the public mind.

This book addresses the central legal question of whether the use and deployment of nuclear weapons is lawful, from two contrasting perspectives. In addition, individual chapters focus on a variety of topical issues. These include nuclear-free zones, the testing of nuclear weapons, the development of the Strategic Defence Initiative ('Star Wars'), nuclear non-proliferation, and the impact of nuclear weapons on the law of the sea. I am grateful to all of the contributors for the scholarly and dispassionate manner in which they have examined their chosen subjects and for their collaboration in this project. Conceived long before Chernobyl entered into our vocabulary and our consciousness, the issues treated in this book have acquired an enhanced significance.

The research for my own chapter, 'Nuclear Weapons and Self-Defence in International Law', was largely undertaken at the Squire Law Library in Cambridge and at the University's Research Centre for International Law, while I was a beneficiary of a research award from the British Academy. I should like to record my thanks to the Centre's Director, Mr E. Lauterpacht, QC, for appointing me a Visiting Fellow of the Centre and for his unstinting help and encouragement. I should also like to acknowledge my debt to Mr Keith McVee, Librarian of the Squire, and to Miss Patricia Farquhar, Librarian at the UN Information

Centre in London, for their generous assistance. Finally, my gratitude is due to Miss Monique Bertoni and to Mrs Rosemary Channing, who efficiently prepared the final manuscript for submission, and to my wife, Ruth, who drew up the index with her customary skill and thoroughness.

The map on p.194, of the Zone of Application of the Treaty of Tlatelolco, is reproduced from the *IAEA Bulletin* with the permission of OPANAL.

Istvan Pogany
Faculty of Law
University of Exeter
August 1986

Abbreviations

ABM	Anti-ballistic Missile
AJIL	*American Journal of International Law*
BYIL	*British Year Book of International Law*
GA	General Assembly
GAOR	General Assembly Official Records
H.C.	House of Commons
H.L.	House of Lords
IAEA	International Atomic Energy Agency
ICBM	Intercontinental Ballistic Missile
ICJ Rep.	*International Court of Justice, Reports*
ICLQ	*International and Comparative Law Quarterly*
ILC	International Law Commission
ILM	*International Legal Materials*
MIRV	Multiple Independently Targetable Reentry Vehicle
SALT	Strategic Arms Limitation Talks
SDI	Strategic Defence Initiative
SIPRI	Stockholm International Peace Research Institute
SLBM	Submarine-launched Ballistic Missile
UKTS	*United Kingdom Treaty Series*
UN	United Nations
UNTS	*United Nations Treaty Series*
UST	*United States Treaty Series*
YBILC	*Year Book of the International Law Commission*

Notes on the Contributors

PATRICIA BIRNIE is a Senior Lecturer in Law at the London School of Economics. She has lectured and published widely on the Law of the Sea and on International Environmental Law. She is the co-editor of *The Maritime Dimension* (1980) and the author of *The International Regulation of Whaling* (2 vols, 1985).

IAIN CAMERON is a Lecturer in Law at the University of Hull. He has written extensively in the fields of Constitutional and International Law.

SCOTT DAVIDSON is a Lecturer in Law at the University of Hull and on the Editorial Committee of the *International Journal of Estuarine and Coastal Law*. He has written extensively on International Law and European Community Law and is the author of *Grenada: a Study in Politics and the Limits of International Law* (1986).

DAVID FREESTONE is a Senior Lecturer in Law at the University of Hull and Managing Editor of the *International Journal of Estuarine and Coastal Law*. He has published widely on European Community Law and International Law, and is the author of the forthcoming *The Institutional Framework of the European Community*. He is currently serving as a Legal Adviser to the Ministry of Economic Development in Antigua.

NICHOLAS GRIEF is a Lecturer in Law at the University of Exeter. He has written extensively on International Law and European Community Law. He is a member of Lawyers for Nuclear Disarmament and has given evidence to British courts concerning the legality of nuclear weapons.

MARK JANIS is a Professor of Law at the University of Connecticut and Chairman of the American Bar Association Law of the Sea Committee. He has written over thirty articles and is the co-editor of *Soviet Law and Economy* (1986). He is the author of *An Introduction to International Law*, which will be published shortly.

ISTVAN POGANY is a Lecturer in Law at the University of Exeter. In addition to numerous articles on constitutional and international law, his publications include *The Security Council and the Arab–Israeli Conflict* (1984) and *The Arab League and Peacekeeping in the Lebanon* (1987). He is co-editor of the forthcoming *Current Issues in International Business Law*.

MALCOLM SHAW is a Reader in Law and Director of the Centre for International Human Rights Law at the University of Essex. During 1986–87, he has been Forcheimer Visiting Professor of Law at the Hebrew University of Jerusalem. In addition to numerous articles, his publications include *International Law* (2nd edn, 1986) and *Title to Territory in Africa* (1986).

JOHN WOODLIFFE is a Senior Lecturer in Law at Leicester University. He has written widely on national, international and European Community aspects of energy and natural resources law, with particular reference to the North Sea continental shelf area. He is currently preparing a monograph on the legal regime governing the peacetime use of foreign military installations.

... and Chairman of the American Bar Association Law of the Sea Committee. He has written over thirty articles and is the author of a book. Professor Lowe's item will be published shortly.

A. V. LOWE is a Lecturer in Law at the University of Exeter. He has published papers on various aspects of international and transnational law. He (with C.M. Schmitthoff) has edited *The Extra-territorial Application of Laws* (1983). He is also editor of the new study suggested for reference to the Vienna (1987) Convention of the Law of the Sea. *Commonwealth Maritime Series*, and is the associate editor of the new *Marine Policy Reports*.

MALCOLM SHAW is a Reader in Law and Director of the Centre for International Human Rights. He is the author of numerous volumes including *Title to Territory in Africa: International Legal Issues* (1986), and has been Ford Foundation Visiting Professor of Law at the University of Michigan. He has published numerous articles, including articles on recent developments in the international law of the sea. He edited *The Law and ...* (1986).

ROBIN WARNER is a Senior Lecturer in Law at Lancaster University. She has written widely on national, international and European Community aspects of energy and marine resources law, with particular relevance to the North Sea continental shelf area. She is currently preparing a monograph on the legal regime governing the protection of marine offshore installations.

1 Nuclear weapons and international law

Malcolm N. Shaw

Introduction

Nuclear weapons have been the subject of intense debate ever since the use of atomic bombs in 1945 opened the door to a new and even more horrific chapter in human enterprises. In recent years, the question of the legality of such weapons has been posed with ever-increasing frequency and intensity.[1]

Because the whole issue is such a pivotal one for humanity, it is hard to disentangle the various threads. Morality and politics are deeply involved in any analysis of nuclear weapons and any attempt to deal solely with the legal aspects is doomed to justifiable accusations of unbalanced consideration of the dilemma that is faced. Nevertheless, the attempt is worthwhile. International law provides a framework, flawed though it may be, within which states conduct their international behaviour, commonly accepting certain reciprocal constraints and regulating expectations raised.[2] It is a normative system, clearly regarded by its adherents as obligatory and possessing a range of sanctions that, while not always effective, are at least acknowledged as existing. States' behaviour is overtly founded upon international law. This is not the case with morality or political considerations.

This chapter accordingly will deal with some international legal aspects of nuclear weapons. It will not touch upon moral considerations or the role of political principles. Whether nuclear weapons are ethically acceptable is not here at issue, nor is the question as to whether the possession of such devices is politically or economically wise.

There is no international treaty banning nuclear weapons as such. Therefore, one must have recourse to the other methods of international law creation to discern whether and to what extent international legal principles regulate the area of nuclear armaments.

International law may be created by one or more of three accepted mechanisms: international treaties, international custom accepted as evidence of the general practice of states or general principles of law accepted by states. Judicial decisions and juridical writings are subsidiary means for determining the law.[3] As will be seen, there is extensive state practice dealing with nuclear weapons, ranging from specific, limited treaties to United Nations General Assembly resolutions to pre-existing customary law. However, it is important to note that not all such practice of itself creates international law binding on all. This is especially true of General Assembly resolutions, which are purely recommendatory only, although this may constitute state practice which together with the necessary obligatory element (the *opinio juris*) may create international customary law.[4]

In the process of law creation through the medium of state practice, it is apposite to note that the impact of states particularly interested in the subject-matter in question will be correspondingly higher. Although all states may contribute to the creation of a new rule of customary law, some states are more equal than others.[5] In the Law of the Sea, for example, the views and practice of the maritime states will be particularly influential and even determinative. Accordingly, in assessing the situation of customary law with respect to nuclear weapons, especial attention must be paid to the opinions of these states actually possessing them.

Article 613 of the US Rules of Naval Warfare, 1955, declares that 'there is at present no rule of international law expressly prohibiting states from the use of nuclear weapons in warfare. In the absence of any express prohibition, the use of such weapons against enemy combatants and other objectives is permitted.'[6] This is reiterated in the manuals of the other US services.[7] The UK view is similar. It is noted that 'there is no rule of international law dealing specifically with the use of nuclear weapons'[8] and that 'in the absence of any rule of international law dealing expressly with it, the use which may be made of a particular weapon will be governed by the ordinary rules and the question of the legality of its use in any individual case will, therefore, involve merely the application of the recognised principles of international law.'[9]

In the light of these unambiguous assertions and the actual possession of nuclear weapons by the USA, UK, USSR, France and China, and in the context of the absence of a binding conventional or customary rule outlawing nuclear weapons, it is hard to demonstrate that the possession of such weapons is in itself unlawful.[10] However the problem is more complex than this, for international law does govern the use of nuclear weapons in a variety of ways, both by virtue of general principles and by specific provisions.

General principles of the laws of war

It is important to appreciate that the lack of specific regulation of each particular weapon and method of warfare is not to be taken as total abstention of control by international legal principles. The famous 'Martens clause', first enunciated in the preamble to the 1899 Hague Convention II, emphasised that, 'in cases not included in the Regulations adopted by them, populations and belligerents remain under the protection and empire of the principles of international law, as they result from the usages established between civilised nations, from the laws of humanity, and the requirements of the public conscience.' This provision is now clearly part of international customary law. It was repeated in the Hague Convention IV of 1907 and in the 1949 Geneva Conventions,[11] the 1977 Protocols to the 1949 Conventions[12] and the 1981 Conventions on Prohibitions and Restrictions on the Use of Certain Conventional Weapons.[13]

There are certain fundamental propositions that are deemed to flow from this and that determine the general field of the laws of war. Much of the discussion concerning the validity of nuclear weapons in fact centres upon how one interprets them. These fundamental propositions attempt to balance the opposing precepts of military necessity and humanity. On the one hand, accepting that a level of violence is, as it must be, permissible in the context of the legitimate use of force, while on the other hand, attempting to keep this to the minimum in the interests of humanity and decency. This balance is not an absolute one. It shifts with each advance in lethality of weapons systems. As the range of horror and destructiveness increases so, inevitably, what is permissible moves to preserve a tenuous median position. In that sense, military technology pulls along the law with it as potential destructiveness rises with each new development. Thus, the shift in acceptability in the law reflects not a weakening or a defect in the law, but rather a dramatic increase in the capacity of new weapons to kill, maim and destroy.

Unnecessary suffering

The preamble to the St Petersburg Declaration of 1868, which banned explosive projectiles under 400g weight, emphasised that 'the only legitimate object which the state should endeavour to accomplish during war is to weaken the military forces of the enemy . . . for this purpose it is sufficient to disable the greatest possible number of men . . . this object would be exceeded by the employment of arms which uselessly aggravate the suffering of disabled men or render their death inevitable.' This balancing attempt was carried forward into the Hague Regulations of 1907, which sought to codify the laws of war. Article

23(b) prohibits the treacherous killing or wounding of enemy soldiers, while Article 23(e) forbids the employment of arms, projectiles or material which is calculated to cause unnecessary suffering. The extent of this concept, however, is controversial.[14] The danger with a wide interpretation is that so much would be covered by it, that it would cease to have any practical value.

The Conference of Experts seeking to add to the 1949 Geneva Conventions discussed the concept of unnecessary suffering and declared that this 'involved some sort of equation between, on the one hand, the degree of injury, or suffering inflicted (the humanitarian aspect) and on the other, the degree of necessity underlying the choice of a particular weapon (the military aspect).' It was noted that this equation was a particularly difficult one to determine.[15] Since the provision in question is so difficult to interpret textually, one must turn to actual state practice. The US Department of the Air Force has noted that the critical factor in the prohibition against unnecessary suffering is 'whether the suffering is needless or disproportionate to the military advantages secured by the weapon, not the degree of suffering itself.'[16]

It is especially emphasised that state practice has determined that it is *per se* illegal to use projectiles filled with glass or other materials inherently difficult to detect medically, to use any substance or projectiles that tend unnecessarily to inflame the wound they cause, to use irregular-shaped bullets as to score the surface or to file off the ends of hard cases of bullets which cause them to expand on contact and thus aggravate the wound they cause.[17] The approach of the UK[18] and US[19] manuals of military law, for instance, is to stress that only state practice can demonstrate what is or is not 'calculated to cause unnecessary suffering'. In other words, a cautious test is here applied. The UK manual, for example, states that Article 23(e) of the Hague Regulations is not intended to apply to the use of explosives contained in mines, aerial torpedoes or hand-grenades. In addition, the use of flame-throwers against military targets is lawful, but not against personnel if it is calculated to cause unnecessary suffering.[20]

This intention-based criterion was reaffirmed in Article 35(2) of Protocol I, 1977, which declares that it is prohibited 'to employ weapons, projectiles and material and methods of warfare of a nature to cause superfluous injury or unnecessary suffering'. This formulation slightly extends the Article 23(e) formula since it specifically refers to 'methods of warfare' also. This addition, however, did not stimulate extensive debate in the Humanitarian Law Conference, despite Australian opposition to it.[21] Thus, quite how far it extends is unclear, although the approach is hardly one to arouse extensive opposition.[22]

Military necessity and the protection of civilians

The preamble to the St Petersburg Declaration emphasises that 'the only legitimate object which states should endeavour to accomplish during war is to weaken the military forces of the enemy.'[23] It was noted in the Nuremberg Tribunal that military necessity 'does not permit the killing of innocent inhabitants for the purposes of revenge or the satisfaction of a lust to kill. The destruction of property to be lawful must be imperatively demanded by the necessities of war.'[24] This approach was adopted by the 1949 Geneva Convention.[25] The XXth International Conference of the Red Cross in 1965 proclaimed in resolution XXVIII that a distinction had to be maintained at all times between persons taking part in the hostilities and members of the civilian population,[26] and this theme was re-emphasised in Article 48, 'the basic rule', of Protocol I, 1977.[27] This stipulates that 'in order to ensure respect for and protection of the civilian population and civilian objects, the parties to the conflict shall at all times distinguish between the civilian population and combatants, and between civilian objects and military objectives and accordingly shall direct their operations only against military objectives.'[28] The extermination of a civilian population, in whole or in part, would be under Article 6(c) of the Nuremberg Charter, a 'crime against humanity'.[29]

Protocol I outlaws indiscriminate attacks, which are defined in Article 51(4) as: (a) those which are not directed at a specific military objective; (b) those which employ a method or means of combat which cannot be directed at a specific military objective; or (c) those which employ a method or means of combat the effects of which cannot be limited as required by the Protocol; and consequently in each such case are of a nature to strike military objectives and civilians or civilian objects without distinction.[30]

Allied to this principle of protecting civilians is the doctrine that the right of the parties to an armed conflict to choose methods or means of warfare is not unlimited. Article 22 of the Hague Regulations specified that the right of belligerents to adopt means of injuring the enemy was not unrestricted; while Article 35 of Protocol I reaffirms this. It is also to be noted that Article 36 stipulates that states are under an obligation to determine whether the employment of a newly-developed weapon would, in some or all circumstances, be prohibited by rules of international law.

The protection of the environment

Increasing concern with the protection of the environment has led to attempts to apply international legal principles. These commenced with

Article 35(3) of Protocol I which states that it is prohibited to employ methods or means of warfare, which are intended, or may be expected, to cause widespread, long-term and severe damage to the natural environment.[31] There are, of course, definitional problems to be faced here, as well as the status of the rule with regard to states not parties to the Protocols.

Neutrality

Hague Convention V, Respecting the Rights and Duties of Neutral Powers and Persons in Case of War on Land, clearly emphasises that 'the territory of neutral powers is unviolable'. This is of relevance to the nuclear weapons issue since the effects of a nuclear blast may well affect neighbouring states that are neutral.[32] Although the Convention has only 34 ratifications to date, most of the nuclear states are parties[33] and the provisions are regarded as part of customary law.[34]

Resort to force in international law

The resort to force under international law is regulated carefully. Article 2(4) of the UN Charter stipulates that states are under a duty to refrain in their international relations from the threat or use of force against the sovereignty, territorial integrity or political independence of any state, or in any other manner inconsistent with the purposes of the UN. The status of war as an instrument of national policy had been proscribed by the 1928 Kellogg–Briand Pact. The only legitimate use of force, under the UN Charter regime, by states is in cases of self-defence under Article 51 'if an armed attack occurs' and until the Security Council has taken action. But to be acceptable, the use of force in self-defence whether under Article 51 or under customary international law has to be proportionate to the action precipitating the valid exercise of the right.[35] The requirement of proportionality is crucial and, as will be seen below, pivotal in an analysis of the legitimacy of the use of nuclear weapons under international legal regulations.

The applicability of the general principles to nuclear weapons

Much of the discussion concerning the legality of nuclear weapons *per se* centres on interpretations of the above principles. However, the threshold issue of the status of the 1977 Protocols must first be faced. This is because several of the provisions of Protocol I, if deemed applicable to nuclear weapons, would severely affect the legality argument, particularly Article 51 and the relatively wide definition of indiscriminate attacks on civilians. It is also to be noted that Article 85 of Protocol

I declares that a grave breach is committed when the civilian population or individual civilians are made the direct object of attack or when an indiscriminate attack affecting the civilian population is launched with the knowledge that such attack will cause excessive loss of life, injury to civilians, or damage to civilian objects in relation to the military advantage anticipated. This approach is to be coupled with the prohibition of reprisals against the civilian population.[36] The provision in Protocol I prohibiting damage to the environment is also relevant in this context. The nature of nuclear weapons and the awesome range of their destructive potential has affected the perception of analysts here.

During the discussions preceding the adoption of the Protocols, there was a tacit understanding among states that the question of nuclear weapons would not be regulated by the new instruments.[37] In addition, both the UK and the US, on signing Protocol I, declared that they did so on the basis 'that the new rules introduced by the Protocol are not intended to have an effect on and do not regulate or prohibit the use of nuclear weapons'.[38] The question is immediately posed as to whether this 'understanding' is a reservation or not. An affirmative answer would, under the terms of the Vienna Convention on the Law of Treaties 1969, mean that legal rights and obligations would therefore flow and the reservation would be binding. A negative answer would have the consequence that no binding element would be involved at all. It seems clear that these 'understandings' were intended to have a legal effect, otherwise there would, in the light of such a crucially perceived issue, be little purpose in raising them. More than a mere interpretative declaration was at issue.

According to Article 19 of the Vienna Convention, a reservation must not be 'incompatible with the object and purpose of the treaty', and it has been argued that a reservation excluding nuclear weapons from the ambit of Protocol I would indeed be incompatible with the objects and purposes of the treaty.[39] Since the Protocol deals with a wide range of issues covering international armed conflicts, it is possible to argue that such a reservation could still be valid, although it is important to note that customary law still operates with respect to nuclear weapons. The fact that such weapons may not come within the direct purview of the Protocol as such cannot be allowed to detract from the situation that customary international law still regulates nuclear armaments. In any event, neither the US nor the UK have ratified the Protocol as yet and thus the reservations argument is still speculative. Nevertheless, the dispute does shed light on one central characteristic of the whole dilemma of nuclear weapons and the law. This is that there is no one binding instrument or rule that clearly and directly outlaws nuclear weapons as such. The arguments in favour of illegality proceed on the basis of analogy and on the developing interpretation of certain existing provisions. This is not necessarily conclusive, but when allied to the overt stand of most of the nuclear weapons states at least, it does have an impact upon the level of evidence required to demonstrate illegality.

The general principles of the laws of war regulate all means and methods of warfare. This clearly includes nuclear weapons. However, one must proceed carefully in analysing the general principles noted in order to assess correctly both their validity and their scope. This applies particularly to the 'unnecessary suffering' concept. It is all too easy to declare that nuclear weapons are illegal since they are eminently capable of palpably and undeniably causing horrific destruction and suffering. But the approach of the laws of war has not been to concentrate as a matter of general principle upon the degree of suffering as such occasioned by particular weapons, but rather to see the issue through the prism of proportionality and relativity to military necessity. The emphasis regarding what is thus prohibited is not simply on weapons of a particular type which of their nature are capable of causing a great deal of suffering, but also upon the particular use of weapons in such a way as to give rise to the reasonable perception that it has been intended to cause unnecessary suffering. In other words, a twofold test is apparent. First, the definition of 'unnecessary' suffering. This will depend upon a balance of military necessity and humanity and will reflect inevitably the technological level of weapons development, since the essence of the balance is predicated on the military tools available to achieve any particular objective and the nature of the opposing forces. This criterion also encompasses weapons that are so constructed as to cause additional and superfluous suffering to persons that have already been incapacitated. One famous example of this would be 'dum-dum' bullets, which unnecessarily inflame wounds occasioned by their use. This element is also difficult to specify precisely for the level of damage inflicted rises with each new technological evolution. What a century ago would have been regarded as 'unnecessary' may not today arouse the same indignation. The second part of the test is the element of calculation or intention. The nature of the weapons themselves or the use to which they have been put must be such as to actually have been calculated to cause the unnecessary suffering.

In the light of these crucial constraining factors, one must examine the problem of nuclear weapons, and this can only be done with an appreciation of the range of such weapons that now exist. From the vast intercontinental ballistic missiles or strategic nuclear weapons capable of obliterating whole cities to the relatively low-yield tactical or battlefield nuclear weapons an array of possibilities now present themselves. In other words, in order to be able to assess the situation, it must be realised that there are distinctions between various types of nuclear weapons. Such distinctions make it hard to characterise these weapons as one single type of weapon. Rather, a family of weapons is involved, with perhaps a common basis but a variety of technical and military characteristics and consequences. The conclusion one must reach in this context is that it is insufficient to deem nuclear weapons as such illegal. One must have regard to the different types of such weapons involved and the framework within which they are being applied. Many weapons have destructive capacities unimaginable a century ago. They are not *per se* unlawful today. Many weapons cause tremendous suffering, not just nuclear ones. Examples one could cite here would include napalm and flame-throwers. What counts for our purposes is not to discount the context in which a particular weapon may be used. The employment of conventional armaments in certain situations would be illegal and the same would certainly be true of nuclear weapons. The context is crucial and it is here that vital elements such as proportionality, military necessity and the distinction between civilians and combatants become relevant.

The illegality of any weapon, nuclear or conventional, will thus depend upon the circumstances of its employment. Accordingly, what would be true in the case of massive strategic nuclear weapons may not necessarily be so for small, tactical, battlefield weapons. The argument that once nuclear weapons of any type have been used, escalation is inevitable, may perhaps be politically viable, but it is of itself, one would submit, insufficient to render all uses or indeed possession of nuclear weapons illegal.[40] Also relevant in this context are rules regarding the protection of the environment[41] and safeguarding the position of neutrals. The capacity of certain types of nuclear weapons by virtue of radiation fall-out to affect the environment and neutral states will be relevant in a consideration of legitimate use, but is not, it is suggested, sufficient to render illegal nuclear weapons as such.[42]

The deployment of nuclear weapons

There are a variety of international agreements that deal with the deployment, or rather limitations thereupon, of nuclear weapons. These all proceed necessarily on the basis of the lawfulness of possession of such weapons, otherwise there would simply be no need for such treaties.

Prohibition treaties

The peace treaties signed by the Allies with Bulgaria, Finland, Hungary, Italy and Romania on 10 February 1947 prohibit the possession, construction or testing of nuclear weapons by the latter states. Similarly, the Austrian State Treaty of 15 May 1955 forbids that state from becoming a nuclear weapons power.[43]

Nuclear-free areas

In addition to the above examples in which specific states by virtue of international agreement are prohibited from possessing nuclear weapons, certain treaties seek to ensure that specific areas are free from nuclear weapons deployment. The Antarctic Treaty of 1959 declares that that area is to be used for peaceful purposes only.[44] Any measures of a military nature are prohibited. The stationing and use of nuclear weapons is banned, as are any nuclear explosions and the disposal of radioactive waste. The Outer Space Treaty of 1967 provides that the contracting parties are not to place in orbit around the earth any objects carrying nuclear weapons and other kinds of weapons of mass destruction. Such weapons are in addition not to be installed on celestial bodies and the parties agreed not to station weapons in outer space in any other manner. The moon and other celestial bodies are to be used by all states parties exclusively for peaceful purposes. By virtue of the Treaty on the prohibition of the Emplacement of Nuclear Weapons and other Weapons of Mass Destruction on the Seabed and the Ocean Floor and in the Subsoil thereof, 1971, the states parties are prohibited from emplanting or emplacing on the seabed or ocean floor beyond the limits of national jurisdiction, any nuclear weapons, structures, launching installations, or any other facilities designed for storing, testing or using nuclear weapons.

By contrast, there exists to date only one treaty in force specifically providing for a nuclear-free zone in an inhabited area. The Treaty for the Prohibition of Nuclear Weapons in Latin America, 1967[45] provides that states parties will not test, use, manufacture, produce or acquire by any means whatsoever nuclear weapons. In Additional Protocol II to the Treaty, the United States agreed not to arm Latin American states with nuclear weapons.[46] A variety of proposals have existed for other geographically determined nuclear-free zones, ranging from the Rapacki Plan proposed by Poland in 1957 and covering Central Europe, to suggestions for such a zone in the Indian Ocean,[47] but none have been successful. The strategic interests of the superpowers have perhaps proved decisive.

Nuclear weapons testing

The Treaty Banning Nuclear Weapons Tests in the Atmosphere, in Outer Space and Under Water was signed in 1963. Under this agreement, states parties agree not to carry out any nuclear weapon test explosion, or any other nuclear explosion in the atmosphere, under water, in outer space, or in any other environment if the explosion would cause radioactive materials to be present outside the testing state's territorial limits. The expressed aim of the treaty was to end the arms race and eliminate the production of testing of weapons, including nuclear weapons.[48]

Arms limitation treaties

The US and the USSR have signed treaties restricting nuclear weapons. The Strategic Arms Limitation Treaty of 1972[49] prohibited the construction of additional fixed, land-based intercontinental ballistic missile launchers. It was decided not to convert land-based launchers for light intercontinental ballistic missiles into heavy land-based launchers. The number of submarine-launched ballistic missile launchers was restricted, as was the number of operational submarines capable of launching such missiles. In 1972, the two superpowers signed the Treaty on the Limitations of Anti-Ballistic Missile Systems, severely restricting the number and type of such systems. Five years later, SALT II was signed limiting strategic offensive arms, but this was not ratified by the US.

The Nuclear Non-Proliferation Treaty[50]

An international agreement on the non-proliferation of nuclear arms was signed in 1968 and came into force two years later. Over 100 states are parties to this treaty, including the US, UK and Soviet Union, but not France and not several powers commonly regarded as being capable of producing nuclear weapons. States parties to the treaty, that do not possess nuclear weapons, undertook not to acquire or produce them and not to engage in nuclear explosions of any kind.

Although none of the above agreements deals with the problems of the use of nuclear weapons, they clearly raise a presumption that the possession of nuclear weapons as such is not contrary to international law. To attempt to regulate what is *per se* absolutely unlawful would be somewhat difficult to reconcile with an international legal order based upon the consent of states.

The testing of nuclear weapons

As can be seen from the above discussion, the testing of nuclear weapons other than in circumstances restricted by treaties and custom would not appear to be illegal. No testing would be permitted contrary to the 1963 treaty, by a state bound by an undertaking not to do the same nor in an accepted nuclear-free area. However, the normal rules of state responsibility continue to operate, so that a state lawfully conducting such tests would be obliged to compensate those suffering thereby. In 1954, a Japanese fishing boat was accidentally contaminated by radiation as a result of an American nuclear test, and the crew suffered radiation sickness. The Japanese government claimed damages and the US government subsequently made an *ex gratia* payment without accepting any legal obligation so to do.[51] The issue of nuclear tests by the US in its Pacific trust territories was raised by the UN Trusteeship Council, but resolutions ultimately adopted, far from criticising as unlawful such tests, declared them to be necessary for the maintenance of international peace and security.[52]

In 1973, Australia and New Zealand instituted proceedings before the International Court of Justice against France, in the light of the latter's conducting of atmospheric nuclear tests in the Pacific.[53] In the event, the Court sidestepped the issue by declaring that France's unilateral declaration to cease such atmospheric testing was binding in the circumstances and that as a consequence the proceedings had no object and no decision on the issue was required.[54] The 1982 Law of the Sea Convention now provides that the high seas are to be used solely for peaceful purposes.[55] Coupled with the evolution of international environmental law upon the basis of the principles of state responsibility for injury to others, it can be stated that only a very restricted type of nuclear testing is now permissible under international law.

The use of nuclear weapons

Illegal per se

A variety of UN General Assembly resolutions have sought to establish that the use of nuclear weapons is *per se* totally illegal. Resolution 1653 (XVI), adopted on 24 November 1961 and entitled 'Declaration on the Prohibition of the Use of Nuclear and Thermo-Nuclear Weapons', stated *inter alia* that 'the use of nuclear and thermonuclear weapons is contrary to the spirit, letter and aims of the United Nations and, *as such*, a direct violation of the United Nations Charter.'[56] In addition, it was declared that any state that did use such weapons not only violated the Charter, but acted contrary to the laws of humanity and committed a crime against mankind and its civilization. Since this resolution, the General Assembly has adopted many others developing the themes, including calling for a conference to be convened to draft a convention prohibiting the use of nuclear weapons.[57] The permanent prohibition of the use of nuclear weapons has been demanded[58] and the view that the use of such weapons would violate the UN Charter and constitute a crime against humanity reaffirmed.[59]

The value of such resolutions in the political field is clear. It demonstrates the mounting concern of states of the dangers of nuclear war and expresses the clear need that something must be done to reduce such risks. However, from the strictly legal point of view, in the context of seeking to establish the relevant binding norms as distinct from moral or political imperatives, the General Assembly resolutions noted are of only limited value. Such resolutions are recommendatory only and do not constitute binding decisions.[60] They are thus unlike Security Council decisions. Nevertheless, General Assembly resolutions can express state practice which may ultimately harden into international customary law. The key point in this process is the *opinio juris* or sense of obligation felt by states in general, with regard to a particular proposition arising out of usage. In order to characterise resolutions in this context, therefore, it is necessary to examine voting figures and the views of states as to the proposition formulated, and in particular those of states especially concerned with the area in question. By this test, it is clear that resolutions proclaiming that any use of nuclear weapons would be of itself a violation of law, do not reflect international law.

Resolution 1653 (XVI), for example, was adopted by 55 votes to 20, with 26 abstentions. Those opposing the resolution included the US, UK and France. A similar pattern has been in evidence with regard to other such resolutions. Therefore, to regard such resolutions as creative of law *simpliciter* is naive and misleading. They reflect widespread concern and political forces and not, as yet at least, a legal consensus. The fact that the leading nuclear powers (with the arguable exception of the Soviet Union) are strongly opposed to such formulations as law is of the greatest importance in the process of customary law formation. It may, of course, be that in the course of time and in the light of modified attitudes on the part of the major nuclear weapons powers, such Assembly resolutions may reflect or constitute a customary rule, but it would be premature to state that this had already occurred.

It has been argued that the use of nuclear weapons is *per se* prohibited since it falls within the ban upon poison or poisonous gas.[61] Article 23(a) of the Hague Regulations forbids the employment of poison or poisoned weapons, while the Hague Declaration of 1899 outlawed 'the use of projectiles the sole object of which is the diffusion of asphyxiating or deleterious gasses'. In addition the Geneva Gas Protocol of 1925 prohibits 'the use in war of asphyxiating, poisonous or other gases and of all analogous liquids, materials or devices'. Several issues arise here. First, and probably most difficult, the definitional question in relation to nuclear weapons. The view has been expressed that the effect of a nuclear explosion cannot be deemed to be analogous to the use of poison. It can also be noted that nuclear weapons operate primarily by intense heat and thermal radiation and that such heat-intensive weapons as napalm and flame-throwers have not been banned as such. As Schwarzenberger has written: 'The fact that modern practice in war has not applied this analogy to the use of fire by way of flame-throwers, napalm and incendiary bombs or fire storms caused by saturation bombing may suggest that the heat effects of nuclear weapons should be assimilated to the use of force rather than that of poisonous substances.'[62] In addition, state practice would appear to demonstrate that chemical gases were not regarded as falling within Article 23(a) of the Hague Regulations. Such weapons were widely utilised in the First World War and were the subject specifically of the 1925 Geneva Gas Protocol, in an attempt to ban practices that perhaps were not unambiguously accepted as being within the purview of the earlier agreement.

However, there is no doubt that nuclear explosions emit radiation, whether immediately upon the blast or as fall-out returning to the earth over an extended period of time. The amount of radiation emitted depends upon the type and tonnage of the weapon, whether the explosion takes place in the air or upon the ground and upon meteorological factors. All nuclear radiation is capable of damaging biological tissue and causing illnesses of varying characteristics. The above provisions therefore do apply to nuclear weapons, although it is unclear whether an absolute prohibition is involved, since the effects of particular nuclear weapons may vary extensively depending upon a range of factors. It is arguable that certain uses of such weapons would not violate the prohibition on poison and poisonous weapons. These might include certain nuclear air bursts where little if any local fall-out is produced (as distinct from surface explosions) and attacks on isolated, military targets, for example, missiles embedded in hardened silos. It would not include enhanced radiation weapons, it would appear.

Although the range of the 1925 Geneva Gas Protocol is considerably broader than earlier instruments and would seem to include the effects of nuclear weapons, two points need to be made. First, the definition of gases is ambiguous as to scope. In particular, it is highly controversial as to whether teargas is included, and in 1970 the UK government declared that 'CS and other such gases' were outside the scope of the Protocol. The US government stated upon ratification in 1975 that control agents and chemical herbicides were not included in the coverage of the 1925 Protocol.[63] These disputes over the range of gases covered weakens to some extent the argument that nuclear weapons fall within the prohibitions enshrined in the Protocol.

Secondly, a relatively large number of states became parties to the instrument subject to a reservation that it would cease to be binding if an enemy or its allies failed to respect the prohibitions therein contained, or in some cases, that the Protocol would only be binding upon the state concerned in relation to other states accepting the same obligations.[64] Accordingly, for a large number of states,[65] the 1925 Protocol constitutes not a total ban upon weapons therein covered (whether or not nuclear weapons are included or, more probably, certain uses of such weapons), but only a prohibition upon first use, at best. In some cases, where a state has made such a reservation, the Protocol would not be operative as the target state is not itself a party to that agreement.[66]

The argument has also been made that the use of nuclear weapons would violate not only the prohibition of crimes against humanity, but also the Convention on the Prevention and Punishment of the Crime of Genocide, 1948.[67] Article 6(c) of the Charter of the Nuremberg Tribunal defined the former as 'murder, extermination, enslavement, deportation and other inhumane acts committed against any civilian population, before or during the war'.[68] Genocide is clearly a violation of customary law, as well as of the 1948 Convention and it is defined in Article II of the latter as any of a number of acts 'committed with intent to destroy, in whole or in part, a national, ethnical, racial or religious group, as such'. Such acts include *inter alia*: (a) killing members of this group; (b) causing serious bodily or mental harm to members of this group; and (c) deliberately inflicting on the group conditions of life calculated to bring about its physical destruction in whole or in part.

Several points need to be stressed. First, the key to the crime is in relation to acts committed 'with intent to destroy' all or part of a group 'as such'. Of course, nuclear weapons could be used to achieve genocide, but it is not an inevitable consequence of their use. The employment of small, low tonnage battlefield nuclear weapons in a tactical fashion to destroy an advancing armoured column, for example, could not be regarded as an act of genocide. That would be fanciful. The key to the crime is not mere suffering or loss of life as such, but the deliberate attempt to destroy a particular group as a group. Genocide would be easier to achieve as a consequence of the possession and employment of nuclear weapons, no doubt, but it is the use made of the weapons in a particular context that will determine whether or not the crime has been committed.

First use

If one accepts that there is no blanket prohibition as such upon the use in all circumstance of nuclear weapons, the next question is whether the first use of such weapons is illegal. Again, one has to keep in mind the pre-existing restrictions upon use that have been noted above, ranging from the establishment of nuclear-free zones to voluntary renunciation of possession and the UN Charter provisions relating to the permissible use of force only in cases of self-defence. The Western Powers have not rejected the first use of nuclear weapons. Indeed, the whole NATO philosophy of deterrence in Europe depends upon the belief that in the event of an overwhelming conventional attack by Warsaw Pact forces, and in the light of the massive superiority in such conventional forces by the Soviet bloc, resort to nuclear weapons is a possibility. To accept a bald no first use proposition would appear to many to question the whole purpose of possessing nuclear weapons as a counterbalance to offset superiority of conventional arms by the opposing forces. This could conceivably lead to an increased conventional arms race and greater instability in the balance of power in Europe. The Special Rapporteur of the International Law Commission, in discussing his second report on the Draft Code of Offences against the Peace and Security of Mankind,[69] in fact made this point. He concluded that nuclear weapons 'were weapons of mass destruction that should not be prohibited, but they should not be used'. This was a careful use of phraseology, but it is clear from the ensuing discussion that the Commission felt that the use of atomic weapons was not *per se* illegal.[70] In the event, the Commission expressed the need for political guidance on such a controversial issue.

Although it is suggested that no prohibition exists as such with regard to first use,[71] such use to be legitimate in the light of the principles of international law discussed above would have to be extremely carefully circumscribed and can only be seriously envisaged in a limited number of scenarios, particularly bearing in mind the requirements as to self-defence, military necessity and proportionality.

Restrictions on use of nuclear weapons

There are a variety of restrictions in force with regard to the use of nuclear weapons, and in the light of the nature and potential of such weapons, they must be broadly interpreted. Many of the restrictions have been noted above. Such use can only be in the framework of a valid exercise of self-defence and this requires that the need for response be instant and overwhelming and that it be proportionate to the precipitating event.[72] This proportionality criterion is axiomatic and central and must be carefully circumscribed, especially where the initial assault is non-nuclear. However, the range of available nuclear armaments is such that graduated responses are now possible. It is not now inevitable that strategic nuclear weapons be employed at an early stage of confrontation, although the risks of this are all too evident and must not be discounted in political and moral calculations.

There are, for example, nuclear mines available with low tonnage and yield capacities that in effect make clear distinctions between nuclear and conventional weaponry increasingly difficult to sustain.[73] It is the existence of such weapons that has altered the legal equation with regard to the use of nuclear arms. Provided that the crucial operating principles of humanity (avoidance of unnecessary suffering, for example), military necessity and proportionality are clearly present and demonstrated, the use of such weapons may be lawful. There exist also a variety of nuclear artillery shells with varying yield capacities that may be fired from howitzers over differing ranges.[74] From this level, one progresses to intermediate missiles with warheads of up to 100 kilotons and beyond, which could devastate areas of at least some 70 miles by 15 miles, although neutron warheads could increase this.[75] These weapons would have such effects on civilians and environment in populated central Europe that their use would almost invariably be unlawful. Such missiles could have ranges up to 1300 miles, and in the case of ground launched cruise missiles, perhaps 2000 miles.[76] However, their use could be legitimate as a response to a prior nuclear attack of the same general level. The same could conceivably be said of the employment of strategic, intercontinental ballistic missiles, that have a devastating capacity, but at this holocaust level of action, surely considerations of basic survival and ethics would take over.

The question of retaliation or proportionate self-defence has often been subsumed under the doctrine of reprisals in wartime. Oppenheim defines the objective of resort to reprisals in terms of compelling a belligerent to abandon illegitimate acts of warfare.[77] The four Geneva Conventions of 1949 prohibited reprisals in specific cases. Convention I, Article 46, outlawed reprisals against the wounded, sick, personnel, buildings and equipment protected by the Convention; Convention II, Article 47, outlawed reprisals against the wounded, sick and shipwrecked persons, the personnel, the vessels and equipment protected by that Convention; Convention III, Article 13, outlawed reprisals against prisoners of war; and Convention IV, Article 37, outlawed reprisals against protected persons and their property. Certainly, the ban on reprisals against civilians in occupied territory would cover nuclear action. However, the 1949 Conventions did not constrain the employment of reprisals against belligerents, or against civilians outside occupied territories.[78] Such provisions are part of customary law.

Protocol I, 1977, however, has expanded radically the scope of protection against reprisals. Article 51(6) declares, for example, that 'attacks against the civilian population or civilians by way of reprisals are prohibited'; while Article 55(2) stipulates that 'attacks against the natural environment by way of reprisals are prohibited'.[79] Such a restriction, it should be noted, would have an immediate consequence in the nuclear situation, since it would prevent retaliation by a nuclear state, after a prior nuclear attack, against targets in populated areas. This is one of the reasons constraining ratification of the Protocol by nuclear states. It would have the effect of undermining the deterrence doctrine, since it would, theoretically at least, enable a nuclear attack to proceed without fear of like retaliation. Accordingly, these provisions cannot be regarded as part of customary law and therefore bind only those states that have signed and ratified Protocol I.

The use of nuclear weapons may, thus be legitimate under international law in certain, severely constrained situations. It must not offend against binding treaty provisions, as discussed above, and must be consistent with customary law. The norms relating to resort to force, in particular self-defence, must be observed and it has been seen that the proportionality criterion at least closely circumscribes employment of nuclear weapons. In addition, the principles of avoidance of unnecessary suffering as defined, general humanity and military necessity must be obeyed.[80] Certain limited uses of such weapons in specific situations, particularly on the battlefield in a restricted tactical fashion may be lawful. Beyond that, the balance of consideration begins to change until the apocalyptical use of strategic weapons against cities is reached.

Notes

1   See e.g. S. Bailey, *Prohibitions and Restraints in War*, 1972; G. Best, *Humanity in Warfare*, 1980; *The New Humanitarian Law of Armed Conflict* (ed. A. Cassese), 1979; F. Karlshoven, *The Law of Warfare*, 1973; G. Schwarzenberger, *The Legality of Nuclear Weapons*, 1958; N. Singh, *Nuclear Weapons and International Law*, 1959; *Nuclear Weapons and Law* (eds Miller and Feinrider), 1984 and *Nuclear Weapons: Report of the Secretary-General of the United Nations*, 1981. See also I. Brownlie, 'Some Legal Aspects of the Use of Nuclear Weapons', 14 *ICLQ*, 1965, p. 437; E. Castren, 'The Illegality of Nuclear Weapons', *University of Toledo Law Review*, 1971, p. 89; R. Falk, L. Meyrowitz and J. Sanderson, 'Nuclear Weapons and International Law', 20 *Indian Journal of International Law*, 1980, p. 541; E. Meyrowitz, 'The Laws of War and Nuclear Weapons', 9 *Brooklyn Journal of International Law*, 1983, pp. 227; J.N. Moore, 'Nuclear Weapons and the Law: Enhancing Strategic Stability', ibid., p. 267 and B. Weston, 'Nuclear Weapons vs International Law', 20 *Indian Journal of International Law*, 1980, p. 541.
2   See generally M.N. Shaw, *International Law*, 2nd edn 1986, Chapter 1.
3   Article 38(1), Statute of the International Court of Justice. This formulation is accepted as authoritative by states in the context of the creation of international law.
4   M.N. Shaw, op. cit., Chapter 3.
5   See e.g. C. De Visscher, *Theory and Reality in Public International Law*, 3rd edn 1960, p. 149.

6 See e.g. R.W. Tucker, *Law and Neutrality at Sea*, 1955.

7 See e.g. *The Law of Land Warfare*, 1956, para 35 (the Army) and *The Conduct of Armed Conflicts and Air Operations*, 1976, para. 6-5 (the Air Force).

8 *The Manual of Military Law: Part III The Law of War on Land*, 1958, para. 113.

9 Ibid., para. 107, n. 1(b). See also the West German Military Manual, 1961, paras 82-5; the Swiss Military Manual, 1963, para. 24 and the Austrian Military Manual, 1965, para. 41.

10 This is, of course, underlined by the international agreements that regulate the actual deployment and use of nuclear weapons, since these clearly operate upon the basis of the denial of the illegality of nuclear weapons as such. See further below.

11 See Article 63 of Convention I on the Wounded and Sick in Armed Forces in the Field; Article 62 of Convention II on the Wounded Sick and Shipwrecked Members of Armed Forces at Sea; Article 142 of Convention III on the Treatment of Prisoners of War, and Article 158 of Convention IV on the Protection of Civilians. See generally, A. Roberts and R. Guelff, *Documents on the Laws of War*, 1982, Chapters 18–21.

12 See Article 1 of Additional Protocol I, 1977, to the 1949 Geneva Conventions, and the preamble to Additional Protocol II, see A. Roberts and R. Guelff, op. cit., Chapters 26 and 27.

13 Ibid., Chapter 29. See also M.N. Shaw, 'The United Nations Convention on Prohibitions on Restrictions on the Use of Certain Conventional Weapons, 1981', 9 *Review of International Studies*, 1983, p. 109.

14 See e.g. P. Robblee, 'The Legitimacy of Modern Conventional Weapons', 71 *Military Law Review*, 1976, p. 95; J. Paust, 'Does your Police Force Use Illegal Weapons?', 18 *Harvard International Law Journal*, 1977, p. 19; A. Cassese, 'Weapons Causing Unnecessary Suffering: Are They Prohibited?', 58 *Rivista di Diritto Internazionale*, 1975, p. 12 and ibid., 'Means of Warfare: The Present and Emerging Law', 12 *Revue Belge de Droit International*, 1976, p. 143.

15 See *Report of the Conference*, 1975, paras 24-7. See also F. Karlshoven, 'Reaffirmation and Development of International Humanitarian Law Applicable in Armed Conflicts: The Diplomatic Conference, Geneva, 1974-1977', Part II, 9 *Netherlands Yearbook of International Law*, 1978, p.107.

16 *The Conduct of Armed Conflicts and Air Operations*, op. cit., Chapter 6, para. 6-3(b)2.

17 Ibid.

18 Op. cit., para. 110.

19 Op. cit., p. 18.

20 Op. cit., para. 110, note 1.

21 See CDDH/III/237; CDDH/III/SR.26, para. 8 and CDDH/III/SR.38, paras 7 and 51.

22 Article 35(2) of Protocol I is reiterated in the preamble to the 1981 Convention.

23 See e.g. J. B. Moore, *International Law*, 1924, viii. See also the *Fundamental Rules of International Humanitarian Law Applicable in Armed Conflicts* drawn up by the Red Cross, A. Roberts and R. Guelff, op. cit., pp. 465-6. Note to the same effect the 1923 Hague Draft Rules on Aerial Warfare, which were not embodied in a treaty, see H. Lauterpacht, op. cit., p. 369.

24 *Law Reports of the Trials of War Criminals* vol. 8, no. 34, 1948, pp. 65-6.

25 See e.g. G. Draper, 'Military Necessity and Humanitarian Concerns', 12 *Revue de Droit Pénal et de Droit de la Guerre*, 1973, p. 141, and H. Lauterpacht, 'The Revision of the Laws of War', 29 *British Yearbook of International Law*, 1952, p. 368.

26 This was reaffirmed in General Assembly resolution 2444 (XXIII) in 1968.

27 See also the slightly weaker formulation in Article 13 of Protocol II, which deals with internal armed conflicts.

28   See also Article 51 of Protocol I.
29   See also the Genocide Convention, 1948, and below.
30   See also Articles 52-6.
31   See also Article 55 and the preamble to the 1981 Convention. Note also the Convention on the Prohibition of Military or any other Hostile Use of Environmental Modification Techniques, 1977.
32   See e.g. Nagendra Singh, op. cit., p. 237. See also L. Oppenheim, *International Law*, vol. 2, 7th edn 1952, p. 674.
33   But not the UK, see A. Roberts and R. Guelff, op. cit., pp. 68-9.
34   See e.g. I. Brownlie, op. cit., p. 444.
35   See generally M.N. Shaw, op. cit., Chapter 17.
36   Article 51(6).
37   See e.g. J. Goldblat, *Arms Control Agreements*, 1983, pp. 84-5. See also *Digest of US Practice in International Law*, 1977, p. 919.
38   See A. Roberts and R. Guelff, op. cit., p. 462.
39   See e.g. E. Meyrowitz, op. cit., p. 253.
40   See e.g. P. Ragone, 'Applicability of Military Necessity in the Nuclear Age', 16 *New York University Journal of International Law and Politics*, p. 701. See further below.
41   The extent to which international law protects the environment is controversial, see generally J. Schneider, *The World Public Order of the Environment*, 1978.
42   But see I. Brownlie, op. cit., p. 444.
43   See also the North Atlantic Treaty (Accession of the Federal Republic of Germany), 23 October 1954.
44   The relevant area is defined in Article IV as the area south of 60 degrees south latitude.
45   The Treaty of Tlatelolco.
46   As did the UK, France, China and the Soviet Union.
47   See A/AC 206/7, 4 May 1981. See also *Encyclopedia of Public International Law*, vol. 4, pp. 38-9. Note, however, the signing in August 1985 of a South Pacific Nuclear Free Zone Treaty, by states in the South Pacific Forum. It is at the moment of writing not yet in force, see 24 *International Legal Materials*, 1985, p. 1440. For a more detailed analogue of nuclear-free zones see Chapter 8, this volume.
48   Note also the US–USSR Treaties of 1974 and 1976 prohibiting certain underground nuclear tests. For a more detailed analysis of nuclear weapons tests see, Chapter 9, this volume.
49   SALT I. This expired formally in October 1977, but is being observed by both sides.
50   For a more detailed analogue of the Treaty see Chapter 5, this volume.
51   See 22 *Bulletin of the State Department*, 1955, p. 90.
52   See e.g. resolutions 1082 (XIV), 15 July 1954, and 1493 (XVII), 20 March 1956.
53   France not having signed the 1963 Treaty.
54   The *Nuclear Tests* case, *ICJ Reports*, 1974, p. 253.
55   See Article 88. For a more detailed analysis see Chapter 7, this volume.
56   Emphasis added.
57   See e.g. resolutions 1801 (XVII), 1909 (XVIII), 2164 (XXI) and 2289 (XXII).
58   Resolution 2936 (XXVII).
59   See e.g. resolutions 33/71B, 35/1520, 36/921, 37/100, and 38/73G.
60   See e.g. Article 11 of the UN Charter. See also M.N. Shaw, op. cit., Chapter 18.
61   See e.g. R. Falk, L. Meyrowitz and J. Sanderson, op. cit., p. 561 *et seq*; I. Brownlie, op. cit., p. 442 and E. Meyrowitz, op. cit., p. 235. See also G. Schwarzenberger, op. cit., p. 27.
62   Ibid., p. 35.

63   See e.g. A. Roberts and R. Guelff, op. cit., pp. 137-8.
64   Ibid., pp. 144-5.
65   Including Australia, Belgium, Bulgaria, Canada, Czechoslovakia, India, Iraq, Nigeria, Pakistan, Romania, UK, USA and USSR, ibid.
66   See also the Convention on the Prohibition of the Development, Production and Stockpiling of Bacteriological and Toxic Weapons, 1972.
67   See e.g. I. Brownlie, op. cit., p. 443; R. Falk, L. Meyrowitz and J. Sanderson, op. cit., p. 568 and E. Meyrowitz, op. cit., p. 247.
68   General Assembly resolution 95(I) affirmed unanimously the principles of international law recognised by the Charter of the Nuremberg Tribunal and the Judgment of the Tribunal. See also the Draft Code of Offences against the Peace and Security of Mankind, 1954.
69   Summary Records of the 36th Session of the ILC, 1984, p. 6.
70   Ibid., p. 26. See also Gross, 'Some Observations on the United Nations Draft Code of Offences Against the Peace and Security of Mankind', 15 *Israel Yearbook on Human Rights*, 1985, pp. 224, 256. See also the discussion in the Sixth Committee, e.g. A/C.6/39/SR.45, para. 30.
71   But see General Assembly resolution 36/100.
72   See generally M.N. Shaw, op. cit., Chapter 17.
73   These are the Medium Atomic Demolition Munition and the Small Atomic Demolition Munition, see e.g. Rogers, *Guide to Nuclear Weapons 1984-5*, 1984, p. 35.
74   Ibid., pp. 34-5.
75   Ibid., p. 33.
76   Ibid., p. 27.
77   *International Law*, vol II, 7th edn 1952, p. 561. See also J. Stone, *Legal Controls of International Conflict*, 1959, p. 354; M.S. McDougal and F.P. Feliciano, 'International Coercion and World Public Order: The General Principles of the Law of War', 67 *Yale Law Journal*, 1958, pp. 771, 833; H. Kelsen, *Principles of International Law*, 1952, p. 23 and F. Karlshoven, *Belligerent Reprisals*, 1971, p. 33.
78   See also Article 4(3), Hague Convention for the Protection of Cultural Property, 1954, prohibiting reprisals against cultural property.
79   See also Articles 53 and 54.
80   Note here the discussion in the *Shimoda* case as to whether the atomic bombing of Hiroshima and Nagasaki by the US was illegal under international law as at 1945. The Japanese Court, in fact, held that such bombings had in the circumstances violated the principles of military necessity and humanity as existing at that date. Particular stress was laid on the fact that the two cities in question were not valid military objectives, see 8 *Japanese Annual of International Law*, 1964, p. 212.

2   The legality of nuclear weapons

Nicholas Grief

Although there are no specific references to nuclear weapons in any of the international agreements on the law of warfare concluded since 1945, it is quite incorrect to draw the conclusion that the deployment and use of nuclear weapons are unregulated, and therefore permitted, by international law. The international law of war is primarily concerned with alleviating the human suffering caused by warfare, and less with regulating the use of particular weapons by name. The United Kingdom *Manual of Military Law*[1] recognises that '[i]n the absence of any rule of international law dealing expressly with it, the use which may be made of a particular weapon will be governed by the ordinary rules and the question of the legality of its use in any particular case will, therefore, involve merely the application of the recognised principles of international law.'[2] This contrasts with the position adopted by the United States, that '[t]he use of explosive nuclear weapons, whether by air, sea or land forces, cannot be regarded as violative of existing international law in the absence of any international rule of law restricting their employment.'[3] In the opinion of the present writer, the use of nuclear weapons is already prohibited by certain rules of customary international law, as well as by certain conventional rules which apply to such weapons by analogy or by implication.

There are two fundamental principles of international humanitarian law which proscribe the use of nuclear weapons. The first of these is that the parties to an armed conflict and the members of their armed forces do not have an unlimited choice of weapons or methods of warfare. They are forbidden to use weapons or methods which are of a nature to cause unnecessary suffering or superfluous injury. This is a long-established principle reflected in several international treaties. It can be traced back to the Declaration of St Petersburg of 1868,[4] which was the first formal agreement prohibiting the use of certain weapons in war.[5] In the light of the development of a bullet which would explode on contact with a soft substance, an International Military Commission was assembled to determine the 'limits at which the necessities of war ought to yield to the requirements of humanity'.[6] Considering that 'the employment of arms which uselessly aggravate the sufferings of disabled men, or render their death inevitable',[7] would exceed the legitimate object of war, the weakening of the enemy's military forces, the Contracting Parties agreed to renounce the use of any projectile weighing less than 400 g which is either explosive or charged with fulminating or inflammable substances.[8]

Although the Declaration was not aimed at weapons of mass destruction, the principle upon which it was based, that a weapon which would be unnecessarily destructive must not be used,[9] is of general application. Indeed, it is unreasonable to condemn the use of such a bullet which would cause excessive suffering to one person at the time of impact, whilst accepting as perfectly legitimate the use of a nuclear weapon, which would cause horrific suffering to many people, combatants and non-combatants, at the time of the blast and even for years afterwards.[10]

The principle is also embodied in the Hague Conventions on Land Warfare of 1899 and 1907.[11] Article 22 of each Convention provides that '[t]he right of belligerents to adopt means of injuring the enemy is not unlimited.' Article 23(e) specifically prohibits the use of weapons which would cause unnecessary suffering: according to the 1899 Convention, it is especially forbidden to employ arms, projectiles or material of a nature to cause superfluous injury; whereas the 1907 Convention forbids the use of arms, projectiles or material calculated to cause unnecessary suffering. Although the 1907 provision appears to demand a subjective test, the authoritative French text confirms that, irrespective of a belligerent's intentions, weapons are prohibited if they are apt to cause unnecessary suffering.[12] It is submitted that these provisions not only prohibit the use of nuclear weapons by states which are parties to them, but have also helped to establish a customary prohibition binding upon all states. Indeed, in 1946 the Nuremberg International Military Tribunal stated that '[t]he rules of land warfare expressed in the (1907) Convention undoubtedly represented an advance over existing International Law at the time of their adoption . . . but by 1939 these rules were recognised by all civilised nations as being declaratory of the laws and customs of war.'[13]

It has been argued by some, however, that the use of nuclear weapons is not regulated by pre-existing customary law or conventions.[14] This argument is based upon the reasoning of the Permanent Court of International Justice in the *Lotus Case*,[15] that 'the rules of law binding upon States . . . emanate from their own free will as expressed in conventions or by usages generally accepted as expressing principles of law.'[16] The argument is not convincing, however. As Falk has argued, it is 'facile and unpersuasive' to extend the *Lotus* reasoning to the drastically different circumstances surrounding the question of the legal status of nuclear weapons.[17] Moreover, according to the judgment of the Tokyo District Court in the *Shimoda Case*,[18] which concerned the legality of the atomic bombing of Hiroshima and Nagasaki, although the use of a new weapon is indeed lawful as long as it is not prohibited by international law, a prohibition must be considered to exist not only where it is expressly provided for, but also where the interpretation and analogical application of existing international law make it necessary, or where the use of a new weapon would be contrary to principles of international law which form the basis of existing law.[19] If this were not so, the overriding purpose of the law of war, the alleviation of suffering, could not be achieved, as prohibitions designed to fulfil this purpose would become obsolete and meaningless as new weapons were developed. The right to life is not lost as new methods of killing are invented.

This is expressly recognized by Protocol I of 1977 Additional to the Geneva Conventions of 1949 and Relating to the Protection of Victims of International Armed Conflicts.[20] Article 36 of the Protocol provides that '[i]n the study, development, acquisition or adoption of a new weapon, means or method of warfare, a High Contracting Party is under an obligation to determine whether its employment would, in some or all circumstances, be prohibited by this Protocol or by any other rule of international law applicable to the High Contracting Party.' Furthermore, the 'Martens clause' in the Preamble of the Hague Conventions on Land Warfare of 1899 and 1907 has a similar effect:

> [u]ntil a more complete code of the laws of war has been issued, the High Contracting Parties deem it expedient to declare that, in cases not included in the Regulations adopted by them, the inhabitants and belligerents remain under the protection and rule of the principles of the law of nations, as they result from the usages established among civilized peoples, from the laws of humanity, and the dictates of the public conscience.[21]

The absence of an express prohibition concerning nuclear weapons cannot therefore be regarded as a licence to use them.

The principle that international law prohibits the use of weapons and methods of warfare which would cause unnecessary suffering was applied by the Japanese court in the *Shimoda Case*.[22] The court concluded, *inter alia*, that 'the act of dropping such a cruel bomb is contrary to the fundamental principle of the laws of war that unnecessary pain must not be given'.[23] It had earlier drawn attention to the particularly cruel effects of the bombing by referring to the radiation sickness which continued to afflict victims of the attacks for many years afterwards. In reaching its conclusion, the court considered whether the bombing 'had an appropriate military effect . . . and whether it was necessary',[24] accepting that humanitarian considerations must be balanced against military considerations in order to determine the limits of legitimate warfare.

The question of what constitutes 'unnecessary suffering' is not straightforward. For every weapon and method of warfare, it is necessary to weigh military advantage against humanitarian demands. For example, it is commonly accepted that if there are two means of achieving the same military advantage, the overpowering of an adversary, the one which would involve the greater suffering must be rejected. If an adversary can be captured without being disabled, injury should not be inflicted. If injury would be sufficient to render him *hors de combat*, he should not be killed.[25] In trying to assess the legality of nuclear weapons, the explosive yield of a weapon and also the context in which it would be used are important. Since their explosive yield is higher, on average, 'strategic' nuclear weapons would almost certainly have more devastating effects than 'tactical' or 'battlefield' nuclear weapons.[26] None the less, given the horrific effects which any nuclear weapon would have upon all who were within range of blast and fall-out, and upon the environment, it is submitted that unnecessary suffering would be caused even if tactical weapons were to be used selectively.[27] No legitimate military advantage could justify the use of weapons which would produce such inhumane effects, not only at the time of an attack and immediately afterwards, but even for future generations.

A more recent international agreement prohibiting the use of weapons which are of a nature to cause unnecessary suffering is Protocol I of 1977.[28] Article 35(1) of the Protocol reiterates the basic rule that in any armed conflict, the right of the parties to the conflict to choose methods or means of warfare is not unlimited. Article 35(2) prohibits the use of weapons, projectiles and material and methods of warfare of a nature to cause superfluous injury or unnecessary suffering. Neither the United States nor the United Kingdom is a party to the Protocol, although both states have signed it[29] and must therefore refrain from acts which would defeat the object and purpose of the Protocol.[30] On signing, each declared its understanding that the rules established by the Protocol were not intended to have any effect on, and do not regulate or prohibit, the use of nuclear weapons.[31] The legal nature and effect of these declarations, which confirmed the understanding on the basis of which the United Kingdom and the United States had participated in the Diplomatic Conference,[32] must be considered. It is clear that the declarations only apply to rules which are *established* by the Protocol, as distinct from provisions which are declaratory of pre-existing customary international law. The rule prohibiting the use of weapons or methods of warfare which are of a nature to cause unnecessary suffering is an example of the latter. Thus, the US and UK declarations do not affect those provisions of the Protocol which are already *lex lata*. The effect of the declarations upon *new* rules introduced by Protocol I will be considered in due course.[33]

The second fundamental principle of international humanitarian law which, in this writer's opinion, prohibits the use of nuclear weapons, is that the parties to an armed conflict must at all times distinguish between civilian objects and military objectives. Weapons which would not permit such a distinction to be drawn, because they are of a nature to strike indiscriminately, may not be used. Indeed, the indiscriminate use of any weapon is also prohibited. This conclusion is strongly supported by the unanimous adoption of resolution 2444 (XXIII) by the United Nations General Assembly on 19 December 1968.[34] Operative paragraph 1 of the resolution affirms resolution XXVIII of the XXth International Conference of the Red Cross held at Vienna in 1965, which laid down, *inter alia*, the following principles for observance by all governmental and other authorities responsible for action in armed conflicts:

> (a) That the right of the parties to a conflict to adopt means of injuring the enemy is not unlimited; (b) That it is prohibited to launch attacks against the civilian population as such; (c) That distinction must be made at all times between persons taking part in the hostilities and members of the civilian population to the effect that the latter be spared as much as possible.

This principle is reflected in the Hague Conventions on Land Warfare of 1899 and 1907,[35] according to which the bombardment of undefended towns, villages, dwellings or buildings is prohibited. The 1907 Convention adds the words 'by any means whatever', to cover attacks from the air.[36] Moreover, all necessary steps must be taken to spare, as far as possible, hospitals and places where the sick and wounded are collected, provided that they are not being used for military purposes.[37]

The Hague Rules of Air Warfare of 1922/23 show how the principle was developed.[38] Although these Rules were never adopted in legally binding form, they have been described as 'an authoritative attempt to clarify and formulate rules of law governing the use of aircraft in war',[39] and were invoked by the Japanese court in the *Shimoda Case*.[40] Article 22 of the Hague Rules lays down the basic rule that aerial bombardment for the purpose of terrorising the civilian population, of destroy-ing or damaging private property not of a military character, or of injur-ing non-combatants is prohibited. Even if aerial bombardment were not carried out *for the purpose of* terrorising civilians or injuring non-combatants, it could still be in violation of the Hague Rules. According to Article 24(1), aerial bombardment is legitimate only when directed at a military objective, defined as an object of which the destruction would constitute a distinct military advantage to the belligerent. Article 24(2) then provides that bombardment is legitimate only when directed exclusively at specified objectives, including military forces and mili-tary establishments. The bombardment of cities, towns, villages, dwel-lings or buildings not in the immediate neighbourhood of land forces is expressly prohibited by Article 24(3), which also requires aircraft to ab-stain from bombardment if the military objectives specified in para-graph 2 are so situated that they cannot be bombarded without the in-discriminate bombardment of the civilian population. In the case of cities, towns, villages, dwellings or buildings which are in the immedi-ate neighbourhood of land forces, Article 24(4) permits bombardment 'provided that there exists a reasonable presumption that the military concentration is sufficiently important to justify bombardment, having regard to the danger thus caused to the civilian population.'

These provisions require comment, particularly in the light of Ad-ditional Protocol I of 1977.[41] This shows beyond doubt that the traditional distinction between civilians and combatants remains valid, despite arguments that it should be regarded as having been abolished through contrary practice.[42] It is clear that international law prohibits attacks upon the civilian population as such, and also upon individual civilians.[43] Attacks must be directed solely against 'military ob-jectives'.[44] Moreover, acts of violence whose primary purpose is to ter-rorise the civilian population are also clearly prohibited.[45]

The position concerning indiscriminate warfare is perhaps less straightforward. Although there is no doubt that indiscriminate attacks are prohibited, there may be differences of opinion as to what this means. Blix has identified three elements which form the essence of the standard required of parties to an armed conflict: (a) targets must be identified with some certainty as military objectives; (b) attacks must be directed against such identified targets; and (c) the weapons and methods of warfare must be such that the target may be hit with some degree of likelihood.[46] These elements are all reflected in Additional Protocol I. Thus, according to Article 57(2)(a), '[t]hose who plan or decide upon an attack shall: (i) do everything feasible to verify that the objectives to be attacked are neither civilians nor civilian objects and are not subject to special protection but are military objectives within the meaning of paragraph 2 of Article 52.'[47] Furthermore, according to Article 51(4),

> [i]ndiscriminate attacks are prohibited. Indiscriminate attacks
> are: (a) those which are not directed at a specific military objec-
> tive; (b) those which employ a method or means of combat which
> cannot be directed at a specific military objective; or (c) those
> which employ a method or means of combat the effects of which
> cannot be limited as required by this Protocol; and consequently,
> in each case, are of a nature to strike military objectives and civil-
> ians or civilian objects without distinction.

Article 51(5) then provides that the following types of attack, among
others, are to be considered as indiscriminate:

> (a) an attack by bombardment by any method or means which
> treats as a single military objective a number of clearly separated
> and distinct military objectives located in a city, town, village or
> other area containing a similar concentration of civilians or
> civilian objects; and (b) an attack which may be expected to cause
> incidental loss of civilian life, injury to civilians, damage to civilian
> objects, or a combination thereof, which would be excessive in re-
> lation to the concrete and direct military advantage anticipated.

The above provisions raise the question whether there are some
weapons which, by their very nature, are incapable of being directed at
a specific military objective or whose effects cannot be limited as required by the Protocol, and are therefore illegal *per se*. Many of the participants at the Diplomatic Conference on Humanitarian Law in Armed
Conflicts, which produced the Additional Protocol, would not admit
that there are any weapons which cannot be directed at a military objective.[48] Blix, himself a participant, surmises that this attitude was
adopted to foreclose any discussion of the question whether nuclear
weapons are inevitably indiscriminate.[49] Whilst it is true that any
weapon can be used indiscriminately and that, in most cases, indiscriminate effects will be the result of the indiscriminate use of a weapon
rather than of the weapon's very nature, the nature of nuclear weapons
makes it virtually inevitable that indiscriminate effects would accompany their use.

Although international law permits the use of weapons and methods
of warfare which have only incidental effects upon civilians and civilian
objects,[50] the extent to which this is tolerated is clearly defined in
Article 51(5)(b) of Additional Protocol I.[51] Indeed, those responsible
for planning or deciding upon an attack are expressly required to

> refrain from deciding to launch any attack which may be expected
> to cause incidental loss of civilian life, injury to civilians, damage

to civilian objects, or a combination thereof, which would be excessive in relation to the concrete and direct military advantage anticipated.[52]

In other words, incidental effects upon civilians and civilian objects are tolerated but subject to the rule of proportionality. As before, therefore, military advantage must be weighed against humanitarian considerations in order to determine the limits of legitimate warfare. Consequently,

> any means – weapons or other devices – or method the normal or typical employment of which results in military objectives and civilians and civilian objects being hit without distinction and in disregard of the rule of proportionality would stand condemned.[53]

The United States has welcomed this 'first codification of the customary rule of proportionality',[54] a rule which follows logically from the principle that civilians as such may not be the object of attack and must be spared as much as possible. Being declaratory of a customary rule, it is not affected by the declarations made by the United States and the United Kingdom on signing the Protocol.[55] It is submitted that, in view of the nature and effects of nuclear weapons, not merely at the time of an attack, but also for the future, their use would almost certainly violate the rule of proportionality, in that the incidental loss of civilian life, injury to civilians and damage to civilian objects would surely be excessive in relation to any direct military advantage.[56] Whilst this is particularly true of strategic nuclear weapons, it could also be true of tactical nuclear weapons intended for battlefield use. Arbess has considered this question in the light of current strategies and weapons' capabilities and suggested that, in each of three different contexts,[57] 'the collateral damage associated with the use of nuclear weapons would most likely outweigh the alleged "military necessity".'[58] He concludes that 'their likely effects and the absence of any mechanism to control the escalatory spiral . . . render virtually any use inconsistent with the fundamental objectives and principles of war.'[59]

Apart from these two fundamental principles of international humanitarian law, there are other international instruments and rules of international law which appear to prohibit the use of nuclear weapons. One such instrument is the Geneva Protocol of 1925 for the Prohibition of the Use in War of Asphyxiating, Poisonous or Other Gases and of Bacteriological Methods of Warfare.[60] Although the Protocol does not refer to nuclear weapons, it is submitted that it applies to them by analogy. It begins by recalling that 'the use in war of asphyxiating, poisonous or other gases, and of all analogous liquids, materials or devices, has been justly condemned by the general opinion of the civilized world'[61] and that 'the prohibition of such use has been declared in Treaties to which the majority of Powers of the world are Parties'.[62] The High Contracting Parties then declare, *inter alia*, that, in so far as they are not already Parties to such Treaties, they accept this prohibition and agree to be bound by it as between themselves.[63]

It is submitted that the Geneva Protocol prohibits the use of nuclear weapons in that they produce effects which are analogous to asphyxiating or poisonous gases.[64] Akehurst's argument that the analogy is not close enough to be absolutely compelling since 'fall-out is only a side-effect of nuclear weapons, whereas poisoning is the main (if not the sole) effect of using poison gas',[65] is, with respect, unconvincing. Nuclear fall-out may not be the sole effect of using nuclear weapons, but it is surely more significant than he suggests.

Several states have made reservations to the Geneva Protocol, including the United Kingdom, the United States and the Soviet Union.[66] According to the two United Kingdom reservations, the Protocol is only binding upon the United Kingdom as regards those states which are themselves Parties to it; and it shall cease to be binding upon the United Kingdom in respect of any enemy state which fails to comply with its prohibitions.[67] In other words, if an enemy state ignores the Protocol, the United Kingdom will do likewise. The United States' reservation is in very similar terms.[68]

The effect of these reservations must be considered. Even with the reservations, the United Kingdom and the United States are under a legal obligation not to be the first in an armed conflict to use weapons which are analogous to asphyxiating or poisonous gases, arguably including nuclear weapons. This is in contrast to NATO's declared intention to use nuclear weapons first if necessary, in response to a conventional attack by the Warsaw Pact.[69] Moreover, if the prohibition of the use of poisonous gas and analogous devices was declaratory of customary international law at the time of the Geneva Protocol's conclusion, the reservations may be ineffective. A state cannot, by formulating a reservation, attempt to exclude or modify a treaty rule which is derived from customary international law.[70] This also raises the question of the permissibility of reprisals in international law since, although the Geneva Protocol may well have been declaratory of customary international law as regards the first use of poisonous gas and analogous devices, the customary prohibition may not have extended to their use in reprisal.[71]

A reprisal is an act which would normally be illegal but which is rendered lawful by a prior illegal act committed by the state against which the reprisal is directed.[72] Some writers have argued that nuclear weapons may lawfully be used in reprisal against an unlawful act itself consisting of the use of nuclear weapons,[73] although others do not insist on retaliation in kind.[74] According to the *Naulilaa Case*,[75] three conditions would have to be satisfied in order to justify the use of force in reprisal: (a) there must have been a previous act in violation of international law; (b) there must have been an unsatisfied demand, since the use of force is justified only if absolutely necessary; and (c) the degree of force used in reprisal must not be disproportionate to the prior illegal act.

Even if the use of force by way of reprisal were still lawful,[76] and even if the principle of proportionality could be respected, the contention that nuclear weapons may be used in this way would meet with certain objections. In the first place, it can be argued that reprisals contemplate a return to legality, not the annihilation of the adversary, and are therefore inapplicable in the context of nuclear warfare. As Brownlie has argued, 'it is hardly legitimate to extend a doctrine related to the minutiae of the conventional theatre of war to an exchange of power which, in the case of the strategic and deterrent uses of nuclear weapons, is equivalent to the total of war effort and is the essence of the war aims.'[77] Secondly, reprisals against persons and property protected by international law are clearly prohibited. In particular, international law prohibits reprisals against all persons and objects protected by the Geneva Conventions of 1949,[78] including the wounded, sick, shipwrecked, and prisoners of war.[79] Medical establishments and personnel are similarly protected.[80] Article 33 of the Fourth Geneva Convention of 1949 relative to the Protection of Civilians in Time of War[81] also prohibits reprisals against protected persons and their property, although this does not mean civilians in general, since 'protected persons' are 'those who, at a given moment and in any manner whatsoever, find themselves, in case of a conflict or occupation, in the hands of a Party to the conflict or Occupying Power of which they are not nationals'.[82] However, the protection against reprisals accorded to civilians and civilian objects has been extended by Additional Protocol I of 1977.[83] Thus, Article 51(6) prohibits attacks against the civilian population or civilians by way of reprisals, and Article 52(1) provides that civilian objects[84] shall not be the object of reprisals. It is also forbidden to make cultural objects and places of worship,[85] objects indispensable to the survival of the civilian population,[86] or works and installations containing dangerous forces[87] the object of reprisals. Attacks against the natural environment by way of reprisals are similarly prohibited.[88]

The prohibition of reprisals against the civilian population expressed in Article 51(6) of the Additional Protocol has been viewed with concern in a report submitted to the US Secretary of State.[89] According to the report's conclusion, it is accepted that some prohibition of reprisals clearly makes sense, but the United States Delegation believes that the Conference has gone unreasonably far in its prohibition of this right in Article 51. It is unreasonable to think that massive and continuing attacks against a nation's civilian population could be absorbed without a response in kind. By denying the possibility of response and not offering any workable substitute, Article 51 is unrealistic and cannot be expected to withstand the test of future conflicts. On the other hand, it will not be easy for any country to reserve, explicitly, the right of reprisal against an enemy's civilian population.[90]

If the prohibition of reprisals against the civilian population or civilians expressed in Article 51(6) of the Protocol is a new rule and not declaratory of customary law, the question of the nature and effect of the declarations made by the United Kingdom and the United States is raised.[91] Are they merely declarations or are they in fact reservations to the Protocol? According to the Vienna Convention on the Law of Treaties, 1969,[92] a reservation is a 'unilateral statement, however phrased or named, made by a State, when signing . . . a treaty, whereby it purports to exclude or modify the legal effect of certain provisions of the treaty in their application to that State'.[93] The name given to a statement is unimportant, therefore. What matters is its effect.

It can be argued that, by means of their declarations, the United States and the United Kingdom are indeed purporting to exclude the legal effect of Article 51(6) of the Protocol with regard to nuclear weapons and that the declarations are therefore reservations. If they are reservations, moreover, are they permissible reservations? As the Protocol is silent concerning the formulation of reservations, Article 19(c) of the Vienna Convention is applicable. Accordingly, a reservation is not permitted if it is incompatible with the object and purpose of the treaty in question. Given that the object and purpose of the Protocol are to protect the victims of international armed conflicts, it is submitted that the reservations are incompatible and thus impermissible. Other states can object to the reservations and even to the entry into force of the Protocol as between themselves and the reserving states.[94] However, the Diplomatic Conference which produced the Additional Protocol seems to have operated throughout on the understanding that the new rules which it established would not apply to nuclear weapons.[95] Consequently, it may be that those rules are irrelevant as far as nuclear weapons are concerned.[96]

Before leaving the subject of reprisals, another point must be considered. According to Article 60(5) of the Vienna Convention on the Law of Treaties,[97] the doctrine of material breach[98] is not applicable to 'provisions relating to the protection of the human person contained in treaties of a humanitarian character, in particular to provisions prohibiting any form of reprisal against persons protected by such treaties.' Paragraph 5 was added at the Vienna Conference, and the provisions of the 1949 Geneva Conventions prohibiting reprisals against protected persons were among the considerations which inspired it.[99]

Although the Vienna Convention applies only to treaties concluded by states after its entry into force for such States, this is without prejudice to the application of any rules in the Convention which apply independently of it.[100] It is submitted that the rule expressed in Article 60(5) is such an example. In the *Namibia Case*,[101] the International Court of Justice referred to 'the general principle of law that a right to termination on account of breach must be presumed to exist in respect of all treaties, except as regards provisions relating to the protection of the human person contained in treaties of a humanitarian character (as indicated by Article 60, para. 5, of the Vienna Convention).'[102] A state which is a party to the Geneva Conventions of 1949 cannot invoke a material breach of the Conventions by another party to justify reprisals against the persons protected by those Conventions, therefore.[103]

Besides specifically prohibiting attacks in reprisal against protected persons, the Geneva Conventions of 1949 also contain other provisions which would appear to render the use of nuclear weapons unlawful, in that the protection guaranteed by the Conventions would be impossible to maintain.[104] For example, bearing in mind that High Contracting Parties have undertaken to respect and ensure respect for the Conventions in all circumstances,[105] Article 12 of the First Convention for the Amelioration of the Condition of the Wounded and Sick in Armed Forces in the Field[106] provides that '[m]embers of the armed forces . . . who are wounded and sick, shall be protected and respected in all circumstances.' Similarly, Article 19 provides that '[f]ixed establishments and mobile medical units of the Medical Service may in no circumstances be attacked, but shall at all times be respected and protected by the Parties to the conflict.' According to Article 24, moreover, '[m]edical personnel exclusively engaged in the search for, or the collection, transport or treatment of the wounded or sick, or in the prevention of disease, staff exclusively engaged in the administration of medical units and establishments, as well as chaplains attached to the armed forces, shall be respected and protected in all circumstances.' Furthermore, Article 14 of the Fourth Convention Relating to the Protection of Civilian Persons in Time of War[107] envisages the establishment and mutual recognition of 'hospital and safety zones and localities so organised as to protect from the effects of war, wounded, sick and aged persons, children under fifteen, expectant mothers and mothers of children under seven.' Indeed, according to Article 16 of the same Convention, the wounded and sick, the infirm and expectant mothers shall be the object of particular protection and respect. Article 18 then provides that civilian hospitals organised to give care to such persons may in no circumstances be the object of attack but shall at all times be respected and protected by the parties to a conflict. It is difficult to see how these and other similar[108] provisions could be honoured if nuclear weapons were used in an armed conflict.

The use of nuclear weapons on any appreciable scale would also violate the territorial integrity and thus the neutrality of states which were not parties to the conflict, on account of the fall-out which would inevitably accompany such use. Indeed, even use on a relatively small scale in Central Europe would be likely to violate the territory of neutral states such as Austria and Switzerland.[109] The obligation to respect the territory of neutral states is laid down in Article 1 of the Hague Convention of 1907 concerning the Rights and Duties of Neutral Powers and Persons in War on Land,[110] but it is also recognised as a principle of customary international law binding upon all states.[111] Furthermore, the violation of neutral territory by nuclear fall-out might infringe Article 2(4) of the UN Charter, which prohibits the use of force against the territorial integrity of any state.

In addition, in view of scientists' warnings about the environmental effects of using nuclear weapons, even on a small scale,[112] it is submitted that their use would be in violation of provisions of international law which require the protection of the environment. According to Article 35(3) of Additional Protocol I of 1977,[113] '[i]t is prohibited to employ methods or means of warfare which are intended, or may be expected, to cause widespread, long-term and severe damage to the natural environment.' This provision is supplemented by Article 55, paragraph 1 of which provides that

> [c]are shall be taken in warfare to protect the natural environment against widespread, long-term and severe damage. This protection includes a prohibition of the use of methods or means of warfare which are intended or may be expected to cause such damage to the natural environment and thereby to prejudice the health or survival of the population.

Although some see these as new provisions which 'might well fill a gap in humanitarian law applicable in armed conflicts',[114] it is submitted that they are evidence of an emerging principle of customary international law,[115] and may indeed already be binding as such.

There are several instruments which suggest that the protection of the environment already belongs to the recognised principles of the laws of armed conflict. These include the United Nations Convention on the Prohibition of Military or Any Other Hostile Use of Environmental Modification Techniques, 1976,[116] and the United Nations Convention on Prohibitions or Restrictions on the Use of Certain Conventional Weapons which may be deemed to be Excessively Injurious or to have Indiscriminate Effects, 1980.[117] The Preamble to the 1980 Convention recalls that it is prohibited to employ methods or means of warfare which are intended, or may be expected, to cause widespread, long-term and severe damage to the natural environment.[118] Furthermore, Principle 26 of the Stockholm Declaration on the Human Environment, 1972,[119] indicates an awareness of the ecological impact of the use of nuclear weapons: '[m]an and his environment must be spared the effects of nuclear weapons and all other weapons of mass destruction.' Also significant is the fact that Article 19 of the International Law Commission's draft articles on state responsibility recognizes that, under certain conditions, causing serious damage to the environment may be regarded as an international crime.[120]

Even if the provisions of Protocol I concerning the protection of the environment are new rather than declaratory of customary international law, it is submitted that the declarations made by the United Kingdom and the United States on signing the Protocol are impermissible reservations with regard to such provisions.[121] The declarations purport to exclude the legal effect of Article 35(3) and Article 55(1) as far as nuclear weapons are concerned, and they are incompatible with the object and purpose of the Protocol which is the protection of victims of international armed conflicts. Again, however, because of the understanding on which the Conference operated, the new rules established by Protocol I may not apply to nuclear weapons.[122]

The legality of using nuclear weapons must also be considered with reference to the United Nations Charter. The use of force against the territorial integrity or political independence of any state, or in any other manner inconsistent with the purposes of the United Nations, is prohibited by Article 2(4). Indeed, it should perhaps be stressed that Article 2(3) requires Members of the United Nations to settle their international disputes by peaceful means in such a manner that international peace and security, and justice, are not endangered. Whilst Article 51 clearly permits a state to use armed force in self-defence if an armed attack occurs against it, and also permits collective self-defence arrangements such as NATO and the Warsaw Pact, any such use of force must be both necessary and proportionate to the prior aggression. A state must show

> a necessity of self-defence, instant, overwhelming, leaving no
> choice of means and no moment for deliberation. It will be for it to
> show, also, that (it) did nothing unreasonable or excessive; since

the act, justified by the necessity of self-defence, must be limited by that necessity, and kept clearly within it.[123]

If deterrence rested wholly on the threat of massive nuclear retaliation, it could be argued that the actual carrying out of the threat would necessarily involve a disproportionate response.[124] Because of the adversary's 'second strike capability',[125] however, a threat to respond to any aggression by using the entire nuclear arsenal is not credible. Current NATO strategy is based upon the theory of 'flexible response', according to which all military options are kept open, including the first use of nuclear weapons on a limited scale in response to a conventional attack by the Warsaw Pact.[126] Nevertheless, it is submitted that the exercise of that particular option would still violate the principle of proportionality. As Brownlie has argued, 'the nuclear weapon is qualitatively different from the conventional weapon in its destructive capacity, effects on the population both at the time of the attack and for the future, and effects on the atmosphere of other States.'[127] Moreover, there would be a real danger of an uncontrollable escalation of the conflict: 'once used, the effect of delivering megaton weapons . . . is so devastating and immediate that there is little time or scope for mediation or negotiation before the State faced with the nuclear attack retaliates with its nuclear weapons.'[128]

The use of nuclear weapons may also involve the commission of genocide which, according to Article 1 of the Genocide Convention of 1948,[129] is a crime under international law whether committed in time of peace or in time of war. Furthermore, it is a crime for which there is individual liability.[130] Article 2 of the Convention defines genocide as

> any of the following acts committed with intent to destroy, in whole or in part, a national, ethnical, racial or religious group, as such: (a) Killing members of the group; (b) Causing serious bodily or mental harm to members of the group; (c) Deliberately inflicting on the group conditions of life calculated to bring about its physical destruction in whole or in part.

This definition calls for comment. First, it is clear that an intention to destroy must be proved in order to establish the crime of genocide, which would not be easy to achieve in the absence of an explicit admission by a government. However, it is submitted that the necessary intention would be present if an act were performed with knowledge of the likely consequences.[131] Moreover, the number of victims could be evidence of intention, as Bryant has suggested:

> [u]nless the intent were express, . . . the intent to destroy the group

would be difficult or impossible to prove, except in those instances where the mere number of people of the group affected was significant. Practically speaking, then, the number of victims may be of evidentiary value with respect to proving the necessary intent.[132]

Secondly, from the ordinary meaning of the text, it appears that an intention to destroy a part of the [national] group would suffice, albeit a substantial part given that the purpose of the Convention is to prevent and punish acts committed against large numbers of people.[133] Thirdly, as Brownlie has observed, the relevance of motive is not entirely clear. A defensive use of nuclear weapons might possibly be justified, although the text does at least create a presumption that their use on a large scale would be illegal.[134]

Besides the possibility of genocide, it is submitted that the use of nuclear weapons could also constitute a crime against peace, a war crime, and a crime against humanity by virtue of Article 6 of the Charter of the International Military Tribunal of 1945, the Nuremberg Charter, under which Nazi war criminals were indicted after the Second World War.[135] According to Article 6 of the Charter,

> [t]he following acts, or any of them, are crimes coming within the jurisdiction of the Tribunal for which there shall be individual responsibility: (a) Crimes against peace: namely . . . initiation or waging of a war of aggression, or a war in violation of international treaties, agreements or assurances . . . ; (b) War crimes: namely, violations of the laws or customs of war. Such violations shall include, but not be limited to, murder, ill-treatment . . . of civilian population of or in occupied territory, murder or ill-treatment of prisoners of war or persons on the seas , . . wanton destruction of cities towns or villages, or devastation not justified by military necessity; (c) Crimes against humanity: namely, murder, extermination . . . and other inhumane acts committed against any civilian population, before or during the war.

In 1946, the General Assembly of the United Nations unanimously adopted resolution 95(I) affirming the principles of international law recognized by the Charter of the Tribunal,[136] and Article 6 may accordingly be considered to represent general international law.[137] Indeed, the International Military Tribunal itself considered that the Charter 'is the expression of international law existing at the time of its creation'.[138] Quite apart from the fact that the imprisonment of Rudolph Hess in Spandau Prison demonstrates the continuing jurisdiction of the Tribunal,[139] therefore, it is submitted that the principles expressed in Article 6 of the Charter are applicable as customary international law, and that they render the use of nuclear weapons unlawful for the following reasons. A war involving nuclear weapons, even if not a war of aggression, would be a war in violation of international treaties, including the Hague Conventions of 1907, the Geneva Protocol of 1925, and the Geneva Conventions of 1949, and thus a crime against peace. Moreover, the use of nuclear weapons would almost certainly involve violations of the laws or customs of war, in particular the two fundamental principles of international humanitarian law discussed earlier, and would therefore constitute a war crime. The argument that only serious violations of the laws or customs of war constitute a war crime can be met by the submission that the use of nuclear weapons would indeed involve serious violations. Finally, if murder or other inhumane acts were committed against a civilian population through the use of nuclear weapons, this would constitute a crime against humanity.[140] Indeed, some writers have expressed the view that the use of nuclear weapons under the doctrine of deterrence is inconsistent with Article 6(c).[141]

The question of the legality of using nuclear weapons must finally be considered in the light of General Assembly resolution 1653 (XVI) on the Prohibition of the Use of Nuclear Weapons for War Purposes.[142] According to this resolution, the use of such weapons is contrary to the spirit, letter and aims of the United Nation and, as such, a direct violation of the UN Charter.[143] Moreover, their use would exceed even the scope of war and cause indiscriminate suffering,[144] and any state using them is to be considered to violate the UN Charter, to act contrary to the laws of humanity, and to commit a crime against mankind and its civilization.[145]

Although most General Assembly resolutions are not of themselves legally binding, they can provide cogent evidence of customary international law.[146] It is true that there was by no means unanimous support for resolution 1653 (XVI): out of 101 states, 55 voted for the resolution, 20 voted against, and 26 abstained. All NATO countries voted against the resolution, except Norway, Denmark and Iceland, which abstained.[147] However, these figures should not be taken at face value. Many representatives did not support the resolution because they did not want to separate the issue of the use of nuclear weapons from the more general question of disarmament. Others considered it inappropriate because it might undermine the efforts to negotiate a nuclear test ban.[148] As Brownlie has observed, representatives generally refrained from challenging the conclusions of law expressed in the resolution, although the representative of the United States did argue that Article 51 of the UN Charter imposes no restrictions on the use of weapons in self-defence.[149] Such an argument fails to appreciate the distinction which must be made between *jus ad bellum*[150] and *jus in bello*.[151] Even if a state has the legal right to use armed force, the law of war imposes restrictions concerning the means and methods of warfare which may be used.[152] Indeed, it is curious that a state which refuses to distinguish between conventional weapons and nuclear weapons in respect of Article 51, should insist upon that very distinction being drawn with regard to Geneva Protocol I of 1977.[153]

Resolution 1653 (XVI) expressed the opinion of many governments that the use of nuclear weapons is unlawful in all circumstances.[154] Other General Assembly resolutions provide further evidence in support of this conclusion.[155] Furthermore, states which voted against resolution 1653 (XVI) cannot regard themselves as 'persistent objectors' and claim that the resolution has no legal effect for them on the ground that they have consistently repudiated the ideas contained in it.[156] Those ideas are based upon principles of international law which predate any objection which they may have made with regard to nuclear weapons. Although new weapons may be developed, the principles of law relating to the conduct of hostilities, based upon humanitarian considerations, remain applicable.

The deployment of nuclear weapons

With regard to the legality of deploying nuclear weapons, it is first necessary to recognize that deployment is far more than simple possession.[157] The nuclear weapons currently deployed by NATO and the Warsaw Pact are ready to be fired at a few minutes' notice. They are not merely being stockpiled in military warehouses: 'the gun has been removed from the holster and pointed at the enemy's head, its trigger cocked.'[158] It is quite true that international law does not clearly forbid the deployment of nuclear weapons, except in certain areas such as outer space[159] and Antarctica,[160] on the seabed more than twelve miles from the coast,[161] and through other treaties establishing nuclear-free zones.[162] There is no express prohibition with regard to a state's national territory, or with regard to the high seas and the superjacent airspace.[163] Nevertheless, it is submitted that the deployment of nuclear wearpons in those areas does violate international law. Indeed, logic would seem to suggest that if actual use would be illegal, an intention to use, coupled with a high risk of use, is also illegal.

The deployment of nuclear missiles is an extremely serious threat to the inherent right to life, the supreme right which is guaranteed by customary international law and by international treaties[164] and which is not subject to derogation, even in time of public emergency threatening the life of the nation.[165] The existence of this threat has been noted by the UN Human Rights Committee.[166] The Committee has declared that states have the supreme duty to prevent wars, and that every effort made to avert the danger of war, especially thermonuclear war, would constitute the most important condition and guarantee for the protection of the right to life.[167]

Instead of averting the danger, the deployment of nuclear weapons makes nuclear war more likely and therefore undermines the right to life. The movement towards first-strike capability[168] has forced the adversary to adopt computer-based 'launch on warning' missile systems which greatly reduce the time available for considered decision-making by political and military leaders.[169] In the words of the Committee,

> the designing, testing, manufacture, possession and deployment of nuclear weapons are among the greatest threats to the right to life which confront mankind today. This threat is compounded by the danger that the actual use of such weapons may be brought about, not only in the event of war, but even through human or mechanical error or failure. Furthermore, the very existence and gravity of this threat generate a climate of suspicion and fear between States, which is itself antagonistic to the promotion of universal respect for and observance of human rights and fundamental freedoms in accordance with the Charter of the United Nations and the International Covenants on Human Rights.[170]

Accordingly, the Human Rights Committee has concluded that the production, testing, possession, deployment and use of nuclear weapons should be prohibited and recognized as crimes against humanity.[171]

Neither should it be forgotten that Article 2(4) of the UN Charter prohibits 'the threat . . . of force against the territorial integrity or political independence of any State, or in any other manner inconsistent with the Purposes of the United Nations.' If a state, purporting to act in accordance with its inherent right of self-defence, threatens to use more force than is permitted by Article 51, it is guilty of an unlawful threat of force. The threat to use nuclear weapons against a conventional attack could thus be in violation of Article 2(4).[172] Indeed, the Member States of NATO and the Warsaw Pact might be charged jointly with violating Article 2(4), in that their deployments of nuclear missiles targeted upon each other's territory constitute a threat of force inconsistent with the primary purpose of the United Nations, the maintenance of international peace and security.[173]

The deployment of nuclear weapons would also appear to be unlawful on other grounds. According to Article 6(a) of the Charter of the International Military Tribunal,[174] which represents customary international law,[175] 'crimes against peace' include 'planning [or] preparation . . . of a war of aggression or a war in violation of international treaties, agreements or assurances, or participation in a common plan or conspiracy for the accomplishment of [either] of the foregoing'. As a war involving the use of nuclear weapons would be in violation of international treaties,[176] it is submitted that to plan or prepare for such a war by deploying nuclear weapons, whether alone or in league with other states, constitutes a crime against peace, regardless of any claim to be acting in self-defence. If so, this gives rise to individual liability under international law, according to Article 6 of the Charter[177] and the judgment of the Tribunal itself:

> the very essence of the [Nuremberg] Charter is that individuals have international duties which transcend the national obligations of obedience imposed by the individual state. He who violates the laws of war cannot obtain immunity while acting in pursuance of the authority of the State, if the State in authorising action moves outside its competence under international law.[178]

Deployment is also in violation of the Genocide Convention of 1948[179] if it constitutes conspiracy to commit genocide,[180] in which case individual liability is similarly involved.[181]

Conclusion

The fundamental distinction which Grotius made between the law of war and the law of peace[182] lies at the heart of any consideration of the legality of nuclear weapons. *Jus ad bellum*, which determines whether a state has the right to use armed force, must be distinguished from *jus in bello*, which determines the means and methods of warfare which may be used by the parties to an armed conflict. International law imposes restrictions upon a state's choice of methods and means of warfare in order to alleviate the suffering caused by armed conflict.

As Additional Protocol I of 1977 and resolutions of the United Nations General Assembly show, the traditional laws of war are not obsolete, in spite of numerous infringements.[183] The practice of the world's most powerful and influential nations in accumulating nuclear weapons and threatening to use them cannot be lightly dismissed, but neither can it be considered to have created new rules of customary international law permitting their deployment and use.[184] As Arbess has argued, such a view 'fundamentally ignores the concept of law as an enterprise tailored toward the realization of certain basic, politically immutable values [including] the sanctity of human life and the prin-

ciple of minimizing losses and suffering in armed conflict which constitute the basis of the entire law of war.'[185] Legal principles cannot be
derived from practice which disregards those values. The rule of law
itself is being seriously undermined. In the judgment of a US War Trials
Tribunal, 'the rules of international law must be followed even if it results in the loss of a battle or even a war. Expediency or necessity
cannot warrant their violation.'[186] It may be possible to imagine situations in which the use of nuclear weapons would not be unlawful but,
as Brownlie has suggested, in view of the fact that the use of such
weapons even on a small scale would necessarily involve a serious risk
of escalation and a concomitant threat to civilization, 'it is ridiculous to
allow refined examples of putatively lawful use to dominate the legal
regime.[187]

The government of the United Kingdom is of the opinion that no aspect of its defence policy is inconsistent with the UK's obligations under
international law.[188] No doubt the governments of the United States
and the Soviet Union have made similar claims about their defence
policies. However, this is not the conclusion drawn by the Nuclear Warfare Tribunal, convened in London in January 1985 to consider the
legal, moral and scientific implications of nuclear weapons.[189] In its Interim Declaration, the Tribunal held that

> current and planned nuclear weapons' developments, strategies
> and deployments violate the basic rules and principles of inter-
> national law both customary and conventional. The procurement
> and use of such weapons involve infringements of the Charter of
> the United Nations, the Hague Conventions of 1899 and 1907 on
> the Law of War, the Geneva Conventions of 1949 and the Geneva
> Protocols of 1977.[190]

The Tribunal was also convinced that the Nuremberg Principles and the
Genocide Convention 'are being violated in the most extreme fashion
by ongoing preparation to wage nuclear war, especially to the extent
that plans include indiscriminate, poisonous and massive destruction of
civilian populations, amounting to a conspiracy to wage aggressive
war.'[191]

In practical terms, such findings may seem unlikely to carry weight
given the attitude of powerful and influential governments that the law
is not being broken, or that it is simply not relevant when it comes to
questions of ultimate power.[192] Nevertheless, it is important that the
continuing validity of the traditional principles of the law of armed conflict should be proclaimed, particularly by jurists,[193] since the opinions
of the most highly qualified publicists constitute subsidiary means for
the determination of rules of law.[194] In this way, governments deploy-

ing nuclear weapons may yet be persuaded to return to the standards of justice, humanity and civilization which those principles embody.

Notes

1   HMSO, 1958, Part III, 'The Law of War on land'.

2   Ibid., para. 107, n.1(b). Cf. para. 113.

3   US Air Force Pamphlet AFP 110–31, 'International Law – The Conduct of Armed Conflict and Air Operations', Department of the Air Force, 1976, s.6-5. At the UN General Assembly in December 1968, however, the US delegation recognized that there are principles of law relating to the use of weapons in warfare and that these principles apply as well to the use of nuclear and similar weapons: E.C. Collier, *International Law on the Use of Nuclear Weapons and the United States Position*, Congressional Research Service Report no. 79-28F, 1979, pp. 19-20.

4   Declaration Renouncing the Use, in Time of War, of Explosive Projectiles under 400 Grammes Weight. The Declaration is reproduced in D. Schindler and J. Toman, *The Laws of Armed Conflict*, 2nd ed., 1981, p. 95.

5   Ibid. See also the Hague Declaration concerning Expanding Bullets, 1899, ibid., p. 103.

6   Declaration of St Petersburg, Preamble, Introduction.

7   Ibid., fourth preambular paragraph.

8   Ibid., operative paragraph 1.

9   Nagendra Singh, *The Legality of Nuclear Weapons*, 1959, pp. 148-52; 'Legal Problems Arising From The Development and Utilisation of Atomic Energy', VIIth Congress of the International Association of Democratic Lawyers, Proceedings of the Second Commission, October 1960, pp.100-1; cf. I. Brownlie, 'Some Legal Aspects of the Use of Nuclear Weapons', *International and Comparative Law Quarterly*, vol. 14, 1965, p. 437 at p. 444; G. Schwarzenberger, *Nuclear Weapons and International Law*, 1958, pp. 15-16, 43-4.

10 Freid, 'First Use of Nuclear Weapons: Existing Prohibitions in International Law', *Bull. Peace Proposals*, 1981, p. 21 at p. 28. On the effects of nuclear weapons, see e.g. 'Comprehensive Study on Nuclear Weapons', UN, New York, 1981; 'Effects of the Possible Use of Nuclear Weapons and the Security and Economic Implications for States of the Acquisition and Further Development of These Weapons', Report of the UN Secretary-General, New York, 1968, Doc.A/6858; A.S. Ginsburg and G.S. Golitsyn, 'Global Consequences of a Nuclear War: A Review of Recent Soviet Studes', Stockholm International Peace Research Institute, *Yearbook*, 1985, p. 107; D.G. Bates, 'The Medical and Ecological Effects of Nuclear War', *McGill Law Journal*, vol. 28, 1983, p. 716; *The Human Cost of Nuclear War*, ed. S. Farrow and A. Chown, Medical Campaign Against Nuclear Weapons, 1983, pp. 16-35; 'The Long-Term Environmental and Medical Effects of Nuclear War', British Medical Association, 1986.

11 Schindler and Toman, op. cit., p. 57.

12 International Committee of the Red Cross, *Weapons That May Cause Unnecessary Suffering Or Have Indiscriminate Effects*, 1973, pp. 12-13.

13 *American Journal of International Law*, vol. 41, 1947, pp. 248-9.

14 See e.g. US Air Force Pamphlet, note 3, above.

15 *France* v. *Turkey* (1927), *PCIJ Reports*, Series A, No. 10.

16 Ibid., p. 18.

17   R.A. Falk, 'Towards a Legal Regime for Nuclear Weapons', *McGill Law Journal*, vol. 28, 1983, p. 519 at p. 527.

18   *Japanese Annual of International Law*, 1964, p. 212. For a discussion of the case, see R.A. Falk, 'The Shimoda Case: A Legal Appraisal of the Atomic Attacks upon Hiroshima and Nagasaki', *AJIL*, vol. 59, 1965, p. 759.

19   Ibid., at p. 235.

20   Adopted by consensus at the Diplomatic Conference on the Reaffirmation and Development of International Humanitarian Law Applicable in Armed Conflicts, Geneva, on 8 June 1977. In force on 7 December 1978. For text, see Schindler and Toman, op. cit., p. 551. There were 55 States Parties to the Protocol on 31 December 1985: see *International Review of the Red Cross*, no. 250, Jan.–Feb. 1986, pp. 72-3. The four Geneva Conventions of 1949 are the First Convention for the Amelioration of the Conditions of the Wounded and Sick in Armed Forces in the Field, Schindler and Toman, op. cit., p. 305; the Second Convention for the Amelioration of the Condition of the Wounded, Sick and Shipwrecked Members of the Armed Forces at Sea, ibid., p. 333; the Third Convention relative to the Treatment of Prisoners of War, ibid., p. 355; and the Fourth Convention relative to the Protection of Civilian Persons in Time of War, ibid., p. 427. 162 States were Parties to the four Geneva Conventions on 31 December 1985. Article 2 common to the Geneva Conventions provides that the Conventions are applicable to all cases of declared war or of any other armed conflict which may arise between two or more High Contracting Parties. According to Article 1(3) of Protocol I, the Protocol is applicable in the same situations. On signing the Protocol, the United Kingdom declared that 'armed conflict' implies a high level of intensity of military operations: *Hansard*, H.C., vol. 941, Written Answers, col. 236-7, 14 December 1977.

21   Hague Convention on Land Warfare, 1907, note 11 above, ninth preambular paragraph. The clause is named after one of the Russian delegates at the Hague Peace Conferences of 1899 and 1907. The Geneva Conventions of 1949, note 20 above, contain a similar provision: see Article 63 of the First Convention; Article 62 of the Second Convention; Article 142 of the Third Convention; and Article 158 of the Fourth Convention. See also Article 1(2) of Additional Protocol I of 1977, ibid.

22   See note 18 above.

23   Ibid., pp. 241-2.

24   Ibid.

25   J. Pictet, *Development and Principles of International Humanitarian Law*, 1985, pp. 75-6.

26   'Strategic' weapons are weapons of intercontinental range. 'Tactical' or 'battlefield' weapons have a range of less than 5500 km. See Stockholm International Peace Research Institute, *Yearbook*, 1985, Glossary. Strategic attack is often defined as aiming at the elimination of the attacked nation as a war-fighting unit. As some of the nuclear weapons for strategic use are themselves regarded as strategic targets, two different strategic modes for nuclear weapon employment have emerged: 'counter-force' against these weapons, and 'counter-value', corresponding to the classic strategic attack. See 'Comprehensive Study on Nuclear Weapons', note 10 above, p. 65, paras. 195-6.

27   D.J. Arbess, 'The International Law of Armed Conflict in Light of Contemporary Deterrence Strategies: Empty Promise or Meaningful Restraint?', *McGill Law Journal*, vol. 30, 1985, p. 89 at pp. 107-21. See also, Singh, op. cit., pp. 151-2. On the effects of nuclear weapons, see note 10 above.

28   See note 20 above.

29   On 12 December 1977. See *AJIL*, vol. 72, 1978, p. 407; and *Hansard*, House of

Commons Debates, vol. 941, Written Answers, cols. 236-7, 14 December 1977.

30   Vienna Convention on the Law of Treaties, 1969, Article 18(a), *International Legal Materials*, vol. 8, 1969, p. 679.

31   See note 29 above.

32   *AJIL*, vol. 72, 1978, p. 406. France participated in the Conference on the same understanding.

33   Below, pp. 32, 35.

34   Schindler and Toman, op. cit., p. 199. See also General Assembly Resolution 2675 (XXV) of 9 December 1970, in Schindler and Toman, op. cit., p. 203.

35   See note 11 above. See also Article 1 of the Hague Convention concerning Bombardment by Naval Forces in Time of War, 1907, ibid., p. 591.

36   See note 12 above.

37   Hague Conventions on Land Warfare, 1899 and 1907, note 11 above, Article 27. The same respect must also be shown to buildings dedicated to religion, art, science, charitable purposes and, according to the 1907 Convention, historic monuments. Such respect is forfeited if the buildings are being used for military purposes at the time of siege or bombardment, however.

38   Schindler and Toman, op. cit., p. 147.

39   Oppenheim, *International Law*, ed. Lauterpacht, 7th edn, vol. 2, p. 519. See also Nagendra Singh, op. cit., note 9, p. 54.

40   See note 18 above.

41   See note 20 above. See generally Part IV of Protocol I.

42   Cf. *The Law of War and Dubious Weapons*, SIPRI, 1976, pp. 32-4.

43   Additional Protocol I, 1977, note 20 above, Article 51(2). 'Attacks' means acts of violence against the adversary, whether in offence or defence: ibid., Article 49(1). Attacks against non-defended localities are prohibited by Article 59, and Article 60 requires agreed demilitarized zones to be respected. If civilians are made the object of attack, this constitutes a war crime. See Articles 85(3)(a) and 85(5).

44   Ibid., Article 48. This is entitled the 'basic rule'. Article 52(2) defines 'military objectives' as 'those objects which by their nature, location, purpose or use make an effective contribution to military action and whose total or partial destruction, capture or neutralisation, in the circumstances ruling at the time, offers a definite military advantage.' According to Article 52(3), moreover, in case of doubt whether an object which is normally dedicated to civilian purposes, such as a place of worship, a house or a school, is being used to make an effective contribution to military action, it shall be presumed not to be so used. However, Article 58 requires the parties to a conflict to take certain precautions against the effects of attacks. These include endeavouring to remove civilians and civilian objects from the vicinity of military objectives, and locating military objectives away from densely populated areas.

45   Ibid., Article 51(2). Threats of violence whose primary purpose is to terrorize the civilian population are also prohibited by this provision. Cf. Article 22 of the Hague Rules of Air Warfare, above, pp. 8-9.

46   H. Blix, 'Area Bombardment: Rules and Reasons', *British Yearbook of International Law*, vol. 49, 1978, p. 31 at p. 48.

47   For the definition of 'military objectives', see note 44 above.

48   Blix, op. cit., p. 50.

49   Ibid.

50   I.C.R.C., above, note 12, p. 13, para. 25. Blix, op. cit., p. 51.

51   Above. On signing the Protocol, however, the United Kingdom declared in relation to Article 51(5)(b) that 'the military advantage anticipated from an attack is intended to refer to the advantage anticipated from the attack considered as a

whole and not only from isolated or particular parts of the attack': Schindler and Toman, op. cit. p. 635.

52   Article 57(2)(a)(iii). See also Article 57(2)(a)(ii). If an indiscriminate attack is launched in the knowledge that it will cause excessive loss of life, injury to civilians or damage to civilian objects, this constitutes a war crime: see Articles 85(3)(b) and 85(5).

53   Blix, op. cit., p. 51.

54   *AJIL*, vol. 52, 1978, p. 406.

55   See above notes 28-33, and the accompanying text.

56   For material concerning the effects of nuclear weapons, see note 10 above.

57   Arbess, op. cit. The three contexts are: (1) a disarming first-strike against ground-launched intercontinental ballistic missiles calculated to force surrender without full-scale war; (2) a decapitating first-strike designed to destroy the adversary's command and control facilities; (3) a selective use of nuclear weapons in battlefields located in Europe or elsewhere, to prevent the collapse of Western forces in the face of an overwhelming attack.

58   Ibid., p. 116.

59   Ibid., p. 121.

60   Schindler and Toman, op. cit., p. 109.

61   Ibid., first preambular paragraph of the Geneva Protocol.

62   Ibid., second preambular paragraph. The treaties referred to include the Hague Conventions on Land Warfare, 1899 and 1907, note 11 above, Article 23(a) of which prohibits the use of poison or poisoned weapons; the Hague Declaration concerning Asphyxiating Gases, 1899, Schindler and Toman, op. cit., p. 99; and the Treaty of Versailles, 1919, 112 British and Foreign State Papers, p. 1. Article 171 of the Treaty provides that 'The use of asphyxiating, poisonous or other gases and all analogous liquids, materials or devices being prohibited, their manufacture and importation are strictly forbidden in Germany.'

63   Geneva Protocol, 1925, operative paragraph 1.

64   Cf. Brownlie, op. cit., p. 442; Nagendra Singh, op. cit., p. 163; Schwarzenberger, op. cit., pp. 37-8.

65   M. Akehurst, *A Modern Introduction to International Law*, 5th ed., 1984, p. 232.

66   For reservations to the Geneva Protocol, 1925, see Schindler and Toman, op. cit., pp. 115-19.

67   Ibid., p. 119. The Soviet Union made the same reservations.

68   Ibid.

69   This is in accordance with NATO's strategy of 'flexible response', according to which all military options would be available in the event of an attack, including a limited use of nuclear weapons.

70   See D.W. Bowett, 'Reservations to Non-restricted Multilateral Treaties', *BYIL*, vol. 48, 1976/77, p. 67 at p. 73; Brownlie, op. cit., p. 446. For the view that the Geneva Protocol was declaratory of customary international law with regard to chemical warfare, see Brownlie, ibid., p.442; Schwarzenberger, op. cit., p. 38. See also General Assembly Resolution 2603 (XXIV) of 16 December 1969, Schindler and Toman, op. cit., p. 125.

71   See Oppenheim, op. cit., p. 344.

72   Akehurst, op. cit., p. 236.

73   Oppenheim, op. cit., p. 351; Nagendra Singh, op. cit., pp. 218-23. This view assumes that the first use of nuclear weapons is illegal, therefore.

74   E.g. Schwarzenberger, op. cit., pp. 40-1, 48.

75   *Portugal* v. *Germany* (1928), 2 *UN Reports of International Arbitral Awards*, p. 1012.

76   The use of armed force in reprisal would appear to be incompatible with Articles

2(3), 2(4), and 51 of the UN Charter. See also the General Assembly Declaration of Principles of International Law concerning Friendly Relations and Co-operation among States In Accordance with the Charter of the United Nations, annexed to Resolution 2625 (XXV) of 24 October 1970. The Resolution, which was adopted without vote, approves the Declaration, which is evidence of the consensus among UN Member States on the meaning of the Charter's principles. It provides, inter alia, that 'States have a duty to refrain from acts of reprisal involving the use of armed force.' See also D.W. Bowett, 'Reprisals Involving Recourse to Armed Force', *AJIL*, vol. 66, 1972, p. 1.

77   Brownlie, op. cit., p. 445. See also, G.I.A.D. Draper, *The Red Cross Conventions*, 1958, p. 99.
78   See note 20 above.
79   See Article 46 of the First Convention; Article 47 of the Second Convention; and Article 13 of the Third Convention.
80   See e.g. Articles 19 and 24 of the First Convention.
81   See note 20 above.
82   Fourth Convention, ibid., Article 4. The provisions of Part II of the Convention are wider in application, however: see note 105, below.
83   See note 20 above.
84   Civilian objects are all objects which are not military objectives as defined in Article 52(2) of the Additional Protocol. See note 44 above.
85   Additional Protocol I, 1977, note 20 above, Article 53(c). See also Article 4(4) of the Hague Convention for the Protection of Cultural Property in the Event of Armed Conflict, Schindler and Toman, op. cit., p. 657.
86   Additional Protocol I, Article 54(4). Such objects include foodstuffs, agricultural areas for the production of foodstuffs, crops and livestock.
87   Ibid., Article 56(4). The works and installations to which the provision refers are dams, dykes and nuclear power stations: see Article 56(1). Reprisals against military objectives located at or near such works or installations are also prohibited.
88   Ibid., Article 55(2). The obligation upon the parties to an armed conflict to protect the natural environment is discussed further below.
89   Report of the US Delegation to the Diplomatic Conference on the Reaffirmation and Development of International Humanitarian Law Applicable in Armed Conflicts, Geneva, 1974–77. See *AJIL*, vol. 72, 1978, p. 405.
90   Ibid., p. 406.
91   Above.
92   See note 30 above.
93   Article 2(1)(d) of the Vienna Convention, 1969.
94   Ibid., Article 21(3).
95   See G.A. Aldrich, 'New Life for the Laws of War', *AJIL*, vol. 75, 1981, p. 764, at p. 781, note 48.
96   Cf. Adam Roberts, 'The Relevance of Laws of War in the Nuclear Age' in *Nuclear Weapons. The Peace Movement and The Law*, 1986, ed. J. Dewar, A. Paliwala, S. Picciotto and M. Ruete, p. 25 at p. 30. Cf. also Hansard, House of Lords Debates, vol. 472, cols. 630-650, 12th March 1986. The Vienna Convention on the Law of Treaties, 1969, provides that a treaty shall be interpreted in good faith in accordance with the ordinary meaning of its terms in their context and in the light of its object and purpose. According to Article 31(2)(a), the context includes 'any agreement relating to the treaty which was made by all the parties in connexion with the conclusion of the treaty'.
97   See note 30 above.
98   According to which the material breach of a multilateral treaty by one party

allows, *inter alia*, another party specially affected by the breach to invoke it as a ground for suspending the operation of the treaty as between itself and the defaulting State: Article 60(2) of the Vienna Convention, 1969. A 'material breach' is defined in Article 60(3) as '(a) a repudiation of the treaty not sanctioned by the present Convention; or (b) the violation of a provision essential to the accomplishment of the object and purpose of the treaty.'

99   U.N. Conference on the Law of Treaties, Official Records, 1969, p. 112, paras. 20-2. Doc.A/Conf.39/11 and Add. 1.

100   Article 4 of the Vienna Convention, 1969.

101   *Legal Consequences for States of the Continued Presence of South Africa in Namibia (South-West Africa) Notwithstanding Security Council Resolution 276*, Advisory Opinion, *ICJ Reports*, 1971, p. 16.

102   Ibid., para. 96 of Opinion.

103   The same applies to Additional Protocol I of 1977, note 20 above. See also Article 51(8) of the Protocol.

104   Cf. Draper, op. cit., pp. 98-100.

105   See Article 1 of each of the four Geneva Conventions, 1949, note 20 above. See also the ICJ's Judgment on the merits in the 'Case concerning Military and Parliamentary Activities in and against Nicaragua', *ICJ Reports*, 1986, p. 14 at pp. 114-15.

106   See note 20 above.

107   Ibid. Articles 13–26 constitute Part II of the Convention, the provisions of which protect the entire populations of the countries in conflict and not merely protected persons as defined in Article 4: above.

108   See e.g. Article 35 of the First Convention; Articles 12 and 36 of the Second Convention; and Articles 20 and 21 of the Fourth Convention, note 20 above.

109   On the distinction between neutrality and neutralisation, see J.G. Starke, *Introduction to International Law*, 9th ed., 1984, pp. 117-19.

110   Schindler and Toman, op. cit., p. 847. The United Kingdom is not a party to the Convention. Cf. Article 1 of the Hague Convention concerning the Rights and Duties of Neutral Powers in Naval War, 1907, ibid., p. 855.

111   Brownlie, op. cit., p. 444.

112   On the effects of nuclear weapons, see note 10 above.

113   See note 20 above.

114   The view expressed by the Australian representative at the Diplomatic Conference, note 20 above. Official Records, vol. XIV, p. 171, para. 2. Doc.CDDH/III/SR.20.

115   Cf. Arbess, op. cit., p. 97.

116   Schindler and Toman, op. cit., p. 131. As at 31 December 1984, 47 states were parties to the Convention, which is in force. Parties include the United Kingdom, the United States and the Soviet Union. The Convention is annexed to General Assembly resolution 31/72 of 10 December 1976, which was adopted by 96 votes to 8 with 30 abstentions. The United Kingdom, the United States and the Soviet Union all voted in favour of the resolution. France abstained and China was absent.

117   *ILM*, vol. 19, 1980, p. 1524. As at 31 December 1984, 24 states were parties to the Convention, which is in force. Parties included the Soviet Union and China, but the United Kingdom, the United States and France had only signed the Convention.

118   Fourth preambular paragraph. According to a French reservation formulated on signature, 'the fourth paragraph of the preamble . . . which reproduces the provisions of Article 35(3) of Additional Protocol I, applies only to States Parties to that Protocol': *Multilateral Treaties Deposited with the*

Secretary-General (Status as at 31 December 1984), p. 717.

119 Report of the UN Conference on the Human Environment, UN Doc.A/ CONF.48/14; *ILM*, vol. 11, 1972, p. 1415. The Stockholm Declaration was adopted by acclamation by the 113 states participating in the Conference. The Soviet Union and other communist states did not attend, however.

120 *Yearbook of the International Law Commission*, 1980, vol. II, (part 2), pp. 26, 32. In its discussion of the draft Code of Offences Against The Peace And Security of Mankind, moreover, the ILC considered that, although not any damage would constitute a crime against humanity, the development of technology and the considerable harm it sometimes did might lead to certain kinds of damage to the human environment being regarded as crimes against humanity. It was pointed out that there are conventions, such as the Nuclear Test-Ban Treaty, prohibiting certain tests which could harm the environment, which seem to have been motivated by the need to protect the environment: UN General Assembly Official Records, 39th Session, Supp. No. 10, Doc.A/39/10, Report of the ILC on the work of its 36th session, p. 27, para. 58.

121 Above.

122 Above.

123 The Webster doctrine from the *Caroline Case* (1841), 29 *British and Foreign State Papers*, pp. 1137-38.

124 Brownlie, op. cit., pp. 446-7.

125 The ability to survive a nuclear attack and launch a retaliatory blow large enough to inflict intolerable damage on the opponent. See SIPRI, *Yearbook*, 1985, Glossary.

126 Ibid. The strategy of 'flexible response' was adopted by NATO in December 1967. See *NATO Handbook* 1985, pp. 26-7.

127 I. Brownlie, *The Use of Force by States in International Law*, 1963, p. 263.

128 Ibid.

129 Schindler and Toman, op. cit., p. 171. The Convention was adopted unanimously by the General Assembly of the United Nations on 9th December 1948. The United States has signed the Convention but not ratified it. However, the prohibition of genocide may be regarded not merely as part of customary international law, but as a rule of *jus cogens*. See I. Brownlie, *Principles of Public International Law*, 3rd ed., 1979, p. 513.

130 Genocide Convention, Article 4. It is submitted that a state can be criminally liable for an act of genocide, as well as an individual. Cf. Article 19 of the International Law Commission's draft articles on state responsibility, note 120 above; *Yearbook of the International Law Commission*, 1976, vol. II (Part 2), pp. 118-19; Barcelona Traction Case, *Belgium* v. *Spain, ICJ Reports*, 1970, p. 3, paras. 33-4 of judgment.

131 Cf. Arbess, op. cit., p. 121.

132 B. Bryant, 'Part I: Substantive Scope of the Convention', *Harvard International Law Journal*, vol. 16, 1975, p. 686 at p. 692.

133 N. Robinson, *The Genocide Convention – Its Origins and Interpretation* (1949), reprinted in Hearings on the Genocide Convention Before a Subcommittee of the Senate Committee on Foreign Relations, 81st Congress, 2nd Session, p. 487 at p. 498 (1950).

134 Brownlie, op. cit., p. 444.

135 Schindler and Toman, op. cit., p. 823.

136 Ibid., p. 833.

137 Brownlie, op. cit., p. 562. Cf. *Hansard*, House of Lords, Debates, vol. 253, col. 831, 2 December 1963. The Nuremberg Principles were formulated by the International Law Commission in 1950: Schindler and Toman, op. cit., p. 835.

138 *Nazi Conspiracy and Aggression, Opinion and Judgment*, US Government Print-
     ing Office, Washington, 1947, p. 48.
139 Hess was sentenced to life imprisonment by the International Military Tribunal
     in 1946. The Soviet Union has consistently refused to agree to his release.
140 The International Law Commission has recently considered whether the use of
     nuclear weapons should be included in the draft Code of Offences Against the
     Peace and Security of Mankind. See *Yearbook of the International Law Com-
     mission*, 1984, vol. I, pp. 35-55.
141 R.A. Falk, L. Meyrowitz and J. Sanderson, 'Nuclear Weapons and International
     Law', *World Order Studies Programme*, Occasional Paper No. 10, Princeton
     University, 1981, pp. 68-9.
142 Adopted on 24 November 1961. Schindler and Toman, op. cit., p. 121.
143 General Assembly Resolution 1653 (XVI), operative paragraph 1(a).
144 Ibid., operative paragraph 1(b).
145 Ibid., operative paragraph 1(d).
146 Brownlie, op. cit., note 9 above, p. 448.
147 Schindler and Toman, op. cit., pp. 122-3.
148 Among the states which considered that the issue should not be separated from
     the general question of disarmament were Australia, Brazil, Denmark, France,
     Italy, Turkey and the United Kingdom. The Canadian representative argued
     that the General Assembly should take no action which might hamper the suc-
     cess of the nuclear test-ban negotiations, a view shared by Pakistan and Thai-
     land. China stated that she had consistently advocated the elimination of nuclear
     weapons but had always voted against proposals for prohibition without control.
     See UN General Assembly, 16th Session, Official Records, First Committee,
     1189th Meeting *et seq.*; Plenary Meetings, 1043rd, 1047th, 1049th and 1063rd
     Meetings.
149 Brownlie, op. cit., note 9 above, p. 449. Italy also argued that Article 51 of the
     UN Charter does not exclude the use of nuclear weapons in self-defence. See
     Italy's proposed amendment to the draft resolution, Doc.A/C.1/L.295, discussed
     at the 1191st-1194th Meetings of the First Committee. Similarly, the United
     Kingdom claimed that the right of self-defence implies the right to use whatever
     force is necessary to repel aggression: First Committee, 1190th Meeting, para. 7.
150 The law which determines whether a state may use armed force.
151 The law which regulates the relations between the parties to an armed conflict.
152 See *The Law of War and Dubious Weapons*, note 42 above, pp. 1-3.
153 At the 1975 Session of the Geneva Diplomatic Conference, note 20 above, the
     representative of the United States asserted that 'rules such as the ones on which
     we are working in this Conference are designed for conventional warfare and
     would not fit in well in the context of the use of weapons of mass destruction.' Cf.
     the comment of the Indian representative at the Conference on Disarmament,
     306th Plenary Meeting, 4th April 1985, UN Doc.DC.PV.306, p. 21.
154 Brownlie, op. cit., note 9, p. 449 above.
155 See e.g. resolution 36/100 of 9 December 1981, Declaration on the Prevention of
     Nuclear Catastrophe, adopted by 82 votes to 19, with 41 abstentions; resolution
     39/63H of 12 December 1984, Convention on the Prohibition of the Use of Nu-
     clear Weapons, adopted by 128 votes to 17, with 5 abstentions.
156 Cf. Akehurst, op. cit., p. 232.
157 This point was well made by Professor Boyle of the University of Illinois in evi-
     dence to the Nuclear Warfare Tribunal in London, January 1985, below. The
     distinction between possession and deployment is also recognized by the UN
     Human Rights Committee, below.
158 Professor Boyle, note 157 above.

159 The Outer Space Treaty, 1967, Article 4. See *UNTS*, vol. 610, p. 205.
160 The Antarctic Treaty, 1959, Article 1. See *UNTS*, vol. 402, p. 71. Article 1 of the Treaty provides for the non-militarization of Antarctica.
161 Treaty on the Prohibition of the Emplacement of Nuclear Weapons and Other Weapons of Mass Destruction on the Sea-bed and Ocean Floor and in the Subsoil Thereof, 1970, Article 1. See *ILM*, vol. 10, 1971, p. 145.
162 E.g. the Treaty of Tlatelolco, 1967, prohibiting nuclear weapons in Latin America, *UNTS*, vol. 634, p. 281; the South Pacific Nuclear Free Zone Treaty, 1985, *ILM*, vol. 24, 1985, p. 1442. See Chapter 8 below.
163 According to Article 88 of the UN Convention on the Law of the Sea, 1982, '[t]he high seas shall be reserved for peaceful purposes'. See *ILM*, vol. 21, 1982, p. 1261. 'Peaceful' is generally understood to mean 'non-aggressive' rather than 'non-military'.
164 See e.g. Article 3 of the Universal Declaration of Human Rights, 1948, UN Doc.A/811. The Declaration is considered by many to have the status of customary international law. See e.g. J.P. Humphrey, 'The Universal Declaration of Human Rights: Its History, Impact and Judicial Character', in *Human Rights Thirty Years After the Universal Declaration*, ed. B.G. Ramcharan, 1979, p. 21 at p. 28. See also Article 6(1) of the International Covenant on Civil and Political Rights, 1966, reproduced in *AJIL*, vol. 61, 1967, p. 870. The United Kingdom and the Soviet Union are parties to the Covenant but the United States is not.
165 International Covenant, above. Article 4(1) and (2).
166 The Human Rights Committee was established under Article 28 of the Covenant to monitor its implementation by states parties.
167 UN General Assembly Official Records, 37th Session, Supp. No. 40 (Doc.A/37/40), Report of the Human Rights Committee, p. 93, Annex V, para. 2.
168 The capability to destroy within a very short period of time all or a very substantial portion of the adversary's strategic nuclear forces, e.g. Intercontinental ballistic missiles and submarine-launched ballistic missiles: see SIPRI, *Yearbook*, 1985, Glossary.
169 Similarly, the development of anti-submarine warfare systems means that submarine-based nuclear missiles are likely to be fired sooner rather than later. In the event of conventional armed conflict, risks would also be inherent in the delegation of decision-making powers to military commanders in the field: the decision to use nuclear weapons could be made earlier than intended by political leaders.
170 General comment 14(23) on Article 6 of the International Covenant on Civil and Political Rights, paras. 4 and 5, adopted on 2nd November 1984: UN General Assembly Official Records, 40th Session, Supp. No. 40, (Doc.A/40/40), Report of the Human Rights Committee, p. 162, Annex VI. The comment gave rise to criticism that the Human Rights Committee had deviated from its mandate: ibid., p. 6, para. 27.
171 Ibid., p. 162, para. 6.
172 Above.
173 Article 1(1) of the UN Charter.
174 Above.
175 Above.
176 Above.
177 Above.
178 *Nazi Conspiracy and Aggression*, note 138 above, p. 53.
179 Above.
180 Conspiracy to commit genocide shall be a punishable act according to Article 3(b) of the Genocide Convention.

181   Ibid., Article 4. It is submitted that a state can be criminally liable for conspiracy to commit genocide, as well as an individual: see note 130 above.

182   *De Jure Belli Ac Pacis*, first published in 1625.

183   The view expressed by the representative of the International Committee of the Red Cross at the Diplomatic Conference, note 20 above, Doc.CDDH/III/SR.2, p. 13, para. 2.

184   Cf. Eugene Rostow, Remarks, *Proceedings of the American Society of International Law*, vol. 76, 1982, p. 25.

185   Arbess, op. cit., p. 103.

186   *Trials of War Criminals before the Nuremberg Military Tribunals under Control Council Law No. 10*, 1950–53, Washington, vol. XI, p. 1272.

187   Brownlie, op. cit., note 9 above, p. 450.

188   *Hansard*, H.C., vol. 81, Oral Answers, col. 293-4, 19 June 1985.

189   The Tribunal was organised by a British group, Lawyers for Nuclear Disarmament. The members of the Tribunal were Sean MacBride (Chairman), Richard Falk, Dorothy Hodgkin, and Maurice Wilkins. The intention of the organizers was to present the Tribunal with the arguments about nuclear weapons policy. Government representatives were invited to attend but declined the invitation. In order to offset their absence, each witness was cross-examined from a viewpoint which incorporated official thinking.

190   London Nuclear Warfare Tribunal, *Interim Declaration*, January 1985, preliminary conclusions, para. 5.

191   Ibid., para. 6.

192   The opinion expressed by Dean Acheson with regard to the Cuban missile crisis: see A. Chayes, *The Cuban Missile Crisis*, 1974, ch. 1.

193   As in the resolution on the Distinction between Military Objectives and Non-Military Objectives, adopted by the Institute of International Law on 9 September 1969. See Schindler and Toman, op. cit., p. 201. The Resolution was adopted by 60 votes to 1, with 2 abstentions.

194   Article 38(1)(d) of the Statute of the International Court of Justice.

3   Do 'laws' regulate nuclear weapons?

Mark W. Janis

Introduction

It is a commonplace that international law is not 'law' like municipal
law. Among other things, international law is often not enforced. This
specific infirmity is nowhere more debilitating than with respect to that
part of international law which relates to armed conflicts. The pages of
history are replete with the wars international law has all too plainly
failed to prevent or even to moderate. This dismal history is all the
more discouraging because there is a greater need today than ever before, as a result of the development of nuclear weapons, to fashion
some sort of effective legal restraint to war.

The legal philosopher, John Austin, in some influential nineteenth
century passages, asserted that what we call international law is not
really 'law' but rather a sort of morality.[1] More recently, H.L.A. Hart
has fashioned a new analytical model for understanding law.[2] This
chapter employs Hart's new model jurisprudence to analyse the nature
of the international laws restraining war and regulating nuclear
weapons. It attempts to answer Austin's question of whether such laws
are really 'law' and, in so doing, moves a little beyond Hart's model in
proposing a 'structural spectrum' which might be helpful in understanding the 'law'-like quality of any purported legal system.

Hart's model and international law

International law plays two roles in Hart's new classic, *The Concept of*
Law. First, it appears alongside primitive law as one of those borderline

53

cases which inspire some people to seek out definitions of the word 'law'.[3] Much more important is international law's second appearance. Hart devotes the tenth and final chapter of his book exclusively to the question of whether international law is properly characterised as 'law'.[4] In a sense, Hart has assumed the mission launched by international law's 'father', Hugo Grotius. Grotius in 1625 wrote that he sought to persuade his readers not to 'believe either that nothing is allowable, or that everything is'.[5] Hart seeks to find a similar middle ground, arguing that while international law is in many ways not like municipal law, it is still 'law'.

The crucial aspect of Hart's proof comes in a playing-off against the great Austrian legal philosopher, Hans Kelsen. Kelsen has argued that a basic norm, a *Grundnorm*, is both a prerequisite for a legal system and extant in international law, but Hart counters that it is entirely possible for a society to 'live by rules imposing obligations on its members as "binding", even though they are regarded simply as a set of separate rules, not unified by or deriving their validity from any more basic rule'.[6] Specifically, Hart maintains 'that there is no basic rule providing general criteria of validity for the rules of international law, and that the rules which are in fact operative constitute not a system but a set of rules.'[7]

This is an important step in Hart's analysis of the nature of international law because he has already postulated that municipal law is definitionally characterized by a union of primary and secondary rules: primary rules being those which impose obligations, and secondary rules being those which recognize, change and adjudicate primary rules.[8] International law, in Hart's eyes, is different from municipal law in that it does not have secondary rules, e.g. it lacks 'the formal structure of . . . a legislature, courts with compulsory jurisdiction and officially organized sanctions.[9] Without a set of secondary rules, international law is really more like primitive law than it is like municipal law.[10] None the less, Hart sees no good reason not to call a legal system composed of only primary rules 'law'.[11] Compared to municipal law, Hart thinks that international law is analogous in content though not in form.[12]

Hart's characterization of international law as 'not a system but a set of rules' is a very useful observation. Its great utility is in the leverage it gives to lift much of the theoretical weight that is usually imposed upon international law by the expectation that any legal system really being 'law' must include effective legislative, adjudicative and administrative structures. Nowhere is this leverage more needed than in contemplating the laws restraining war.

Laws, war and nuclear weapons

The most problematic rules of international law are those dealing with international conflict. Despite 3000 years, we seem little further along the road to international peace than when Isaiah prophesied:

> And they shall beat their swords into ploughshares
> And their spears into pruning hooks;
> Nation shall not lift up sword against nation,
> Neither shall they learn war any more.[13]

There have long been laws purporting to regulate international conflict. For example, in the fourth century BC, India's *Book of Manu* instructed that:

> When [the King] fights with his foes in battle, let him not strike with weapons concealed [in wood], nor with [such as are] barbed, poisoned, or the points of which are blazing with fire.
> Let him not strike one who [in flight] has climbed on an eminence, nor a eunuch, nor one who joins the palms of his hands [in supplication], nor one who [flees] with flying hair, nor one who sits down, nor one who says 'I am thine';
> Nor one who sleeps, nor one who has lost his coat of mail, nor one who is naked, nor one who is disarmed.[14]

In medieval Europe, too, there were attempts to moderate the military cruelties of the day. One legal device employed by the Church was the 'Peace' such as the one imposed by the Archbishop of Arles in 1035 for parts of the south of France:

> This is the peace or truce of God which we have received from heaven through the inspiration of God, and we beseech you to accept it and observe it even as we have done; namely, that all Christians, friends and enemies, neighbours and strangers, should keep true and lasting peace one with another from vespers on Wednesday to sunrise on Monday, so that during these four days and five nights, all persons may have peace, and, trusting in this peace, may go about their business without fear of their enemies.[15]

In the sixteenth century, Spanish jurists – Vitoria, Ayala and Suarez – began to collect and explicate Biblical and classical sources to fashion a theory of the laws of wars: when and how nations should fight. These works in turn served as a foundation for the writings of the Dutchman, Hugo Grotius, who is generally acknowledged as the principal creator of what we now know as international law. Grotius' seminal book, *De Jure Belli ac Pacis (The Law of War and Peace)*, is an impressive collection of authority, drawn from Greek and Roman literature. What most concerned Grotius, an active diplomat as well as a scholar, was the horror of the Thirty Years War. Between 1618 and 1648 large parts of Central Europe were laid waste; millions of Europeans were slaughtered in battle and in sack. Grotius lamented:

> I have had many and weighty reasons for undertaking to write upon this subject. Throughout the Christian world I have observed a lack of restraint in relation to war, such as even barbarous races should be ashamed of; I observed that men rush to arms for slight causes, or no cause at all, and that when arms have once been taken up there is no longer any respect for law, divine or human; it is as if, in accordance with a general decree, frenzy had openly been let loose for the committing of all crimes.[16]

Grotius sought to set a middle course between those who thought that states and sovereigns were subject to no laws and those who had 'come to the point of forbidding all uses of arms to the Christian, whose rule of conduct above everything else comprises the duty of loving all men.'[17] Grotius thought that war was inevitable and even proper in some circumstances, but that there were natural and positive (state-imposed) legal limits to the declaration and conduct of war.

At the conclusion of the Thirty Years War and for a century and a half thereafter Europe entered a period of what might be termed 'reasonable' wars. Conflicts in Europe were generally set-piece battles waged by professional armies fighting for fixed and limited political objectives. Civilian populations (often perceived as prizes) were usually left more or less unharmed by military forces. Talleyrand could write to Napoleon in 1806:

> Three centuries of civilization have given to Europe a law of nations, for which . . . human nature cannot be sufficiently grateful. This law is founded on the principle, that nations ought to do to one another in peace, the most good, and in war, least evil possible.[18]

Into the early nineteenth century, the laws of war continued to develop and, to a considerable extent, to progress. Especially notable were treaties concluded to limit war or to remove its causes. For example, in 1815, the principal European powers agreed to the perpetual neutrality of Switzerland, a pact respected to this day.[19] In 1817, the United States and the United Kingdom agreed to limit their naval forces on the Great

Lakes, a settlement eventually leading to the demilitarization of the United States–Canadian border.[20]

The effort to codify and develop the laws of war and control the use of arms became even more earnest as the late nineteenth century unfolded. There were profound hopes that war might eventually be abolished now that civilization had become so advanced. In 1856, Great Britain, Austria, France, Prussia, Russia, Sardinia and Turkey signed the Declaration of Paris, hoping to settle outstanding differences concerning the rights of neutral shipping in times of war.[21] In 1864, Switzerland, Baden, Belgium, Denmark, Spain, France, Hesse, Italy, the Netherlands, Portugal, Prussia and Würtemberg signed the Geneva Red Cross Convention, protecting hospital and ambulance crews.[22] In 1868, seventeen countries including Great Britain, Austria, Hungary, France, Italy, Prussia, Russia and Turkey, signed the Declaration of St Petersburg, renouncing the use of certain explosive projectiles.[23]

Between 1899 and 1907, in the highest tide of idealism, there issued the various and detailed Hague Conventions. The Conventions were the product of the two Hague Peace Conferences called in 1898 by Tsar Nicholas II of Russia who declared 'that the present moment would be very favorable for seeking, by means of international discussion, the most effectual means of insuring to all peoples the benefits of a real and durable peace, and above all, of putting an end to the progressive development of the present armaments.'[24] The very listing of the Hague Conventions illuminates the aspirations of the time: on the Pacific Settlement of Disputes (1899); on the Laws and Customs of War and Land (1899); on the Adaption to Maritime Warfare of the Principles of the Geneva Convention of 1864 (1899); on Prohibiting Launching of Projectiles and Explosives from Balloons (1899); on Prohibiting Use of Expanding Bullets (1899); on Prohibiting Use of Gases (1899); on the Exemption of Hospital Ships from Taxation in Time of War (1904); on the Pacific Settlement of International Disputes (1907); on the Limitation of Force for Recovery of Contract Debts (1907); on the Opening of Hostilities (1907); on the Laws and Customs of War on Land (1907); on the Rights and Duties of Neutral Powers and Persons in War on Land (1907); on the status of Enemy Merchant Ships at the Outbreak of Hostilities (1907); on the Conversion of Merchant Ships into War Ships (1907); on the Laying of Automatic Submarine Contact Mines (1909); on Bombardment by Naval Forces in Time of War (1907); on the Application to Maritime Warfare of Principles of the Geneva Convention (1907); on Restrictions with regard to Right of Capture in Naval War (1907); on the Establishment of an International Prize Court (1907); on the Rights and Duties of Neutral Powers in Naval War (1907); and on prohibiting Discharge of Projectiles and Explosures from Balloons (1907).[25]

However, the great hopes behind the many Hague and like conventions came to nothing. Joseph Choate, a delegate of the United States to the Second Hague Peace Conference, wrote in 1913 that there were preparations for a Third Hague Conference in 1915 and plans set 'to celebrate the completion of a century of unbroken peace between ourselves and the all the other great nations of the earth'.[26] No third Conference was held; the century of unbroken peace was missed by a year. Beginning in 1914, Europe fought a war with great savagery; aerial bombardment and poison gas played new roles. Mankind had apparently not progressed all that far. The warring nations issued learned volumes in the midst of the conflict accusing their enemies of destroying the fabric of international law.[27] The truth was that international law had neither kept the peace nor much mitigated the slaughter. What was to be done?

Post-war reactions to the failure of international law were curious. On the one hand, many foresook international law as a path to world peace. Some academics, for example, left the discipline of international law to fashion new disciplines called international relations and international politics in the belief that only by integrating politics, economics, sociology, history and other scholarly perspectives could they adequately identify the causes of conflicts and prevent future wars.[28] Others turned all the more fervently to international law, thinking that the cause of the Great War was that the laws of war had heretofore been too loosely drafted. Indeed, though the laws of war had attempted to moderate and reduce the chances of conflict, war itself remained legal when undertaken to defend rights in international law.[29]

It was in the spirit of new and prohibitive laws of war that diplomats representing Germany, the United States, Belgium, France, Great Britain, Italy, Japan, Poland and Czechoslovakia concluded the Kellogg–Briand Pact of 27 August 1928.[30] The parties condemned 'recourse to war for the solution of international controversies, and renounce[d] it as an instrument of national policy in their relations with one another.'[31] They agreed 'that the settlement or solution of all disputes or conflicts of whatever nature or of whatever origin they may be, which may arise among them, shall never be sought except by pacific means'.[32] But the Pact was an exercise in futility. The scholars in this case had been more prescient than the statesmen. Germany and Japan utterly disregarded their pledge not to use force. A Second World War soon ensued even more dreadful than the First. Grotius himself could well have been shocked by the new barbarities visited on Europe and across the globe. Between 1939 and 1945, the gap between the theory of the laws of war and the realities of international practice was wider than ever before. The laws of war and peace stood, and to a sad degree still stand, discredited and in disarray.

The discredit and disarray comes at a time when the desire to limit war with law is all the greater because of the development of nuclear weapons and other advanced means of destruction. There have been countless pleas for arms control and disarmament.[33] Yet, the record is dismal. Since the end of the Second World War in 1945, there have been more than 100 new wars and more than 25 million more fatalities.[34] Though for 'forty years the nations of the world have been obsessed with nuclear weapons and the need to abolish them, [t]he results have been pitiful.'[35]

'Law' and the structural spectrum of legal systems

If Hart is right about international law, then the laws regulating nuclear weapons and warfare, like other rules of international law, are primary rules linked to no secondary rules. Describing such a situation, Hart says that primary rules without secondary rules are afflicted with three sorts of 'defects', defects which inspire societies to develop secondary rules. He writes that primary rules, standing alone, tend to be uncertain, static and inefficient.[36] Let us test these theoretical defects against the realities of the laws mentioned above.

Hart seems to be most right about efficiency. He says that a 'simple form of social life' has 'no agency specially empowered to ascertain finally, and authoritatively, the fact of [a law's] violation.'[37] Ideas about efficacy are included in this defect: '[i]t is obvious that the waste of time involved in the [simple] group's unorganized efforts to catch and punish offenders, and the smouldering vendettas which may result from self help in the absence of an official monopoly of "sanctions", may be serious.'[38]

This is a fair, even gentle, characterization of the disturbing realities of the efficiency of the laws restraining war or of the laws regulating nuclear weapons. How very true it is that the Hague Conventions were 'inefficiently' applied in moderating the slaughter of the First and Second World Wars. How equally true it is that the Kellogg-Briand Pact and the Charter of the United Nations have been 'inefficient' in preventing the outbreak of hundreds of wars, large and small. Nor has the Treaty on the Non-Proliferation of Nuclear Weapons succeeded in arresting the spread of nuclear arms.[39]

It is at this stage that Hart's model of international law is particularly useful. The laws restraining war and regulating nuclear weapons certainly look like rules, but perhaps they are only primary rules unable authoritatively to ascertain 'the fact of violation' and 'to catch and punish offenders'.[40] It is indeed helpful to think of such international laws as primary rules lacking secondary rules.

Yet the model does a little less well with Hart's other two defects. Hart writes that primary rules without secondary rules are also uncertain and static. With respect to uncertainty, how true is it to assert that international law, like a 'simple form of social control', has trouble settling doubts 'as to what the [primary] rules are or as to the precise scope of some given rule?'[41] Or, with respect to their static nature, how right is it to say that international law is a simple society which has as its 'only mode of change in the rules known to [it] . . . the slow process of growth, whereby courses of conduct once thought optional become first habitual or usual, and then obligatory.'[42]

Hart's assertions about international law's uncertainty and static form seem to founder on the rocks of the many treaties framed to prohibit and regulate armed conflicts and nuclear weapons. Such treaties are often quite detailed and are usually generated rapidly rather like municipal legislation.[43] Can it be said that international conferences play a role in international law rather similar to that played by secondary rules in a municipal system? Is it right to characterize international law being unlike municipal law because it is bereft of secondary rules?

It may make more sense to visualize any legal system, international or domestic, as placed somewhere along a structural spectrum. The place of each legal system depends on the degree to which the legal system has settled secondary rules and institutions responsible for and capable of fixing, changing and enforcing the system's primary rules.

Not only do various sorts of international law fall at different places along the spectrum but so, too, do various sorts of municipal law. For example, some municipal systems, e.g. that in the Soviet Union, may well assign less authority to its legal system (and more to its bureaucratic/administrative structures) than would another society. This would not make the Soviet legal system any less a legal system, it only means that a proper description of the Soviet legal system would explain the degree to which legal structures (and not other mechanisms) are actually employed to regulate specific aspects of that society.[44]

Similarly, the nature of any sort of international law varies along the structural spectrum. International law is not monolithic. Rather, there are a great variety of international legal systems, some more structured than others. For example, the international legal systems embodied in European economic law or European human rights law are much more structured with effective institutions and secondary rules than are other aspects of international law,[45] such as the laws restraining wars.

The answer, then, to the question of whether or not the laws restraining war and regulating nuclear weapons are really 'law' is that they are certainly 'law' in so far as 'law' means a collection of rules defining obligations. Whether these rules also constitute a legal system is a second question. Hart seems to say that they are not because of the absence of secondary rules. However, it is arguable that there are, in fact, secondary rules available even to these most frail of international laws, i.e. in the international conferences which frame treaties and give them certainty and modernity. Nonetheless, such secondary rules fall far short of the structures we associate with much more developed legal systems like those in Britain and the United States or even those in more developed parts of international law like European regional law.

Notes

1   J. Austin, *The Province of Jurisprudence Determined*, 1st ed. 1832, pp. 207-8.
2   H.L.A. Hart, *The Concept of Law* (1961) [hereinafter cited as 'Hart'].
3   Ibid., pp. 3-4. This first notion is ultimately rejected by Hart. He argues that there are more fundamental problems, intrinsic even to ordinary municipal law, which in truth trigger the definitional perplexities. Ibid., pp. 4-17. The unimportance of international law in this respect is best seen at p. 77.
4   Ibid., pp. 208-31.
5   H. Grotius, *Prolegomena to the Law of War and Peace* 21 (1957 ed. trans. Kelsey) (hereinafter cited as 'Grotius').
6   Hart, op. cit., p. 228.
7   Ibid., 230-1.
8   Ibid., 77-96.
9   Ibid., 226.
10 Ibid., 209.
11 Hart is satisfied that international law may be 'law' without an Austin-like sovereign's sanction; ibid., 211-21, and even though some may confuse international law with morality; ibid., 221-26.
12 Ibid., pp. 226-31.
13 2:2, 4.
14 L. Friedman (ed.), 1 *The Law of War: A Documentary History* 3, 1972, (hereinafter cited as 'Friedman').
15 T.N. Dupuy and G.M. Hammerman (eds.), *A Documentary History of Arms Control and Disarmament* 6, 1973, (hereinafter cited as 'Dupuy and Hammerman').
16 Grotius, op. cit., p. 21.
17 Ibid.
18 Translated in T.D. Woolsey, *International Law* 306, 1st edn 1860.
19 See Dupuy and Hammerman, pp. 38-9.
20 Ibid., 39-41.
21 Friedman, op. cit., pp. 156-7.
22 Ibid., 187-91.
23 Ibid., 192-3.
24 Quoted in J.H. Choate, *The Two Hague Conferences* 5, 1913, (hereinafter cited as 'Choate').
25 Freidman, op. cit., pp. 204-56, 270-397.
26 Choate, op. cit., p. 92.
27 See French Foreign Ministry, *Germany's Violations of the Laws of War* (1915 edn, trans. Bland).
28 See R.L. Buell, *International Relations* vii, 2nd edn 1929.
29 See 2 Oppenheim, *International Law* 177-8, 7th edn 1952.
30 46 Stat. 2343, T.S. 796.

31   Ibid., Art. I.
32   Ibid., Art. II.
33   See 'Disarmament Resolution adopted by the General Assembly', UN Doc. A/AC187/29 (1978).
34   B.H. Weston, R.A. Falk and A.A. D'Amato, *International Law and World Order* 259 (1980).
35   L.B. Sohn, 'How to Obtain Peace, Security and Justice', 19 *International Lawyer* 599 (1985). For a detailed discussion of attempts to regulate the use, deployment, proliferation and testing of nuclear weapons see Chapters 1 and 2 above and Chapters 5, 7, 8 and 9 below.
36   Hart, op. cit. pp. 89-91.
37   Ibid., p. 91.
38   Ibid.
39   See, generally, J. Woodliffe, 'Nuclear Weapons and Non-Proliferation: the Legal Aspects', Chapter 5, this volume.
40   Hart, op. cit., p. 91.
41   Ibid., p. 90.
42   Ibid.
43   See, for example, the Treaty on the Non-Proliferation of Nuclear Weapons 1968; the Treaty on the Limitation of Anti-Ballistic Missile Systems 1972; the Treaty Banning Nuclear Weapons Tests in the Atmosphere, in Outer Space and Under Water 1963. These are, examined, respectively, in Chapters 5, 6 and 9.
44   For example, the Soviet economy, though plainly governed by municipal law, is much more subject to administrative fiat than the market economies of the West. O.S. Ioffe and M.W. Janis (ed), *Soviet Law and Economy*, 1986.
45   M.L. Jones, 'The Legal Nature of the European Community: A Jurisprudential Analysis Using H.L.A. Hart's Model of Law and a Legal System', 17 *Cornell International Law Journal* 1, 1984. Jones argues that EEC law is so developed it is no longer really international law, pp. 50-7. I prefer to challenge Hart's municipal/international distinction and to use both EEC and European human rights law as examples of how developed international law may become. M.W. Janis, 'Individuals as Subjects of International Law' 17 *Cornell International Law Journal* 61, 64-71, 1984.

4 Nuclear weapons and self-defence in international law*

Istvan Pogany

The development of nuclear weapons has had a twofold impact on the concept of self-defence as understood by international law. The unprecedented destructive power of such weapons has caused some lawyers to question whether states may lawfully use or deploy nuclear devices, even in self-defence.[1] In addition, the impossibility of adopting defensive measures *after* a strategic ballistic missile attack has been launched has prompted speculation as to whether preventive action is lawful.[2] A number of scholars have concluded that anticipatory self-defence is essential so that a state confronted by an imminent nuclear attack may take steps immediately to ensure its national survival.[3]

This chapter examines the assertion that preventive action is permissible under contemporary international law.[4] It also evaluates the strategic assumptions underlying calls for the retention of anticipatory self-defence. Even if preventive measures are lawful, it is by no means clear that the doctrine is relevant to any realistic scenario involving the use of nuclear weapons. Of necessity, strategic theories have evolved in accordance with successive changes in the variety, payload and distribution of nuclear weapons.[5]

Anticipatory self-defence: Strategic aspects

International lawyers have generally avoided elaborate discussion of the strategic premises underpinning their arguments in favour of anticipatory self-defence. For the most part, they have treated as obvious the proposition that a state wishing to defend itself against a nuclear ballistic missile attack must initiate protective measures *before* the attack has been launched. Thus, Professor Friedmann has contended:[6]

> The ability of missiles with nuclear warheads, to paralyse and destroy the nerve centres even of vast countries such as the U.S.S.R. or the U.S.A., and to kill or maim major parts of their populations in one blow, may make it a form of suicide for a state to wait for the actual act of aggression before responding . . . the right of self-defence must probably now be extended to the defence against a clearly imminent aggression, despite the apparently contrary language of Article 51 of the Charter.

Similarly, McDougal and Feliciano dismiss as 'romanticism' attempts to proscribe the right of anticipatory self-defence in an era where states are confronted by the spectre of nuclear annihilation:[7]

> In case of delivery by ballistic . . . missiles, whose trajectory is traversed in a matter of minutes and against which effective repulsion measures have yet to be devised . . . to require postponement of response until after 'the last irrevocable act' is in effect to reduce self-defence to the possible infliction, if enough defenders survive, of retaliatory damage upon the enemy.

However, these seemingly commonsensical arguments rest on two, rarely scrutinised, premises. First, the arguments presuppose that a nuclear attack involving ICBMs, or other strategic nuclear weapons, could occur *at the inception* of an armed conflict. If hostilities were already in progress, a state which *was exercising* its right of self-defence would have no need to rely on the controversial doctrine of anticipatory self-defence to preempt an attack by nuclear weapons.[8] Instead, it would be sufficient for it to demonstrate that such measures were necessary and proportionate.[9] Second, the arguments assume that there are credible counter-measures that a state can take to protect itself from an imminent ballistic missile attack. If protection is, in fact, unavailable, counter-measures would assume the character of forcible reprisals rather than of genuine anticipatory self-defence.[10]

Both premises were widely regarded as suspect in the 1960's, when McDougal and Friedmann were writing, at least with respect to a possible conflict between the superpowers, each of whom already possessed a 'second-strike' capability.[11] In the opinion of most commentators the premises are even more doubtful in the 1980s, as neither the United States nor the Soviet Union can hope to launch a successful 'first strike'.[12]

As long as both superpowers possess a 'second-strike' capability, most analysts believe that neither state is *likely* to initiate a US/Soviet armed conflict with strategic nuclear weapons although, of course, a conventional conflict between the superpowers could escalate into all-out nuclear war. Even if one of the superpowers were to decide to launch a strategic nuclear attack against the other, the possession of 'second-strike' weapons by both states would prevent the intended victim from assuring its defence by pre-empting the attack.[13]

In these circumstances, it is necessary to re-examine the proposition, advanced by Waldock, McDougal, Friedmann and others, that anticipatory self-defence has assumed an unprecedented importance as a result of the development of nuclear ballistic missiles. As noted above, this thesis is open to doubt, at least with respect to a possible conflict between the superpowers. However, the argument may be more obviously applicable, for example, to hostilities between smaller nuclear powers.

In assessing the relevance of anticipatory self-defence to a conflict involving the use of nuclear weapons, three contrasting scenarios will be examined: (a) a conflict between the superpowers; (b) a conflict between smaller nuclear powers or between a smaller nuclear power and a non-nuclear power; (c) a conflict between a superpower and a smaller nuclear power or a non-nuclear power.[14] Finally, the functions and capabilities of warning and intelligence systems will be analysed, in so far as they affect the applicability of the doctrine of anticipatory self-defence to conflicts involving the use of nuclear weapons.

A conflict between the superpowers

As noted above, it is widely accepted that the possession of a 'second-strike' capability by both superpowers severely reduces the likelihood of a US/Soviet armed conflict *commencing* with a strategic nuclear attack.[15] This view is confirmed by a number of recent studies.[16]

Nevertheless, the possibility that one superpower may launch a surprise attack, involving strategic nuclear weapons, against the other cannot be discounted completely. Indeed, it is one of the criticisms of 'deterrence theory' that it assumes an excessive rationality on the part of governments, particularly during periods of heightened international tensions.[17]. It has also been argued that , while *civilian* analysts generally believe that neither superpower would use its strategic nuclear arsenal *at the inception* of an armed conflict, because of the risk of nuclear retaliation, *military* strategists instinctively favour the first use of nuclear weapons, as soon as an armed confrontation seems inescapable:[18]

The common operating premise among U.S. war planners . . . is
that the United States would never permit itself to be hit first . . .
Deterrence is accepted, but this does not rule out pushing the
button first in a grave crisis if deterrence wobbles and appears to
be failing. The entire history of conventional conflict shows that
surprise carries with it a large advantage. The effects of a nuclear
'second strike' may seem sufficiently devastating to cancel out the
hypothetical gain from getting in the first blow, at least in the
minds of many civilians. But this 'fact', which is supposed to dominate thinking about warfare in the nuclear age, does not reflect
the military's established outlook.

However, even if this scenario is plausible, it does not enhance the
relevance of preventive measures. As noted previously, while both the
United States and the Soviet Union possess a 'second-strike' capability,
the pre-emption of a strategic nuclear attack by one superpower against
the other would invite retaliation. Thus, the utility of anticipatory self-
defence is open to doubt.

Changes in nuclear weapons technology may, naturally, upset such
assumptions. The Strategic Defence Initiative ('Star Wars') would, if
effective, provide the United States with a shield against ballistic missile attack.[19] In such circumstances, the United States could, with relative impunity, resort to preventive measures. However, the likelihood
of a Soviet strategic nuclear attack on the United States would be reduced, still further, if the US possessed an effective antiballistic missile
(ABM) system. Thus, the relevance of anticipatory self-defence to a
nuclear conflict between the superpowers remains open to doubt.

*A conflict between smaller nuclear powers or between a smaller nuclear
power and a non-nuclear power*

In addition to the United States, the Soviet Union, Great Britain,
France and China, all of whom are known to possess nuclear
weapons,[20] a number of states are believed to have the necessary technology to assemble nuclear weapons at short notice. These include
Israel, South Africa and India.[21] In addition, there is compelling evidence that other states, notably Pakistan and Iraq, have embarked on
ambitious programmes with a view to acquiring the materials and
'know-how' necessary to manufacture nuclear weapons.[22] More dis-
turbingly still, Libya has shown an interest in acquiring a nuclear military capability.[23]

Many of these states are involved in long-running disputes which
have intermittently flared into armed conflict. The disputes between
India and Pakistan, between Iraq and Iran, and between Israel and the

Arab states, may be cited as examples. In addition, a number of these countries have been governed, or may be governed in the future, by volatile rulers inspired by uncompromising ideologies.[24] Thus, the possibility exists that such a state, having acquired a rudimentary nuclear weapons capability, may decide to launch a surprise attack.

Such a decision will be made easier by the knowledge that the 'enemy' state, if its possesses nuclear weapons at all, is unlikely to have an effective 'second-strike' capability. The adversary's delivery system[s] will comprise long-range bombers or relatively unprotected surface-to-surface missiles,[25] both of which are vulnerable to a surprise attack. Moreover, a radical regime, imbued by an 'extremist' ideology, is less likely to be deterred from launching a nuclear attack, by the fear of nuclear retaliation, than a stable government.[26]

If a smaller nuclear power believed that a comparable adversary were about to launch a nuclear attack, it might regard anticipatory self-defence as a realistic option. Even a non-nuclear power might consider it militarily feasible to use conventional means to pre-empt a nuclear attack by a smaller nuclear power whose delivery systems, as noted above, are unsophisticated and hence vulnerable to a first strike.

Some states may be reluctant to allow their adversaries to acquire nuclear weapons at all, and to have to rely on their ability to pre-empt an impending attack. Thus, in June 1981, Israeli jets destroyed an Iraqi nuclear facility which, according to Israeli sources, was to have been used to produce fissionable material.[27] Israeli spokesmen argued that their action constituted a legitimate, albeit novel, application of the doctrine of anticipatory self-defence.[28]

A conflict between a superpower and a smaller nuclear power or a non-nuclear power

Hypothetically, a strategic nuclear attack by a superpower on either a non-nuclear state or on a smaller nuclear power is possible, as is a nuclear attack by a state with a limited nuclear capability on a superpower. However, these need not detain us here. While a nuclear attack by a superpower on a lesser power is certainly conceivable,[29] there would be little point in the target state attempting a pre-emptive strike in view of the relative invulnerability of the aggressor's submarine-launched ballistic missiles (SLBMs). In such circumstances, recourse to preventive measures would not significantly reduce the risk of nuclear annihilation.

The likelihood of a smaller nuclear power launching a nuclear strike on a superpower, while theoretically possible, must be so remote as to obviate the need for detailed analysis. As a commentator has observed, with comparative understatement, 'the risk of carrying out such a threat to a superpower would be extraordinary'.[30] China, France and the United Kingdom may be equated with the superpowers, in this context, as each of these states has a significant 'second-strike' capability.

In so far as a nuclear attack by a smaller nuclear power on a super-power, or on a middle-ranking nuclear power, is even conceivable, it is *least* likely to occur at the inception of an armed conflict, quite simply because of the awesome danger to which it would expose the attacking state.[31] Thus, the issue of anticipatory self-defence is largely irrelevant.

Warning and intelligence systems

The functions and capabilities of warning and intelligence systems must also be analysed, in so far as they affect the applicability of the doctrine of anticipatory self-defence to conflicts involving the use of nuclear weapons. As understood by its protagonists, the doctrine may only be exercised in circumstances which satisfy the requirements of *necessity, imminence* and *proportionality*.[32]

'Proportionality' need not concern us here, as this criterion relates to the permissibility of the *degree* of force which is employed, rather than to the validity of the decision to resort to preventive measures.[33] The 'necessity' of pre-empting a nuclear attack, where practicable, is self-evident. However, the feasibility of determining whether an armed attack is 'imminent' may be a source of genuine difficulty in the context of nuclear weapons.

There is considerable doubt as to whether even the superpowers have the means to establish whether a ballistic missile attack is imminent. It should be emphasised that states with sophisticated intelligence-gathering systems, such as the United States, the United Kingdom and Israel, have failed to discover that a *conventional* assault was impending. Israel obtained only a few hours' forewarning of the attack by Egypt and Syria, in October 1973.[34] The United Kingdom was taken completely by surprise, in April 1982, when Argentinian forces occupied the Falklands. The United States apparently failed to learn, in advance, of either of these attacks, or of the 1968 Soviet military intervention in Czechoslovakia.[35]

In comparison with an impending nuclear ballistic missile attack, there are often copious indications of an imminent conventional assault.[36] Troop levels are reinforced, tanks and artillery are brought up to the forward lines and, where appropriate, pontoons and landing-craft are assembled in readiness for the attack. Such relatively cumbersome preparations are generally detectable by a variety of means including aerial reconnaissance, interception of radio signals, and by orbiting spy satellites.

By contrast, a surprise attack involving nuclear weapons would be much more difficult to anticipate. Intercontinental ballistic missiles (ICBMs) are housed in underground silos. No incontrovertible physical activity is identifiable until the actual moment of use. The precise location of an adversary's ballistic missile submarine fleet is difficult to establish, while preparations for firing submarine-launched ballistic missiles (SLBMs) are, obviously, concealed from view. Thus, no readily observable operations are involved in the run-up to a ballistic missile attack.

Whether there are other, more sophisticated means by which evidence of an impending nuclear attack can be discovered cannot be established on the basis of unclassified material. However, there were reports in the mid-1970s that the United States had succeeded in intercepting Soviet 'high-level military messages'.[37] If true, this suggests that the US would have had forewarning of a Soviet surprise attack. However, it is impossible to state, with certainty, whether either superpower has the ability, at present, to determine if a strategic nuclear attack is imminent.

It is clearly conceivable that one or both powers can monitor the volume, and perhaps some part of the content, of the other's military communications. However, in view of the repeated failure of technologically sophisticated states in the past to discover that a *conventional* attack was impending, it should not be assumed too readily that either the United States or the Soviet Union has the ability to establish, with complete confidence, that a nuclear attack is 'imminent'.

Failure to anticipate a surprise attack would deprive the victim of the opportunity to take preventive measures, where available. However, in the absence of incontrovertible evidence of an imminent attack, the doctrine of anticipatory self-defence can scarcely be invoked to justify a massive use of armed force.

The preceding analysis has been confined, very largely, to the superpowers, whose nuclear arsenals are characterised by a high degree of sophistication. There may be more tangible evidence of preparations for a surprise attack where the aggressor is a smaller nuclear power, relying on a relatively crude delivery system such as long-range bombers. In these circumstances, the criterion of 'imminence' may be easier to satisfy where the potential victim can demonstrate, for example, that planes which had been assigned a strategic nuclear function were being prepared for an attack.

Nevertheless, the intrinsic difficulty of establishing that an attack is 'imminent' should not be underestimated. The failure of Israel to anticipate the attack by Egypt and Syria, in October 1973, suggests how hard it is to evaluate the significance of military preparations, even where these are readily observable.

Anticipatory self-defence: Legal aspects

Self-defence prior to the UN Charter

The concept of self-defence, as understood by general international law in the nineteenth and early twentieth centuries, was enunciated by US Secretary of State Webster, following the *Caroline* incident of 1837. Webster declared that a state is entitled to take forcible measures in self-defence, where it can demonstrate a 'necessity . . . instant, overwhelming, leaving no choice of means and no moment for deliberation'.[38] In addition, Webster cautioned that 'the act justified by the necessity of self-defence, must be limited by that necessity and kept clearly within it'.[39]

Although the *Caroline* formula does not *expressly* sanction preventive measures, it *implicitly* recognises a right of anticipatory self-defence where the requirements of a 'necessity . . . instant, overwhelming etc.' are satisfied. In the opinion of a significant body of jurists the Webster doctrine, incorporating a right of preventive action, remained an authoritative definition of self-defence at least until the conclusion of the UN Charter.[40] In the interwar period, a number of states argued for a wider construction of the concept of self-defence, going beyond even the *Caroline*. Thus, in a reservation to the 1928 Kellogg–Briand Pact, the US Secretary of State affirmed that the Treaty did not:[41]

> restrict or impair . . . the right of self-defence. That right is inherent in every sovereign State and is implicit in every treaty. Every nation is free at all times and regardless of treaty provisions to defend its territory from attack or invasion and it alone is competent to decide whether circumstances require recourse to war in self-defence.

The impact of the UN Charter

The impact of the UN Charter on the doctrine of self-defence has given rise to a protracted controversy. Certain jurists have argued that Article 51 of the Charter is *constitutive* of the right of self-defence. For example, Professor Brownlie contends:[42]

> even as a matter of 'plain' interpretation the permission in Article 51 is exceptional in the context of the Charter and exclusive of any customary right of self-defence . . . the prohibition in Article 2(4) is in absolute terms and the delegations at San Francisco regarded it in this light.

Others, including Professors Bowett and Stone, have argued with equal conviction that the UN Charter has left the customary law right of self-defence largely unimpaired. Thus, Professor Bowett maintains:[43]

> We must presuppose that rights formerly belonging to member states continue except in so far as obligations inconsistent with those existing rights are assumed under the Charter . . . It is, therefore, fallacious to assume that members have only those rights which the Charter accords to them: on the contrary they have those rights which general international law accords to them except and in so far as they have surrendered them under the Charter.

This 'academic' controversy has obvious implications for the concept of self-defence and, in particular, for the permissibility of preventive measures. Article 51 provides:

> Nothing in the present Charter shall impair the inherent right of individual or collective self-defence if an armed attack occurs against a Member of the United Nations, until the Security Council has taken measures necessary to maintain international peace and security . . .

Thus, a literal interpretation of the Charter, as favoured by Brownlie, Akehurst and others, would *exclude* measures of self-help involving resort to armed force except in response to an antecedent armed attack. By contrast, customary international law, as noted above, was widely recognised as permitting recourse to anticipatory self-defence, in accordance with the strict requirements of the *Caroline*.[44]

The intractable character of this controversy is, in part, a consequence of the inconclusiveness of the Charter's *travaux préparatoires*. There are, on the one hand, unequivocal statements by delegates, at the San Francisco Conference, affirming the intention of the parties to achieve a comprehensive prohibition of the unilateral use of armed force. Thus, during a committee discussion of the text of Article 2(4) of the Charter, the US delegate stated:[45]

> the intention of the authors of the original text was to state in the broadest terms an absolute all-inclusive prohibition; the phrase 'or in any other manner' was designed to ensure that there should be no loopholes.

Similarly, the summary of an earlier discussion of Article 2(4) noted: '[i]t was felt . . . that paragraph 4 should be reworded so as to provide that force should not be used by any member state except by direction of the world Organization'.[46]

However, there is some evidence to suggest that the delegates at San Francisco may have believed that self-defence was exempt from the general prohibition of the unilateral use of armed force. Thus, Committee 1 of Commission I observed '[t]he use of arms in legitimate self-defence remains admitted and unimpaired'.[47] The choice of the term 'legitimate self-defence', in preference to a more obviously restrictive formulation, has led some commentators to conclude that the understanding at San Francisco was that there would be no curtailment of the concept of self-defence as traditionally understood.[48]

It is also important to note that Article 51 was *not* introduced in the Charter in order to define the right of individual self-defence. The provision was drafted *solely* to 'accommodate regional security organizations . . . within the Charter's scheme of centralized, global collective security, and to preserve the functioning of these regional systems from the frustration of vetoes cast in the Security Council'.[49] This emerges clearly from the *travaux préparatoires*. Following the decision of Commission III to insert the text of Article 51 in the draft UN Charter, the US delegate noted 'we have found a sound and practical formula for putting regional organizations into effective gear with the global institution which we here erect on behalf of the world's peace and security'.[50]

Similarly, the Venezuelan delegate observed, '[t]hrough difficult negotiations we have endeavoured to fulfil two main purposes . . . to preserve on the one hand the working of regional systems and, on the other hand, to maintain the supreme authority of the world Organization'.[51] Finally, the French delegate commented, 'I would . . . like to express my gratitude to all the nations of America who wanted this amendment *in order to safeguard their fecund Pan American Union*, which for years has prevented or avoided war in your continent.'[52] There is no suggestion, in any of these statements, that Article 51 was intended to confine the exercise of the right of self-defence to situations in which there had been a prior armed attack.

It is, therefore, doubtful whether an unequivocal view emerges from the *travaux préparatoires* as to whether the Charter precludes resort to force in anticipatory self-defence. Quotations can be produced, with equal facility, to support *either* construction.[53]

Subsequent practice

The practice of states, judicial decisions and the teachings of publicists have failed to resolve the controversy as to whether anticipatory self-defence is permitted by international law.

The teachings of publicists As noted previously, publicists have arrived at diametrically opposed conclusions on this issue. Whereas western scholars are divided in their views concerning the permissibility of anticipatory self-defence, 'socialist' international lawyers are united in their rejection of the doctrine.[54] However, the teachings of even the most highly qualified publicists are merely a 'subsidiary means' for the determination of rules of law.[55]

State practice State practice, encompassing both the conduct and public utterances of governments, reveals a similar lack of consensus concerning the permissibility of anticipatory self-defence. It is striking how *rarely* states have invoked the doctrine, in the post-war period, to justify the use of armed force.[56] Even where the facts might have supported an argument based on the need to take preventive measures, states have sometimes preferred to rely on the contention, however implausible, that they were the victim of an armed attack. Thus, in June 1967, after launching a pre-emptive strike against Egypt, Israel claimed that its resort to self-help was in response to a prior Egyptian attack.[57]

The evident reluctance of states to invoke the doctrine of anticipatory self-defence is indicative, at the very least, of an awareness that the concept does not command universal support. Although Israel argued, in June 1981, that its attack on the Iraqi nuclear reactor 'Osirak' was in exercise of the right of anticipatory self-defence, this justification was prompted by necessity rather than conviction. In view of the limited progress made by Iraq, in its attempts to acquire nuclear weapons, Israel could scarcely contend that its operation was in response to a prior Iraqi 'attack'. Moreover, in the absence of even an 'imminent' nuclear threat from Iraq, the Israeli action cannot serve as an instance of anticipatory self-defence, at least as understood by the *Caroline*.[58]

Nevertheless, while the Security Council unanimously adopted a resolution in which it condemned the Israeli operation against Iraq as a 'clear violation of the Charter of the United Nations and the norms of international conduct', it did not reject anticipatory self-defence as such.[59] Moreover, during the Security Council debate, a number of delegates, representing the United States, the United Kingdom, Sierra Leone, Niger and Israel, made statements recognizing a right of preventive action. Thus, the United Kingdom delegate, Sir Anthony Parsons, contended that the Israeli operation violated international law *in so far as* '[t]here was no instant or overwhelming necessity for self-defence'.[60] This formulation, taken almost verbatim from the *Caroline*, amounts to an implicit recognition of the permissibility of preventive measures, *provided that* the requirements of the Webster doctrine are satisfied. The US representative, Ambassador Kirkpatrick, observed, 'our judgement that Israeli actions violated the United Nations Charter is based solely on the conviction that Israel failed to exhaust peaceful means for the resolution of this dispute.'[61] Ambassador Kirkpatrick's statement constitutes a clear affirmation of a right of self-defence in circumstances that do not amount to an 'armed attack'.

More surprisingly, perhaps, the representative of Sierra Leone quoted approvingly from the *Caroline*: '[a]s for the principle of self-defence, it has long been accepted that, for it to be invoked or justified the necessity for action must be instant, overwhelming and leaving no choice of means and no moment for deliberation.'[62] In very similar terms the representative of Niger condemned the attack on the Iraqi nuclear facility 'because Israel was in no way facing an imminent attack, irrefutably proved and demonstrated'.[63] Thus, both statements allowed for the possibility of anticipatory self-defence, in accordance with the strict requirements of the *Caroline*.

Other delegates, representing Uganda, Algeria, Brazil, Spain, Ireland, Romania, Syria, Guyana, Mexico and the USSR, condemned both the Israeli operation and also the doctrine of anticipatory self-defence. Thus, the representative of Uganda stated:[64]

> In his attempts to justify Israel's action the Israeli representative quoted the provisions of Article 51 of the Charter. But, as has been stated by many members, in order to bring his case under that umbrella, he had to prove an armed attack.

The Mexican delegate, speaking in his capacity as the representative of Mexico rather than as the Security Council President,[65] but nevertheless claiming to summarise the 'convergence of views' amongst delegates, stated:[66]

> It is inadmissible to invoke the right to self-defence when no armed attack has taken place. The concept of preventive war, which for many years served as justification for the abuses of powerful States, since it left it to their discretion to define what constituted a threat to them, was definitively abolished by the Charter of the United Nations.

In similar terms, the Soviet Ambassador rejected legal arguments based on the 'doctrine of preventive war'.[67] Nevertheless, in evaluating Soviet 'practice' it is important to recognize that, while Soviet legal theory has consistently rejected the permissibility of preventive measures,[68] Soviet military strategy has intermittently called for resort to preemptive strikes.[69] In these circumstances, it is scarcely possible to conclude that Soviet 'practice' indicates, unequivocally, that anticipatory self-defence is unlawful.[70]

The lack of consensus amongst states as to whether preventive measures are lawful is reflected in the reticence, or ambivalence, of key UN resolutions. Thus, the General Assembly's 1970 Declaration on the Principles of International Law, widely regarded as an authoritative elaboration of the principles of the Charter, fails to specify the scope of legitimate self-defence.[71]

The General Assembly's 1974 Definition of Aggression relies on deliberate obfuscation. Article 2 states, with reasonable clarity, that '[t]he first use of armed force by a State in contravention of the Charter shall constitute *prima facie* evidence of an act of aggression'.[72] However, Article 2 notes that 'the Security Council may, in conformity with the Charter, conclude that a determination that an act of aggression has been committed would not be justified in the light of other relevant circumstances.' Moreover, Article 6 states: '[n]othing in this Definition shall be construed as in any way enlarging or diminishing the scope of the Charter, including its provisions concerning cases in which the use of force is lawful.'

Judicial decisions

The Nuremburg and Tokyo Tribunals   The Nuremburg and Tokyo International Military Tribunals, which were constituted after the Second World War to try German and Japanese war criminals respectively, found that anticipatory self-defence is permitted by international law. While rejecting the contention that the German occupation of Norway amounted to anticipatory self-defence, the Nuremburg Tribunal held: 'preventive action in foreign territory *is* justified only in case of an instant and overwhelming necessity for self-defence, leaving no choice of means, and no moment of deliberation.'[73] Similarly, the Tokyo Tribunal held that a state 'threatened with impending attack' may resort to force in self-defence.[74]

Although the Nuremburg and Tokyo Tribunals were concerned with the legality of offences committed *before* the establishment of the United Nations, their findings were perceived as applicable to international law *after* the war. Thus, on 11 December 1946, the UN General Assembly unanimously adopted a resolution in which it affirmed 'the principles of international law recognized by the Charter of the Nuremburg Tribunal and the judgment of the Tribunal'.[75]

Iranian Hostages Case   In the *Iranian Hostages Case* the International Court of Justice did not address itself directly to the legal implications of an abortive attempt by the United States to rescue its hostages in Tehran.[76] However, in dissenting opinions, Judges Morozov and Tarazi emphasised that self-defence, which had been invoked by the United States as justifying its rescue operation, could only be exercised 'if an armed attack occurs against a Member of the United Nations'.[77]

Morozov and Tarazi were concerned with the *illegality*, as they saw it, of the use of force to rescue nationals abroad. Nevertheless, their emphasis on the existence of an 'armed attack', as a precondition for self-defence, would exclude resort to preventive measures.

Military Activities Against Nicaragua Case   The *Military and Paramilitary Activities in and Against Nicaragua Case* is of fundamental importance, in this context, as it represents the first occasion on which the World Court has considered the right of self-defence in detail. For jurisdictional reasons, the Court was compelled to confine its analysis to the relevant rules of general international law, as distinct from Article 51 of the Charter.[78] However, the Court found that, although the 'areas governed by the two sources of law . . . do not overlap exactly, and the rules do not have the same content',[79] the 'differences which may exist between the specific content of each are not, in the Court's view, such as to cause a judgment confined to the field of customary international law to be ineffective or inappropriate'.[80]

Ostensibly, the Judgment does not concern itself with the permissibility of preventive measures:[81]

> In view of the circumstances in which the dispute has arisen, reliance is placed by the Parties only on the right of self-defence in the case of an armed attack which has already occurred, and the issue of the lawfulness of a response to the imminent threat of armed attack has not been raised. Accordingly, the Court expresses no view on that issue.

Nevertheless, the Court went on to note '[i]n the case of individual self-defence, the exercise of this right is subject to the State concerned having been the victim of an armed attack'.[82] Despite the Court's earlier protestations, this passage may be read as an implicit condemnation of anticipatory self-defence.

In his Dissenting Opinion, Judge Schwebel drew attention to the Judgment's ambivalence on this question:[83]

> The Court rightly observes that the issue of the lawfulness of a response to the imminent threat of armed attack has not been raised in this case, and that the Court accordingly expresses no view on that issue. Nevertheless, its Judgment may be open to the interpretation of inferring that a State may react in self-defence, and that supportive States may react in collective self-defence, only if an armed attack occurs.

Judge Schwebel continued:[84]

> I wish, *ex abundanti cautela*, to make clear that, for my part, I do not agree with a construction of the United Nations Charter which would read Article 51 as if it were worded: 'Nothing in the present Charter shall impair the inherent right of individual or collective self-defence if, and only if, an armed attack occurs. . .' I do not agree that the terms or intent of Article 51 eliminate the right of self-defence under customary international law, or confine its entire scope to the express terms of Article 51.

Although Judge Schwebel declined to mention the *Caroline*, or to expressly uphold a right of anticipatory self-defence, his Opinion is an affirmation of the 'broad' view of self-defence, as understood before the establishment of the United Nations, which encompassed a right of preventive action. Moreover, as the Court disclaimed any intention to comment on the legality of preventive measures, it would be a misreading of the Judgment to construe it as an unambiguous rejection of the lawfulness of anticipatory self-defence.

Finally, while allowing for discrepancies between customary law and the provisions of the UN Charter, governing the exercise of self-defence, the two are now closely integrated.[85] Accordingly, it is doubtful whether the findings of either Judge Schwebel, or of the Court, would have been significantly different had they been able to address themselves directly to the Charter.

Conclusion

The present writer expressed the opinion, in an earlier volume, that 'neither state practice, nor the writings of jurists, demonstrate conclusively that anticipatory self-defence no longer exists as a permissible category of self-help'.[86] Analyses of the *travaux préparatoires* of the UN Charter, and of the jurisprudence of the World Court strengthen that conclusion, despite the contrary arguments of some jurists, notably from developing and socialist states.

Nevertheless, as emphasised earlier in this chapter, it is doubtful whether the doctrine has much relevance to a nuclear conflict between the superpowers. In view of the 'second-strike' capability of the United States and the Soviet Union, it is widely considered *unlikely* that either state would mount a surprise attack on the other with nuclear ballistic missiles and *impossible* for the victim, if such an attack were imminent, to take meaningful defensive measures. International lawyers have largely ignored the strategic realities that have eroded the utility of anticipatory self-defence.

As noted above, the doctrine has greater potential relevance to conflicts between smaller nuclear powers, or between smaller nuclear
powers and non-nuclear powers, where the aggressor's delivery-system
may be vulnerable to a first strike, and where he lacks a second-strike
capability.

However, the doctrine of anticipatory self-defence, in so far as it is
recognised by international law, permits the use of force only where an
attack is *imminent* and where there is a *necessity* of self-defence.[87] This
is clearly desirable, from the perspective of the international community, which has a collective interest in the preservation of world
peace and in the limitation of unilateral resort to armed force. However, a state such as Israel may have genuine grounds for believing that
an adversary is attempting to acquire nuclear weapons and may be
understandably reluctant to rely on its ability to anticipate an imminent
attack. In such circumstances, the temptation to take 'defensive' measures long before an attack is imminent may, as in the past, prove
irresistible.

Notes

* An earlier version of this chapter was presented by the author at a seminar at the
  Faculty of Law, University of Hull, in November 1985. I am grateful to all of those
  who participated in the seminar, particularly to Mr Iain Cameron, for their valu-
  able and stimulating comments.
1 For contrasting views see M.N. Shaw, 'Nuclear Weapons and International Law',
  Chapter 1, this volume, and; N.J. Grief, 'The Legality of Nuclear Weapons',
  Chapter 2, this volume.
2 On the impossibility of defending oneself *after* a ballistic missile attack has been
  launched see e.g. I. Cameron, 'Anti-Ballistic Missile Systems and International
  Law', Chapter 6 this volume, esp. notes 5–8, and the accompanying text. Of
  course, the Strategic Defence Initiative ('Star Wars') is intended to provide effective protection in the event of such an attack. However, the feasibility of such a
  system remains doubtful. According to Professor John Darlington of London University: '[t]he breakthroughs needed in computer technology are just not possible.
  They are tens, hundreds and in some cases thousands of times more complex than
  even the most advanced systems which exist at the moment.' See *The Times*, 28
  June 1986, p.2.
3 See e.g. H. Waldock, 'The Regulation of the Use of Force by Individual States in
  International Law', Hague, *Recueil des Cours*, vol. 81, 1952, Part II, p.455, at
  p.498; M.S. McDougal and F.P. Feliciano, *Law and Minimum World Public Order*, 1961, pp.238–40; M.S. McDougal, in *Proceedings of the American Society of
  International Law*, 1963, p.164; W. Friedmann, *The Changing Structure of International Law*, 1964, pp.259–60; T.M. Franck, 'Who Killed Article 2(4)?',
  American Journal of International Law, vol. 64, 1970, p.809, at pp.820-3. Without
  referring expressly to nuclear weapons, Professor Bowett has argued: '[n]o state
  can be expected to await an initial attack which, in the present state of armaments,

may well destroy the state's capacity for further resistance and so jeopardize its very existence.' D.W. Bowett, *Self-Defence in International Law*, 1958, pp.191-2. Israeli spokesmen argued, following Israel's attack on an Iraqi nuclear facility in June 1981, that preventive measures can be taken even where a nuclear attack is not considered to be imminent. See note 58 below.

An alternative approach has been to argue that self-defence is permitted by the UN Charter in the event of an 'armed attack' (Article 51) and that the term should be interpreted broadly in the context of a possible nuclear attack. Thus, in 1946, the US contended that 'an "armed attack" is now something entirely different from what it was prior to the discovery of atomic weapons' and that it includes 'not simply the actual dropping of an atomic bomb, but also certain stages in themselves preliminary to such action'. See *International Control of Atomic Energy: Growth of a Policy*, US Department of State, Publication No. 2702 (1946), p.164. The text is reproduced in P. Jessup, *A Modern Law of Nations*, 1952, pp.166-7. For a similar conclusion see for example N. Singh, *Nuclear Weapons and International Law*, 1959, pp.127-8. However, such arguments are potentially destabilising. It is unclear what criteria should be employed to determine whether an 'armed attack' has commenced if no missiles have been launched, for example. By contrast, anticipatory self-defence, as understood by almost all of its protagonists, is subject to stringent requirements. Preventive measures are only legitimate if there is a necessity of self-defence 'instant, overwhelming, leaving no choice of means and no moment for deliberation'. See note 38 below and the accompanying text.

4   This chapter does not attempt to deal with the complementary question of which weapons, notably nuclear weapons, may be used in self-defence. This question is discussed in some detail in Chapters 1 and 2, above.

5   See e.g. J.H. Barton and L.D. Weiler (eds), *International Arms Control*, 1976, p.123.

6   Friedmann, op. cit., pp.259-60. For very similar observations see Franck, op. cit., p.820; Waldock, op. cit., p.498. Article 51 provides: '[n]othing in the present Charter shall impair the inherent right of individual or collective self-defence if an armed attack occurs against a Member of the United Nations, until the Security Council has taken measures necessary to maintain international peace and security. . .'

7   McDougal and Feliciano, op. cit., p.240.

8   A state already exercising the right of self-defence does not need to show that every military initiative which it takes, during the course of hostilities, is in response to an individual armed attack. See e.g. C. Greenwood, 'The Relationship Between *Ius ad Bellum* and *Ius in Bello*', *Review of International Studies*, vol. 9, 1983, p.221, at p.224.

9   In its recent Judgment in the *Military Activities Against Nicaragua Case*, the ICJ emphasised that measures taken in self-defence must satisfy the criteria of 'necessity' and 'proportionality'. *ICJ Reports*, 1986, p. 14 at p. 93. These criteria have long been recognised by general international law.

10   On the distinction between self-defence and forcible reprisals see e.g. D.W. Bowett, 'Reprisals Involving Recourse to Armed Force', *American Journal of International Law*, vol. 66, 1972, p.1, at pp.2-3.

11   Barton and Weiler, op. cit., pp.126-8. The term 'second-strike' capability has been defined as '[a] strategic concept which excludes preemptive and preventive actions before the onset of a war. . . . In general nuclear war, this implies the ability to survive a surprise first strike and respond effectively.' J.M. Collins, *U.S.–Soviet Military Balance, 1980–1985*, 1985, p.311.

12   On the current 'strategic nuclear stand-off' see e.g. Collins, op. cit., p.59; Cameron, op. cit., notes 55-62, and the accompanying text. The term 'first-strike' im-

plies, in the context of a general nuclear war, 'the ability to eliminate effective retaliation by the opposition'. Collins, op. cit., p.305. Of course, the *possibility* that one superpower may initiate hostilities against the other with a strategic nuclear attack cannot be discounted altogether. However, the *probability* of such an attack has been reduced considerably, in the opinion of most commentators, because both sides possess, and are known to possess, an effective 'second-strike' capability. For a forceful critique of 'deterrence theory' see note 18 below, and the accompanying text.

13   It is by no means clear that either power could be certain of destroying all of its adversary's ICBMs in a pre-emptive strike. However, *merely to attempt to do so*, might lead the opposing side to launch its submarine-launched ballistic missiles (SLBMs) in retaliation.

14   For details of states possessing, or likely to possess, nuclear weapons see notes 20-3 below and the accompanying text.

15   It should be emphasised that not all American analysts accept the premise that the US possesses, or can expect to retain, an effective 'second-strike' capability. See e.g. Cameron, op. cit., notes 50-4, and the accompanying text. Note, however, the author's scepticism concerning the claims for a Soviet 'first-strike' capability. Ibid., notes 55-62, and the accompanying text.

16   See e.g. Collins, op. cit., p.53. For a summary of a recent study of Soviet strategic thinking, which concludes that Soviet strategy aims at achieving a conventional victory, while avoiding all use of nuclear weapons, see *The Guardian*, 13 January 1986, p.8.

17   Barton and Weiler, op. cit., pp.129-30.

18   D. Ford, *The Button: the Nuclear Trigger-does it work?*, 1986, p. 234. The author concludes that Soviet military planners also favour an offensive strategy. Ibid., p. 237.

19   See note 2 above.

20   On the acquisition of nuclear weapons by the US, the USSR, the United Kingdom, France and China, see e.g. J. Woodliffe, 'Nuclear Weapons and Non-Proliferation: the Legal Aspects', Chapter 5 this volume, notes 5-19, and the accompanying text.

21   On Israel, India and South Africa see ibid., notes 33, 55, 128, and the accompanying text. On Israel see also *The Sunday Times*, 5 October 1986, p.1.

22   See e.g. T.F. Dorian and L.S. Spector, 'Covert Nuclear Trade and the International Nonproliferation Regime', in Holroyd, op. cit., p.137, at pp.147-63.

23   Ibid., p.164, notes 9, 10.

24   See, generally, L.A. Dunn, 'Nuclear Proliferation: What Difference Will it Make?', in Holroyd, op. cit., p.118, at pp.118-20.

25   Ibid., p.121.

26   Ibid., pp.118-19.

27   See, generally, on the Israeli raid and its background, A. Perlmutter, M. Handel and U. Bar-Joseph, *Two Minutes Over Baghdad*, 1982.

28   See note 58 below.

29   The Soviet Union apparently considered a nuclear strike against China in the late 1960s. See e.g. Dunn, op. cit., p.123.

30   Ibid., p.128.

31   Thus, the ability of a smaller nuclear power to launch a limited nuclear strike against a superpower has been characterised as a '*last-resort* capability'. Ibid. (my emphasis).

32   See notes 38-40 below and the accompanying text.

33   On the complementary question of whether the *use* of nuclear weapons may ever be proportionate see Chapters 1 and 2, this volume.

34   See e.g. I. Pogany, *The Security Council and the Arab-Israeli Conflict*, 1984, p.115.
35   Bracken, op. cit., p.172.
36   The problem may be one of *evaluating* the signs, rather than of *discovering* them.
37   Bracken, op. cit., p.181.
38   *British Foreign and State Papers*, vol. 30, p.193.
39   Ibid.
40   See e.g. Waldock, op. cit., pp.476-8; J.L. Brierly, *The Law of Nations*, 6th edn, 1963, pp.409-11; Bowett, op. cit., pp.142-4. Others, notably Professor Brownlie, argue that the ambit of the customary law right of self-defence underwent successive modifications in the interwar period. See I. Brownlie, *International Law and the Use of Force by States*, 1963, pp.274-5, 279-80. In particular, Brownlie argues that these had the effect of removing a right of anticipatory self-defence.
41   The text of the Secretary of State's Note to the Signatory Governments, dated 23 June 1928, is reproduced in J. Stone, *Aggression and World Order*, 1958, p.32, note 29.
42   Brownlie, op. cit., p.273. For a similar conclusion see e.g. H. Kelsen, *Recent Trends in the Law of the United Nations*, 1951, p.914; Singh, op. cit., p.126; K. Skubiszewski, 'Use of Force by States', in M. Sørensen, *Manual of Public International Law*, 1968, p.739, at pp.766-7; M. Akehurst, *A Modern Introduction to International Law*, 5th edn 1984, p.222.
43   Bowett, op. cit., pp.184-5. See also, Stone, op. cit., pp.94-8; Waldock, op. cit., pp.496-8; McDougal and Feliciano, op. cit., p.235.
44   See, however, the argument of Professor Brownlie that the *content* of the customary law right of self-defence underwent successive modifications in the inter-war period. See note 40 above.
45   *Documents of the United Nations Conference on International Organisation*, vol. VI, 1945, p.335 (hereafter cited as UNCIO). Article 2(4) of the Charter provides: 'All Members shall refrain in their international relations from the threat or use of force against the territorial integrity or political independence of any State, or in any other manner inconsistent with the Purposes of the United Nations.'
46   UNCIO, vol. VI, p.304.
47   Ibid., p.459.
48   See e.g. Stone, op. cit., p.44, note 13. See also, McDougal and Feliciano, op. cit., pp.235-6.
49   McDougal and Feliciano, op. cit., p.235.
50   UNCIO, vol. XI, p.52.
51   Ibid., p.55.
52   Ibid., p.58 (my emphasis).
53   In any event, the proceedings of the San Francisco Conference are only of *secondary* importance. Thus, Article 32 of the Vienna Convention on the Law of Treaties, which is generally regarded as declaratory of customary law, describes the preparatory work of a treaty as a 'supplementary means of interpretation' and states that recourse '*may* be had' to such materials (my emphasis). See, generally, I. Sinclair, *The Vienna Convention on the Law of Treaties*, 2nd edn 1984, pp.141-7.
54   See e.g. G.I. Tunkin, *Theory of International Law*, W.E. Butler, trans., 1974, p.52; J. Zourek, *l'Interdiction de l'Emploi de la Force en Droit International*, 1974, p.106; H. Bokor-Szegö, 'The Attitude of Socialist States Towards the International Regulation of the Use of Force', in A. Cassese (ed.), *Current Legal Regulation on the Use of Force*, 1986, p.453, at p.465.
55   Thus, Article 38(1) of the Statute of the International Court of Justice refers to 'the teachings of the most highly qualified publicists', together with 'judicial decisions', as 'subsidiary means for the determination of rules of law'.
56   This may well be because the majority of states, particularly developing and social-

ist states, have generally contended that the right of self-defence may only be exercised in the event of an 'armed attack'. See, generally, R. Higgins, *The Development of International Law Through the Political Organs of the United Nations*, 1963, pp.199-203; L.M. Goodrich, E. Hambro and A.P. Simons, *Charter of the United Nations*, 3rd rev. edn 1969, pp.347-8; J.-P. L. Fonteyne, 'Forcible Self-Help by States to Protect Human Rights: Recent Views from the United Nations', in R. B. Lillich (ed.), *Humanitarian Intervention in the United Nations*, 1973, p.197, at pp.211-13. See, also notes 60-7 below and the accompanying text.

57   For details, see e.g. Pogany, op. cit., pp.90-1.

58   The Israeli Ambassador to the United Nations, Dr Blum, contended that the Israeli operation constituted legitimate self-defence. See e.g. Security Council Verbatim Records 2280th meeting, 12 June 1981, pp.37, 52-5 (hereafter cited as S/PV. etc.). Dr Blum argued, in addition, that the principles governing the exercise of self-defence cannot remain unchanged despite fundamental developments in weapons technology:

> To assert the applicability of the Caroline principles to a State confronted with the threat of nuclear destruction would be an emasculation of that State's inherent and natural right of self-defence. . . . Indeed, the concept of a State's right to self-defence has not changed throughout recorded history. Its scope has, however, broadened with the advance of man's ability to wreak havoc on his enemies. Consequently the concept took on new and far wider application with the advent of the nuclear era. Anyone who thinks otherwise has simply not faced up to the horrific realities of the world we live in today, and that is particularly true for small States whose vulnerability is vast and whose capacity to survive a nuclear strike is very limited.

See S/PV. 2288th meeting, 19 June 1981, pp.32-6.

59   Security Council Resolution 487, 19 June 1981.

60   S/PV. 2282nd meeting, 15 June 1981, p.42.

61   S/PV. 2288th meeting, 19 June 1981, p.60.

62   S/PV. 2283rd meeting, 15 June 1981, p.57.

63   S/PV. 2284th meeting, 16 June 1981, p.5.

64   S/PV. 2288th meeting, 19 June 1981, p.53. See, also, statement of representative of Algeria, S/PV. 2280th meeting, 12 June 1981, pp.80-1; statement of representative of Brazil, S/PV. 2281st meeting, 13 June 1981, p.21; statement of representative of Uganda, S/PV. 2282nd meeting, 15 June 1981, pp.6-7 (this can be read as supporting a limited right of anticipatory self-defence under general international law, although not under the Charter); statement of representative of Spain, ibid., p.27; statement of representative of Ireland, S/PV. 2283rd meeting, 15 June 1981, pp.10-11; statement of representative of Romania, ibid., p.43; statement of representative of Syria, S/PV. 2284th meeting, 16 June 1981, p.22; statement of representative of Guyana, S/PV. 2286th meeting, 17 June 1981, pp.11-12.

65   On the dual functions of the Security Council President see e.g. I. Pogany, 'The Role of the President of the UN Security Council', *International and Comparative Law Quarterly*, vol. 31, 1982, p.231, esp. at pp.234-5.

66   S/PV. 2288th meeting, 19 June 1981, pp.42, 46.

67   S/PV. 2283rd meeting, 15 June 1981, p.23.

68   See e.g. Stone, op. cit., pp.69-72. See, also, J. Stone, *Conflict Through Consensus*, 1977, p.198, note 20.

69   In the 1950s and early 1960s, Soviet military analysts advocated resort to a pre-emptive strategic nuclear strike if an attack by the United States was thought to be imminent. See D. Holloway, "Thinking About Nuclear War: the Soviet View", in

Holroyd, op. cit., p. 45, esp. at pp. 52, 71. At present, according to some analysts Soviet military doctrine envisages the early, and possibly preemptive, use of theatre nuclear weapons in order to "paralyze opponents physically and psychologically at every operational, logistical, and control level". See Collins, op. cit., p. 67. See, also, note 18 above for the argument that Soviet military planners favour an offensive nuclear strategy. For a contrary view, i.e. that Soviet strategy currently seeks to avoid all use of nuclear weapons relying, instead, on Soviet conventional superiority see note 16 above.

70   There is, thus, a not unfamiliar methodological problem in that what states declare to be the law may conflict with their actual, or probable, behaviour.

71   General Assembly Resolution 2625 (XXV), 24 October 1970.

72   General Assembly Resolution 3314 (XXIX), 14 December 1974. However, this formulation still leaves open the question of whether every 'first use of armed force by a State' is necessarily 'in contravention of the Charter'.

73   The passage is reproduced in G. Schwarzenberger, *International Law as Applied by Courts and Tribunals*, vol. II, 1968, pp.28-9.

74   Ibid., p.71.

75   General Assembly Resolution 95 (I), 11 December 1946.

76   See, generally, N. Ronzitti, *Rescuing Nationals Abroad Through Military Coercion and Intervention on Grounds of Humanity*, 1985, pp.41-9. The Court confined itself to the observation that, as the US had already submitted its dispute with Iran to the ICJ, the rescue operation was 'of a kind calculated to undermine respect for the judicial process in international relations'. *ICJ Reports*, 1980, p.3, p.43.

77   Ibid., pp.56-7, 64. This is, in fact, a quote from Article 51 of the Charter.

78   The US acceptance of the ICJ's jurisdiction, deposited on 26 August 1946, *excluded* 'disputes arising under a multilateral treaty, unless (1) all parties to the treaty affected by the decision are also parties to the case before the Court, or (2) the United States of America specially agrees to jurisdiction'. Neither condition was satisfied in the present case. See *ICJ Reports*, 1986, p. 14 at pp. 21-38.

79   Ibid., p. 94.

80   Ibid., p. 97.

81   Ibid., p. 103.

82   Ibid.

83   Ibid., p. 347.

84   Ibid., pp. 347-8.

85   Ibid., p. 94.

86   Pogany, op. cit., p.7

87   Thus, a state may only resort to force in self-defence if there are no satisfactory peaceful means by which it can assure its defence. See note 9 above.

5 Nuclear weapons and non-proliferation: The legal aspects

John Woodliffe

Within months of the first demonstration of the awesome destructiveness of the atom bomb, the General Assembly of the fledgling United Nations Organization had agreed unanimously to the establishment of an Atomic Energy Commission (AEC), whose task was to examine the problems raised by the discovery of atomic energy.[1] The AEC was charged with drawing up proposals on four key issues. First, the free exchange of basic scientific information for peaceful ends; second, control of atomic energy to the extent necessary to ensure its use only for peaceful purposes; third, the elimination of atomic weapons from national armaments; and fourth, the creation of effective inspection procedures to ensure compliance with the normative framework established. Forty years later such an agenda seems positively utopian. Nuclear disarmament remains a chimera; and the spiralling growth in the world's nuclear armoury fuelled by the arms race[2] has had a debilitating effect on progress in harnessing nuclear energy for peaceful ends.

These failings notwithstanding, it is possible to discern some modest progress over the past four decades towards the realisation of the goals set out in that first resolution of the General Assembly.[3] Some of the evidence is to be found in the discussion elsewhere in this book of specific treaty regimes limiting the testing and deployment of nuclear weapons. These measures may be viewed as links in a chain that supports the overarching policy of the international community to prevent the spread of nuclear weapons. The cornerstone of this policy of non-proliferation, as it is now commonly called,[4] and the main focus of this chapter, is the Treaty on the Non-Proliferation of Nuclear Weapons 1968 (NPT). It has been reinforced by supplementary measures, some formal, others informal, adopted by the international community, regional organizations, individual states, and groups of states. The most important of these measures are referred to below.

The chapter is organized under the following headings: the genesis of a global non-proliferation regime; the rights and duties assumed by states parties to the NPT; the effectiveness of these norms over the fifteen years since the treaty entered into force; measures aimed at strengthening non-proliferation policies; and finally, an estimate of the treaty's long-term prospects. Although the emphasis is on the legal framework governing non-proliferation of nuclear weapons that framework cannot be understood in isolation from the dominant political and economic forces that have conditioned it.

The evolution of a global policy on non-proliferation, 1945–68[5]

The hopes raised by the radical nature of the AEC's terms of reference, described above, soon fell victim to the emergent Cold War between East and West. The revolutionary proposal put to the AEC by the American statesman Bernard Baruch in June 1946,[6] would have created an international atomic energy authority entrusted with exclusive responsibility for monitoring all phases of the development and use of atomic energy. Upon successful implementation of this plan the US (then the sole possessor of the atomic bomb) undertook to destroy its stocks of atomic weapons. Within days the Soviet Union had tabled counter-proposals outlawing the production and use of atomic weapons and calling for the destruction of existing stocks of such weapons. Unlike the US plan, that envisaged supervision by an international body, the Soviet proposal was based on self-regulation by individual states. In May 1948, the AEC announced that talks had reached an impasse; the 'first attempt to achieve international nuclear disarmament had failed'.[7] Not long after, the US monopoly was ended when the Soviet Union exploded its first atomic bomb. The United Kingdom's entry into the nuclear club followed in 1952. These developments signalled the failure of the US Atomic Energy Act 1946[8] which had imposed an absolute ban on the dissemination of information on the technology of atomic power. Furthermore, both Canada and France had started significant civil nuclear programmes. At this stage, the only countries officially to have renounced the possession, manufacture and testing of atomic weapons had been compelled to do so as part of the post-war peace settlement.[9]

It was the Soviet thermonuclear explosion in 1953 that finally prompted the US to seek a fresh initiative to halt the growing threat of an increase in the number of nuclear weapons states. In December 1953, President Eisenhower unveiled his Atoms for Peace plan to the

UN General Assembly.[10] In essence, the plan involved the lifting of the US moratorium on atomic cooperation with other states. In return for sharing US know-how, the beneficiary states would have to undertake not to divert any assistance received towards military ends. This obligation was to be made verifiable by a system of safeguards including on-site inspection by international officials. The Atoms for Peace approach did not explicitly incorporate non-proliferation objectives since it did not bar peaceful nuclear assistance to states which might be developing nuclear power for military purposes independently.[11] The creation in 1957 of the International Atomic Energy Agency (IAEA), an independent intergovernmental organization within the UN system,[12] set the seal on the general philosophy underlying the Eisenhower proposals.

An amendment to the McMahon Act in 1954 opened the way for the US – then the indisputable leader in the development of civil nuclear power[13] – to fulfil its pledge to provide materials, equipment and information to the many states who desired to embark on peaceful nuclear programmes. Commencing in 1956, the US concluded numerous bilateral cooperation agreements under which the state receiving assistance permitted US inspectors to enter its territory to administer safeguards. Safeguards were designed to provide verification of the uses to which the transferred nuclear material or equipment were put. These bilateral agreements were doubly significant. On the one hand, they 'represented the first successful major effort to subject undertakings among nations to verification by outside authorities in place of the historic reliance on the good faith of each nation'.[14] On the other hand, safeguards adhered solely to the material and equipment received, and in no way required the assisted state 'to abandon any form of nuclear military program . . . provided it was carried out in installations and with materials totally distinct from those provided by the US.'[15]

A truly international system of safeguards had become imperative now that other industrialised nations had begun to export nuclear know-how and technology under bilateral cooperation agreements similar to those concluded by the US. The IAEA, however, needed more time to build up its own safeguards system[16] and to train its personnel for on-site inspection of nuclear facilities. It was only in 1963 when the Soviet Union dropped its opposition to the idea of internationally administered safeguards, that the IAEA was in a position to start to operate the new system. Thereafter, the safeguards responsibilities of the supplier states under existing bilateral agreements were transferred to the IAEA – sometimes only with the reluctant consent of the assisted state – by means of what became known as 'safeguards transfer agreements'.[17] Any bilateral cooperation agreement concluded since 1963 has invariably incorporated a standard provision according the IAEA responsibility for establishing and administering safeguards under the agreement. This is effected by the negotiation of a separate agreement (known as a 'trilateral safeguard agreement') between the IAEA and the two states concerned. Although the detailed arrangements will vary from case to case, the general structure of these safeguard agreements will be modelled on guidelines laid down by the IAEA.[18]

By the mid-1960s the two superpowers, while unable to agree on measures to curb the nuclear arms race, were united in their concern that nuclear weapons might spread beyond the five states with a proven nuclear weapons capability.[19] The ability to pursue, whether overtly or covertly, an indigenous or other unsafeguarded route to the acquisition of nuclear weapons was now within the reach of a growing number of states.[20] A more hopeful sign was the voluntary renunciation by three leading industrial states of any intention to develop a nuclear weapons programme.[21] The momentum towards some formal agreement limiting the spread of nuclear weapons had been given a significant boost in 1961 when the UN General Assembly set up the Eighteen Nation Disarmament Committee (ENDC).[22] This body was to play a vital role in the lengthy negotiations that culminated on 1 July 1968, in the signing by over 50 States of the Treaty on the Non-Proliferation of Nuclear Weapons (NPT).[23]

The Treaty on the Non-Proliferation of Nuclear Weapons[24]

The treaty in perspective

The unique achievement that the NPT represents should not be underestimated:

> For the first time in history, nations have unilaterally renounced the manufacture of the most powerful armament known, even though the manufacturing process was within their technical and financial capacity. For the first time also, they have agreed to guarantee the peaceful character of certain of their industrial installations – and even to submit these installations to international control.[25]

This should not, however, be allowed to obscure the underlying reality. At bottom, the Treaty is no more than a 'collateral'[26] means to an end, namely, general and complete disarmament, rather than an end in itself.[27] Non-proliferation of nuclear weapons is intended simply as a device for buying time while the nuclear weapons states (NWS) tackle in decisive manner the issue of nuclear disarmament. The Treaty does indeed explicitly recognize the linkage between the two issues.[28] It is the lack of progress on the arms control issue, highlighted by the non-nuclear weapon states (NNWS) at the NPT review conferences convened in 1975, 1980 and 1985[29] that undoubtedly constitutes the gravest threat to the treaty's survival into the next decade. In addition to these 'non-proliferation' and 'disarmament' strands, the treaty contains another strand which has also received close scrutiny at the above mentioned review conferences. To many NNWS the treaty is a straightforward bargain by which in return for their undertaking to refrain from making or acquiring nuclear weapons, they are to be afforded every assistance by the NWS to develop nuclear energy for peaceful purposes.[30] What emerges from the three review conferences is a clear division among states as to the treaty's primary purpose. There are those who regard non-proliferation as its *raison d'être*; there are others – probably a majority – who regard the elements of non-proliferation, disarmament and promotion of nuclear energy for peaceful purposes as interdependent obligations of equal importance. It is the strictly non-proliferation provisions of the NPT to which attention is now turned. As will be seen, their drafting leaves much to be desired from the point of view of clarity and precision.

Analysis of the non-proliferation obligations of the contracting parties[31]

Any realistic analysis of the intention of the states parties to the NPT cannot but fail to heed the comments of the US Secretary of State at the time the treaty was negotiated: 'the Treaty deals only with what is prohibited – not with what is permitted.'[32]

Obligations relating to the ban on the transfer, receipt and manufacture of nuclear weapons

Here, as throughout the treaty, a fundamental distinction is drawn between the obligations imposed upon nuclear weapon states (NWS) and those imposed upon non-nuclear weapon states (NNWS).

1.   Obligations of nuclear weapon states   For the purposes of the NPT, a nuclear weapon state is defined as one which has manufactured and exploded a nuclear weapon or other nuclear explosive device prior to 1 January 1967.[33]

The central undertaking of NWS is contained in Article I, the first part of which provides:

> Each nuclear weapon State Party to the Treaty undertakes not to transfer to any recipient whatsoever nuclear weapons or other nuclear explosive devices or control over such weapons or explosive devices directly or indirectly. . .

Attention is drawn to two preliminary points concerning the interpretation of the phrase 'any recipient whatsoever'. First, it embraces not only states, whether or not parties to the treaty, but arguably also such non-state entities as a military alliance[34] or an international organization.[35] Secondly, transfers of weapons or control thereof made by one NWS to another NWS are clearly caught by the prohibition in Article I. On the other hand, as between two NWS there is no bar on the transfer of delivery systems such as missiles or aircraft that are merely capable of being equipped with nuclear warheads.[36] There is likewise no bar on the transfer of a nuclear reactor intended to provide the propulsion system for a submarine or warship. These conclusions would seem warranted given the absence from the Treaty of any definition of the terms, nuclear weapon and nuclear explosive device.[37] This is also the interpretation of Article I adopted by the US and is one that has not been challenged, at least publicly, by other parties to the NPT.

It must also follow that the 'special relationship' between the US and the UK regarding cooperation on matters connected with the military use of nuclear power remains unaffected by the NPT. The legal basis of this cooperation is to be found in an important agreement concluded in 1958.[38] This provides, *inter alia*, for exchanges of nuclear equipment and materials and of information on the development of nuclear weapons and of delivery systems for such weapons; it stipulates, however, that 'there will be no transfer by either Party of atomic weapons'.[39] Accordingly, assistance, however substantial, that falls short of actual transfer of nuclear weapons is not contrary to the NPT. This is illustrated by the exchanges of letters in July 1980[40] and March 1982[41] relating to the purchase by the UK of Trident missiles from the US, 'less only the warheads themselves'.[42] In what is clearly a reference to the NPT, the text of the letter from the British Prime Minister to the US President avers: 'it is my understanding that cooperation in the modernization of the UK deterrent in this way would be consistent with the present and prospective international obligations of both parties.'[43]

The prohibition on the transfer of 'control', either 'directly' or 'indirectly', had a long and complicated drafting history that requires only a brief comment here.[44] Essentially, this form of words was intended to legitimize arrangements among the member states of the North Atlantic Treaty Organization (NATO) concerning the release in time of crisis of tactical nuclear weapons deployed since the late 1950s[45] in the territories of several NATO states in Europe. The warheads for these weapons, as opposed to the delivery systems, remain under US legal ownership and in the physical custody of its forces stationed in Europe.[46] Although these weapons are within NATO's formal procedures for joint consultation and planning on nuclear policy, in which both NWS and NNWS members participate, the generally accepted view is that the procedures in no way involve the transfer of control by the former to the latter group of states. The reason is that any final decision to release and/or to fire these European-based weapons would rest with the nuclear state that owned them. The US would not therefore be surrendering 'control' over these decisions in the sense of allowing other states a 'finger on the trigger'.[47]

The decision taken by NATO in December 1979[48] to modernize its long-range theatre nuclear forces in Europe with cruise and Pershing missiles does not represent any change in the legal position set out above. The missiles will remain under US ownership and control.

In this connection, it should be noted that in contrast with the NPT, the Treaty for the Prohibition of Nuclear Weapons in Latin America 1967, whose primary aim is the military denuclearization of that continent, places an absolute ban on the diffusion, storage, installation or deployment of nuclear weapons irrespective of who owns or controls them.[49]

Finally, the reference in Article I to transfers that are 'indirect' possibly contemplates the situation where the nuclear weapon or device is channelled through the intermediary of a third state which may or may not be a party to the NPT.[50]

Further obligations are imposed on NWS by the second part of Article I, namely:

> not in any way to assist, encourage or induce any non-nuclear-weapon State to manufacture or otherwise acquire nuclear weapons or other nuclear explosive devices or control over such weapons or explosive devices.

The foregoing obligation of NWS has been described as a 'long ladder with many rungs'.[51] It purports to proscribe a range of activities in language so vague as to be 'susceptible only of subjective appraisal. . . . Almost any kind of international nuclear assistance is potentially useful to a nuclear weapons program. Indeed most nuclear activity is objectively ambiguous.'[52] What would be the position, for example, of a NWS that in all good faith provided training in nuclear physics to students from a state not a party to the NPT and suspected of wanting to manufacture its own nuclear weapons? Fortunately, some element of objectivity is furnished by the requirement in Article III.2 considered below, that safeguards be attached to the categories of peaceful nuclear assistance therein specified.

It is manifest that the obligation of NWS to withhold assistance or other forms of encouragement, in respect of the manufacture or control of nuclear explosives applies to *all* NNWS. Otherwise there would be little incentive for a NNWS to become a party to the NPT.

2.   *Obligations of non-nuclear weapon states*   In terms of their meaning and scope the obligations on NNWS have been said to raise fewer problems than those incumbent on NWS.[53] The triad of obligations set out in Article II is the logical counterpart to those imposed by Article I upon NWS. Article II provides:

> Each non-nuclear-weapon State Party to the Treaty undertakes (1) not to receive the transfer from any transferor whatsoever of nuclear weapons or other nuclear explosive devices or of control over such weapons or explosive devices directly or indirectly; (2) not to manufacture or otherwise acquire nuclear weapons or other nuclear explosive devices; and (3) not to seek or receive any assistance in the manufacture of nuclear weapons or other nuclear explosive devices.

Many of the phrases used mirror those in Article I, and their meaning has been considered when discussing that Article. Article II, however, diverges from Article I in several important respects. First, the second of the prohibitions imposed on a NNWS applies equally to the manufacture or acquisition of nuclear weapons accomplished by means of indigenous resources and without any outside assistance. On the other hand, Article II in no way prohibits research and development in the nuclear field. Accordingly it has been suggested that a NNWS party to the NPT may quite legally conduct all the preparations for the 'manufacture' of a nuclear device barring the final stage of assembly, that is, up to the point where 'the last screw has been turned'. Until then, or until a successful test is carried out, the device is arguably not transformed into a 'nuclear weapon or nuclear explosive device.'[54] Whichever interpretation of Article II is correct, many commentators believe that a NNWS wishing to acquire nuclear weapon status will prefer this 'bomb in the basement' route to the less ambiguous route of a nuclear detonation.[55] Secondly, Article II, when read with Article I, would not appear to preclude a NWS receiving from a NNWS assistance that pertains to the manufacture of nuclear weapons; *a fortiori* a NNWS is free to give that assistance to a NWS.[56]

There remains a potentially even more serious lacuna in Article III. Nowhere in that Article is there a specific ban on assistance provided by one NNWS party to the treaty to another NNWS that is not a party, in connection with a nuclear weapons programme in the latter. This possibility was raised during negotiation of the NPT by the erstwhile United

Arab Republic. Other states considered this as no more than a 'theoretical loophole'. Both superpowers expressed their unwillingness to reopen discussion on the point, not least because the assisting state would have no reason to afford the assisted state advantages that it had itself forsworn. If a NNWS party to the NPT were to provide such assistance then the natural inference was that its actions were intended to promote the development of nuclear weapons for its own benefit.[57]

The system of safeguards[58]

As will be explained shortly safeguards play a pivotal role in the operation of the NPT. Once more, the burden of safeguards lies almost entirely on NNWS. In marked contrast, the treaty makes no provision for the verification of the obligation of NWS in Article I nor for inspection of civil nuclear facilities in those states.

1.   Nature and scope of safeguard obligations   By Article III.1, each NNWS undertakes to accept safeguards

> for the exclusive purpose of verification of the fulfilment of its obligations assumed under this Treaty with a view to preventing diversion of nuclear energy from peaceful uses to nuclear weapons or other nuclear explosive devices.

In order to achieve that aim safeguards are to attach to

> *all* source or special fissionable material in *all* peaceful nuclear activities within the territory of such State, under its jurisdiction, or carried out under its control anywhere.[59]

This constitutes an unequivocal commitment to accept 'full-scope' safeguards, so called for the reason that they apply to a state's entire peaceful nuclear programme both now and in the future.[60]

Article III.2 reinforces this primary obligation of NNWS by requiring that all international transactions involving the supply to any NNWS for peaceful purposes of source or special fissionable material[61] or of equipment or material especially designed or prepared for the processing, use or production of special fissionable material, 'shall be subject to the safeguards required by the Article'. It follows that upon the sale of 'equipment' within the meaning of Article III.2, for example a reprocessing or uranium enrichment plant, safeguards would prospectively attach to special fissionable material used, produced or processed therein.[62] *Prima facie*, then, the reach of the obligation in respect of NNWS is unlimited; it applies to the supply of material or equipment by any state party, whether NWS or NNWS, to any NNWS, whether a party to the NPT or not. It follows therefore that a non-party state will find itself obliged, as a condition of receiving assistance, to agree to safeguards. There remain, nevertheless, several situations outside the reach of mandatory safeguards. First, where otherwise safeguardable material is transferred for peaceful use to a NWS by a NNWS.[63] Secondly, the discrimination against NNWS built into the NPT is especially marked in the context of safeguards, since NWS are under no obligation to apply them to their own peaceful nuclear activities. The official reason given for this immunity was that verification within NWS of the non-diversion to weapons obligation could serve no non-proliferation purpose whatsoever. The unofficial reason was the Soviet Union's opposition to any international inspection of its civil nuclear activities.[64]

2. What safeguards can and cannot achieve The Director-General of the IAEA, Dr Hans Blix, himself an international lawyer, has enunciated the role of safeguards within the framework of the NPT as follows:

> [It] constitutes a monitoring system providing confidence that monitored activities are purely peaceful. Safeguards are therefore a confidence building measure . . . to generate confidence, they must be capable of detecting possible breaches of commitments with such promptness that other States would have time to mobilize means of inducing respect for the non-proliferation pledge. . . . States do not invite inspection to deter themselves from diversion, but to achieve verification confirmation.[65]

In a subsequent address, Dr Blix spelt out the limits of safeguards in the sense of what they cannot and – despite public preconceptions to the contrary – were never intended to accomplish.

> Safeguards cannot prevent a violation of obligations – the diversion of fissile material – any more than bank or company audits can prevent a misappropriation of funds. All they can do is expose infringements or arouse suspicions, in effect, sound the alarm. The inspectors are not public officers with physical powers of prevention. All they can do is report. If they should be denied admittance they can only report the fact. . . . Another limitation in IAEA safeguards . . . is that it can make no predictions regarding the possible future intentions of an inspected State. The . . . system reports on the current situation.[66]

Thus safeguards alone are incapable of providing an impenetrable barrier to proliferation of nuclear weapons. The major barrier is the political judgement of a state to abjure nuclear weapons expressed by its commitment to the NPT or to some analogous agreement.[67]

3.   The mode of implementation of NPT safeguards undertakings by NNWS   Article III.1 requires each NNWS party to the treaty to negotiate and conclude with the IAEA a 'safeguards agreement' whose terms must accord with the Agency's Statute and with its safeguard system.[68] It should be noted that the Agency is not a party to the NPT and accordingly cannot enforce the obligations assumed by States who are parties to it: 'obligations owed to the Agency by NPT States arise under consequential safeguard agreements which the NPT obliges them to conclude with the Agency'.[69]

The Agency's 'statutory' system of safeguards is based on its Statute and on an outline agreement drawn up in 1965.[70] This system, since it applied only to plants and facilities specifically agreed with the state concerned, was not equipped to deal with the different situation under the NPT which required the safeguarding of all nuclear activities in a state. To cover the latter situation, the Agency in 1971 produced a detailed model agreement.[71] Any departure from this agreement requires the approval of the IAEA's Board of Governors.[72] Constraints on space prevent more than a cursory discussion of the model agreement, many of whose provisions are highly technical in character. For the most part, they reinforce and amplify the skeletal framework of obligations set out in the NPT. The document defines the objective of safeguards thus:

> The timely detection of diversion of significant quantities of nuclear material from peaceful nuclear activities to the manufacture of nuclear weapons or of other nuclear explosive devices or for purposes unknown and deterrence of such diversion by the risk of early detection.

In order to secure this objective, the safeguards agreement should prescribe as 'the safeguards measure of fundamental importance', the use of 'material accountancy . . . with containment and surveillance as important complementary measures'.[73]

The Agency's team of inspectors perform a vital role in policing the operation of the safeguards system. The methods used include on-site measurements and observations. These are then checked against the data in reports and records that each state is obliged to maintain and to supply to the IAEA.[74] The necessary data is collected under each state's national system for controlling and accounting for nuclear material within its territory.

Article III.3 of the NPT provides that the implementation of safeguards shall be 'in a manner designed to comply with Article IV of the Treaty and to avoid hampering the economic or technological development of the Parties or international co-operation in the field of peaceful nuclear activities'. These considerations are echoed in INFCIRC/153 which, in addition, stipulates that the Agency must take the utmost care to protect commercial and industrial secrets and other confidential information coming to its knowledge as a result of its safeguard functions.[75]

4. Sanctions for breach of the non-diversion obligation in a safeguards agreement   The NPT is silent on the legal consequences of a finding, following a visit by IAEA inspectors, that a state has diverted nuclear material. To deal with such a contingency, INFCIRC/153 confers important functions on the Board of Governors of the IAEA. Where the Board, after examination of relevant information reported to it by the Director General, finds that the Agency 'is not able to verify that there has been no diversion of nuclear material required to be safeguarded under the Agreement to nuclear weapons or other nuclear explosive devices', then the Board may activate the procedures laid down in Article XII of the Statute.[76] These may ultimately lead to the reporting of the defaulting state to the Security Council and General Assembly of the UN.[77] The IAEA having sounded the warning bell, responsibility for further action – including political or economic sanctions – against the transgressor state thus passes to the UN. Experience suggests that whether such action by the Organization would be forthcoming is highly problematic.[78] The criticism that the IAEA lacks credible sanctions of its own is misplaced and in any event disregards the Agency's primary role which is the promotion of the peaceful uses of atomic energy.

Reinforcement of the NPT: Subsequent practice of the state parties and of the IAEA

The preceding section identified several structural weaknesses in the NPT regime. The purpose of this section is twofold. First, to consider some of the measures taken by the community of states to strengthen the legal barriers against proliferation in the decade and a half following the treaty's entry into force in 1970. Secondly, to determine how far these measures have succeeded.

The Nuclear Suppliers Group

The 'peaceful nuclear explosion' carried out by India in May 1974 drew attention to the fragility of safeguard arrangements which do not embrace the totality of peaceful nuclear activities within a state – an obligation which is limited to states parties to the NPT. A related concern was that unregulated competition among industrialised states to sell nuclear technology to developing Third World states – particularly those who had not adhered to the NPT – would lead to a 'bargaining down' of safeguard requirements.[79] The response by those states who are the world's major suppliers of nuclear equipment and nuclear fuel was to draw up strict guidelines for the transfer of items of sensitive technology. This action also served to amplify Article III.2 of the NPT which, as noted above, sanctions transfers of such items as part of normal commercial nuclear relations between states.[80]

The guidelines, drawn up initially in London in 1975 by the fifteen states members of the Nuclear Suppliers Group (NSG),[81] include the following interrelated principles: (1) the application of IAEA safeguards as a precondition of the transfer either of items on a 'trigger list'[82] or of certain kinds of technology[83] (2) the exercise of 'restraint' by suppliers in the transfer of sensitive facilities, technology and weapons-usable materials (3) in the case of a transfer made in accordance with principles (1) and (2), any subsequent retransfer by the recipient state of 'trigger-list' items or of sensitive technology must satisfy two conditions. First, the consent of the supplier state must be obtained. Secondly, the new transferee must give the supplier assurances identical to those given by the original transferee. (4) the recipient state must undertake to accept IAEA safeguards on any facility constructed by it during an agreed period where that facility is of the same type as one transferred to it by the supplier, or is one that the supplier and recipient states jointly identify as using transferred technology.[84]

However well-intentioned may have been the motives of the NSG, the guidelines have prompted a hostile response from NNWS who view them as a *démarche* that runs counter to the letter and spirit of Article IV of the NPT.[85] Resentment has been compounded by the realization of NNWS parties to the NPT that states remaining outside the NPT have for all practical purposes received no less favourable treatment from supplier states, their non-acceptance of 'full-scope' safeguards notwithstanding. This unsatisfactory situation led the first NPT Review Conference, held in 1975, to urge that 'in all achievable ways common export requirements relating to safeguards be strengthened, in particular by extending the application of safeguards to all peaceful nuclear activities in importing states, not parties to the Treaty'.[86] In the long-term, the 'policy of denial' embodied in the NSG guidelines may prove counterproductive by encouraging states to achieve a nuclear fuel cycle that is wholly independent of outside assistance,[87] thereby weakening non-proliferation objectives.[88]

In the past few years, several new supplier states who are neither parties to the NPT nor members of the NSG, have entered the international nuclear market. They include Argentina, Brazil, China, India and South Africa.[89] There is concern that these 'second-tier' suppliers could undermine the NSG guidelines, particularly in relation to the spread of sensitive nuclear technology. It has been suggested that these states could be attracted by the prestige and status that an offer of membership of the NSG might be seen to confer.[90]

The effectiveness of the guidelines is difficult to gauge, not least because their promulgation coincided with a general economic recession which resulted in large scale downward revision of earlier forecasts about the scale of development of nuclear power programmes for the remainder of the twentieth century.[91] However, some commentators are predicting an upturn in the fortunes of the nuclear industry in the late 1980s. One indication of this may be the recently declared intention of the People's Republic of China (PRC) to develop a substantial civil nuclear power programme. The PRC is reported to have concluded cooperation agreements with several supplier states including the UK, the German Federal Republic, Belgium, Argentina and the US.[92]

The PRC–US agreement for cooperation concerning peaceful uses of nuclear energy,[93] was transmitted to Congress on 24 July 1985. Attached to it was a Presidential message affirming that the agreement satisfied the requirements of US nuclear non-proliferation policy. In this connection considerable reliance was placed on assurances given by the Chinese Prime Minister and subsequently endorsed by the National People's Congress.[94] The gist of the first of these assurances was that the US 'can expect' that the PRC's undertaking not to assist a NNWS to acquire nuclear explosives will be implemented 'in a manner consistent with non-proliferation practices common to the US and other suppliers'.[95] The second assurance concerned an undertaking, in conjunction with the PRC joining the IAEA in January 1984, to apply IAEA safeguards to all future nuclear exports to NNWS.[96] These assurances notwithstanding, the agreement has met considerable opposition within Congress on the ground that its text adopts a lax approach to the issue of non-proliferation.

Criticism has focused on the ambiguity of two key provisions. The first states that 'in the event that a party would like at some future time' to undertake either enrichment to 20 per cent or above, or reprocessing of, material transferred under the agreement, the parties 'will promptly hold consultations to agree on a mutually acceptable arrangement'. In so doing they must bear in mind that such activities are to be considered 'favourably'.[97] As the agreement is between two nuclear weapon states it is expressly provided that bilateral safeguards are not required. Instead, 'diplomatic channels' leading to the establishment of 'visits' to material and facilities covered by the Agreement are stipulated as the means for determining whether its provisions are being 'effectively carried out'.[98]

'Voluntary offers' of safeguards by nuclear weapon states

It has already been seen that under Article III of the NPT, safeguards are not required on peaceful nuclear activities within NWS. In addition to the overt discrimination that this immunity created between NWS and NNWS, it was felt by several of the latter states that by accepting safeguards they had put themselves at a commercial and economic disadvantage. Two reasons were proffered. First, additional financial burdens would be placed upon plant operators. Secondly, the risk of industrial espionage would be accentuated by reason of the multinational composition of the IAEA inspectorate.[99] To counter these criticisms and to induce acceptance of the NPT by those states voicing concern, the US and the UK both declared their willingness during discussions preceding the conclusion of the NPT, to accept inspection by IAEA personnel of all peaceful nuclear activities within their territories.[100] However, over ten years elapsed before these 'voluntary offers'[101] to accept safeguards were transformed into formal agreements.[102] Since then, France, though not a party to the NPT, has submitted a similar 'voluntary offer' to the IAEA.[103] The Soviet Union, which is a party to the NPT, is the latest NWS to allow inspection of its civilian nuclear activities under a 'voluntary offer' agreement.[104]

All four of the above-mentioned safeguards agreements are closely modelled on those applying to NNWS pursuant to the provisions in INFCIRC/153. Each NWS is free, however, at any time, to exclude from the scope of the agreement any facilities having national security significance.[105] This has led one commentator to compare these 'voluntary' agreements 'to the attitude of a traveller who has a right to show the customs officials which of his suitcases should be examined'.[106] Others see these inspection arrangements as providing the IAEA with invaluable experience of applying safeguards to advanced types of nuclear facility not yet in widespread use by NNWS.[107] Furthermore, though of little more than psychological value in terms of curbing 'horizontal' proliferation, the agreements may yet come to assume longer term significance as a prototype for tackling the issue of 'vertical proliferation'. In September 1985, the PRC which refuses to accede to the NPT on the ground of what it regards as the Treaty's discriminatory character, announced at the Annual Conference of the IAEA its willingness to conclude a 'voluntary offer' agreement permitting inspection of some of its civilian nuclear facilities.[108]

In the early stages of their nuclear weapons programmes, all the

NWS are believed to have relied on plutonium produced in civil reactors.[109] Though the commingling of civilian and military nuclear facilities and programmes by NWS is not expressly proscribed by the NPT, there are today sound political reasons why such activities should cease. First, they set a bad precedent in terms of promoting non-proliferation policy goals; secondly, they undermine what little credibility 'voluntary offer' agreements are perceived to have. The decision of the Reagan administration to modernise and expand US strategic nuclear forces[110] has given the issue some prominence. This follows reports that the US was contemplating for this purpose, the use of plutonium from British civil reactors,[111] transferred under the 1958 US–UK Defence Agreement[112] and stockpiled since then in the US. The British government strenuously denies that any of the plutonium bartered for US enriched uranium[113] between 1964–71 has been used in the manufacture of US nuclear weapons and cites long-term assurances to that effect given by the US in 1964, and repeated in 1984.[114] Nevertheless, a Bill[115] introduced in 1984 in the House of Representatives, sought to prohibit the use of civil nuclear material of UK origin.

The British government has frequently affirmed that no plutonium derived from civil power stations has been or will be used in the production of nuclear weapons, whether in the UK or abroad.[116] The use of plutonium for this purpose is in any case prohibited under the terms of the 'voluntary offer' agreement concluded in 1976 between the UK, Euratom, and the IAEA.[117]

Evaluation of the non-proliferation regime

The record so far

In 1963, the late President Kennedy ventured to prophesy that the 1970s might well presage a world in which up to 25 nations possessed nuclear weapons.[118] Happily, since 1964 no new nuclear weapon state has emerged[119] and an overwhelming majority of states have solemnly forsworn the acquisition of nuclear weapons. Thus, by the end of 1975, 97 NNWS had become parties to the NPT. By July 1985, immediately prior to the third NPT Review Conference, there were 128 parties.[120] As of the same date, the IAEA had negotiated safeguards agreements with 84 of the NNWS' parties to the NPT.[121] This picture is incomplete, however, since it excludes two other categories of safeguard agreement; those concluded pursuant to the Tlatelolco Treaty[122] and those based on INFCIRC 66/Rev 2 entered into by states with significant nuclear activities who are neither parties to the NPT nor to the Tlatelolco Treaty.[123] There are at present ten NNWS in this latter category and in six of those, *all* operating and planned nuclear activities of which the IAEA is *aware* are under IAEA safeguards, thereby creating in each state a system of *de facto* full-scope safeguards.[124] Nevertheless they are inferior to *de jure* full-scope safeguards in several important respects: they do not preclude unsafeguarded nationally independent nuclear facilities being set up in the future; nor will the mosaic of agreements which comprises the *de facto* system contain uniform undertakings on such matters as the duration of the agreement and its application to subsequent generations of nuclear material.[125]

It is estimated that 98 per cent of all nuclear facilities outside the NWS are now under IAEA safeguards of one type or another.[126] Moreover, the IAEA Secretariat, when submitting its latest annual Safeguards Implementation Report to the Board of Governors in June 1985, was able to state, as in previous years, that no diversion of fissile material from a safeguarded facility had been identified.[127] Finally, no state has withdrawn from the NPT or terminated any non-NPT safeguard agreement; nor, since the mid-1970s, has there been any major failure of the NSG guidelines on the transfer of nuclear technology.

According to critics of the NPT reality is somewhat different. There remains in four non-NPT states[128] at least one significant nuclear activity that is non-safeguarded and capable of producing nuclear weapons-grade material. Yet, as shown above, these states would be acting quite lawfully in building facilities that fall outside the scope of such safeguard arrangements as are binding on them. The term 'threshold state' is commonly used to refer to a state that keeps its 'nuclear options' open in this way. The adamant refusal of these states to accede to the NPT must, therefore, 'raise questions about the plans of the country concerned'.[129] Suspicion is fuelled further when these same states are observed to have opted for advanced forms of nuclear technology which given the absence of any civil nuclear power programme in those states, can serve no immediate commercial purpose.[130]

Long-term prospects

Very few of the ten NNWS with a significant nuclear activity who remain outside the NPT regime, can be expected to accede to it.[131] Many of the ten states have recorded objections in principle to the NPT, the most common being the treaty's discriminatory character in as much as it condones the continued possession of nuclear weapons by the NWS.[132] Whether evidence of real progress by NWS in reducing their nuclear stockpiles would induce new accessions to the NPT is likely to remain an untested hypothesis. It is no coincidence that the 'threshold states' who are least likely to yield on this issue are to be found in regions of high political tension where considerations of national security will be overriding. Accordingly, the prospects of gaining new adherents are unpromising. A hard core of states is likely to remain outside the treaty and will not prove susceptible to blandishments, entreaties or quiet diplomacy let alone coercive threats.[133] Experience has shown that these 'hold-out' states will find the means to circumvent any barriers imposed by way of embargoes or similar measures aimed at denying them access to nuclear materials and equipment. Policies of denial, whether imposed nationally or internationally, have enjoyed very limited success[134] and may, perversely, serve only to strengthen the embargoed state's resolve to achieve an independent nuclear fuel cycle.[135] The preceding discussion confirms, it is submitted, the proposition made at the beginning of this chapter that ultimately the effectiveness of the barriers against proliferation of nuclear weapons depends far more on political rather than on legal or technical[136] considerations.

What are these political factors? First, a state that crossed the 'threshold' would pay a heavy price for its newly acquired status and would be treated as a pariah by the international community. Consequently, a sudden unravelling of non-proliferation norms, whether in the form of widespread denunciation of the NPT, or of some public manifestation of nuclear weapons status by non-party states, seems improbable. At the same time, the international trade in materials and equipment necessary for harnessing civil nuclear power will continue to grow; increasingly, new, simpler techniques, not reliant on reactors and resistant to traditional safeguards systems will emerge, thereby increasing proliferation risks.[137] The most ominous possibility is the clandestine weapons programme that produces 'a world of bombs without tests'.[138] This would effectively render obsolete the definition of proliferation in the NPT based on the detonation of a nuclear device.

These factors provide a constant reminder that while the NNWS parties to the NPT have undertaken not to make or acquire nuclear weapons, they have not undertaken to renounce the acquisition of the prerequisites or capability – in the form of materials and technology – for so doing. The stark reality, however, is that the non-proliferation regime is a fragile construct, vulnerable to vicissitudes in relations among states, more especially between the two nuclear superpowers. The strongly worded commitment to enhancing the effectiveness of the NPT, expressed in the Joint Statement issued after the Gorbachev–Reagan meeting in November 1985,[139] provides hope that the treaty will survive not only a Fourth Review Conference in 1990 but also the ultimate test in 1995 when a decision on whether to renew the treaty must be made.[140] The final outcome will depend largely on how far the NWS, as called upon by the Final Declaration adopted at the Third Review Conference of the NPT in September 1985, can be seen to have made 'greater efforts to ensure effective measures for the cessation of the nuclear arms race at an early date (and) for nuclear disarmament',[141] a pledge reaffirmed by the USSR and the US in November 1985.[142] Without progress on these matters the political legitimacy of nuclear weapons will be accentuated. Less comforting is the verdict of a foremost historian of the nuclear age: the two superpowers' achievement, unprecedented on such a scale, in imposing a 'nuclear Yalta' under which the world is permanently divided into those states with and those without nuclear weapons, runs counter to the course of history.[143]

Notes

1   UN GA Resolution (I), 24 January 1946. The Commission was composed of the five permanent members of the Security Council plus Canada.

2   See M. Kidron and D. Smith, *The War Atlas*, 1983, Maps 9 and 10.

3   Evidenced not least by the non-use of nuclear weapons in the 300 instances of international conflict recorded since 1945: *The War Atlas*, note 2, Introduction and Maps 1–4.

4   The term is thought to have been first used officially in 1965 when it appeared as the title of a UN GA Resolution. Res/2028 (XX).

5   See generally, W. Epstein, *The Last Chance*, 1976, Ch.1.

6   Extracts from his speech are produced in 11 *Digest of International Law* (ed. Whiteman), pp. 536-8.

7   B. Goldschmidt, *The Atomic Complex. A Worldwide Political History of Nuclear Energy*, 1982. (This is a substantially revised and updated version of the author's *Le Complexe Atomique*, 1980.)

8   Otherwise known as the McMahon Act.

9   See provisions in peace treaties with Bulgaria, Finland, Hungary, Italy and Romania concluded in 1947: *UNTS*, Vol. 41, p. 21; Vol. 48, p. 228; Vol. 41, p. 135; Vol. 42, p. 3; Vol. 49, p. 126.

10   UN GAOR 8th Sess. Plenary Meetings. Vol. 1, 470th Meeting, 8 Dec. 1953, p. 450.

11   B. Goldschmidt and M. Kratzer, *Peaceful Nuclear Relations: A Study of the Creation and Erosion of Confidence*, 1978, The Rockefeller Foundation/The Royal Institute of International Affairs, p. 6.

12   See Article I of the Relationship Agreement between the UN and the IAEA, 1957. UNTS, Vol. 281, p. 369. The text of the Statute of the IAEA is in *UNTS*, Vol. 276, p. 3; it has been amended subsequently. *UNTS*, Vol. 471, p. 334.

13   The US also had a virtual monopoly over the supply of enriched uranium to the western world.

14   Goldschmidt and Kratzer, op. cit., p. 9.

15   Goldschmidt, op. cit., pp. 117-18.

16   The safeguards functions of the Agency are set out in Articles III (A) 5, XI (F) 4 and Art. XII of the Statute.

17   Made pursuant to Article III (A) (5).

18   The guidelines are set out in Agency Document INFCIRC/66, April 1965 (text reproduced in *4ILM* (1966) p. 512) as revised in 1966 and 1968 (8 *ILM* (1969) p. 893). The content of safeguards agreements is highly technical and outside the

scope of the present discussion. For a useful summary see Edwards, 'International Legal Aspects of Safeguards and the Non-Proliferation of Nuclear Weapons', 33 *ICLQ* (1984) 1, at pp. 5-8. Some general observations on the system of safeguards established under the Non-Proliferation Treaty 1968, are made below.

19   France and China had established themselves as nuclear weapons states in 1960 and 1964 respectively.

20   Doubts were already being expressed about the sincerity of the peaceful nuclear intentions of Israel and India. Goldschmidt, op. cit., p. 185.

21   Switzerland in 1962, following a referendum on the issue; Canada in the 1950s; Sweden in 1965. In addition, Japan, Italy and Germany had had nuclear abstinence imposed on them by the post-World War II peace settlement. It has been suggested that the example set by these six states to the rest of the world, gained precious breathing space for the launch of efforts to conclude an international agreement to prevent the spread of nuclear weapons. Goldschmidt, op. cit., pp. 183-5.

22   Res/1722 (XVI) 1962. Membership of the Committee was subsequently enlarged to 31 states and its name changed to the Conference of the Committee on Disarmament (CCD). Over the period 1959–68, the General Assembly adopted 13 resolutions specifically concerned with the prevention of the wider dissemination of nuclear weapons. See list in *A Short History of Non-Proliferation*, 1976, IAEA, Annex 11.

23   For differing accounts of the negotiations that preceded the Treaty see: Epstein, op. cit., Ch.5: G. Fischer, *The Non-Proliferation of Nuclear Weapons*, 1971, Ch. 3: E. Young, *A Farewell to Arms Control*, 1972, Ch. 6.

24   Text set out in *UNTS*, Vol. 729, p. 169; 7 *ILM* (1968) p. 811; UK Treaty Series. No. 88 (1970) Cmnd. 4474. The nuclear weapons-free zone provides another route for achieving non-proliferation goals. Currently, the only legally binding regime is the Treaty for the Prohibition of Nuclear Weapons in Latin America 1967 (hereafter Treaty of Tlatelolco) *UNTS*, Vol. 634, p.281. For further details on nuclear-free zones, see Chapter 8, this volume.

25   Goldschmidt, op. cit., Foreword p.xii.

26   Young, op. cit., p. 82.

27   See preambular paras 9–12 of the Treaty.

28   Article VI.

29   See Article VIII.3. This stipulates that the parties to the Treaty shall review its operation five years after its entry into force and at intervals of five years thereafter if a majority so decides. The text of the Final Declaration of the First Review Conference is reproduced in Appendix B, *Nuclear Energy and Nuclear Weapon Proliferation*, SIPRI, 1979. For summaries of the second and third Review Conference see *IAEA Bulletin*, Vol. 23, March 1981, pp. 28-31, and Vol. 26. Winter 1985, pp. 64-5, respectively.

30   See Article IV and preambular paras 4, 5, 6 and 7.

31   See M. Willrich, 'The Treaty on Non-Proliferation of Nuclear Weapons: Nuclear Technology Confronts World Politics', 77 *Yale L.J.* (1968), p. 1447; E. Firmage, 'The Treaty on the Non-Proliferation of Nuclear Weapons', 63 *AJIL* (1969), p. 711; G. Fischer, *The Non-Proliferation of Nuclear Weapons*, 1971, Chs 4–7. The discussion in the text assumes that the controlling principles of treaty interpretation are those set out in Articles 31–3 of the Vienna Convention on the Law of Treaties 1969.

32   Testimony of US Secretary of State, Dean Rusk, to Hearings on the NPT before the Senate Committee on Foreign Relations, 90th Cong. 2nd. Sess. (1968), cited in Firmage, *loc. cit.* p. 723.

33   Article IX.3. The only states to satisfy this definition are: China, France (neither of whom is a party to the Treaty), the US, USSR and UK – all of whom are parties. India, who in 1974, exploded a nuclear device for peaceful purposes is therefore regarded as a non-nuclear weapon state and would remain so even if it were to accede to the NPT. For an examination of the legality of the Indian explosion see Epstein, op. cit., Ch. 16.

34   For example, the North Atlantic Treaty Organization.

35   For example, the United Nations.

36   It has been questioned whether an anti-ballistic missile system could be transferred without breaching the NPT, on the ground that it is impossible to distinguish the offensive and defensive character of weapon systems. Fischer, op. cit., p. 57. The Greenpeace Organization is reported to have challenged the compatibility of President Reagan's Strategic Defence Initiative with the NPT, in so far as it (i) involves joint research between the US and its allies into X-ray lasers powered by nuclear explosions and (ii) envisages the transfer of a successfully completed system to the Soviet Union. *The Guardian*, 25 June 1985.

37   The Treaty of Tlatelolco is the only treaty to contain a definition of nuclear weapon, namely; 'any device which is capable of releasing nuclear energy in an uncontrolled manner and which has a group of characteristics that are appropriate for use for warlike purposes. An instrument that may be used for the transport or propulsion of the device is not included in this definition if it is separable from the device and not an indivisible part thereof' (Article 5). In contrast with the NPT, Article V of which unambiguously equates 'nuclear explosive device' – even though intended for peaceful purposes – with nuclear weapon, the Treaty of Tlatelolco has been construed by some Latin American states as sanctioning peaceful nuclear explosions. The US position is that the NPT imposes an absolute ban on such explosions 'unless someone can someday invent a nuclear explosive which cannot be used as a nuclear weapon' (quoted in Willrich, op. cit., p. 1465). Article V of the NPT is all but a dead letter. See Final Document of the Third NPT Review Conference, Doc. NPT/CONF. III/64/I p 10. Geneva 1985.

38   Agreement for cooperation on the uses of atomic energy for mutual defence purposes 1958, *UNTS*, Vol. 326, p. 3. The agreement has been amended several times.

39   Article 5. It has been argued that any form of cooperation between NWS that goes beyond scientific exchange of information, such as the transfer of fissile material intended for military use or research is now incompatible with Article I of the NPT. Fischer, op. cit., p.66 n.42. *Contra*, Willrich, op. cit., p. 1447. See also below.

40   Cmnd. 7979.

41   Cmnd. 8517. This 1982 agreement – which in every other respect is identical to the 1980 agreement – was made necessary by the US decision to phase out the Trident I missile specified in the earlier agreement and to replace it with a Trident II version.

42   That is, the UK will build its own submarines and nuclear warheads.

43   See also H.C. Deb. Vol. 73, col. 478 (Written Answer) 20 February 1985.

44   See Willrich, op. cit., pp. 1465-74; Fischer, op. cit., pp. 70-8.

45   Under agreements for cooperation on the uses of atomic energy for mutual defence purposes. See e.g. US – Turkey agreement, *UNTS* Vol. 355, p. 341.

46   Under the so-called dual-key mechanism.

47   *NATO-Facts and Figures* (10th edn 1981), p.153. See also statement by US President Johnson that 'the release of nuclear weapons would come by Presidential decision alone'. 51 *US Department of State Bulletin* (1964), pp. 458-9. The UK government has expressed the view that there is no incompatibility between

these NATO arrangements and the NPT. H.C. Deb. Vol. 768, cols. 6–7, 8 July 1968.

48 Communiqué of NATO Ministers, 12 December 1979, reproduced in *NATO-Facts and Figures*, op. cit.

49 Article I.

50 Fischer, op. cit., p. 58.

51 Statement of Swedish representative at 1966 session of the ENDC, cited in Willrich, op. cit., p. 1475.

52 Ibid., p. 1476.

53 Fischer, op. cit., p. 59.

54 Epstein, op. cit., pp. 89-90.

55 Israel and South Africa are frequently cited as examples of states that have already taken the bomb in the basement route.

56 When supplying uranium oxide ('yellow cake') to NWS, both Australia and Canada insist on safeguards. Curiously, the only obligation under the NPT safeguards system is to inform the IAEA of shipments of such materials. This is less strict than non-NPT safeguards under INFCIRC/66/REV. 2, note 18 above and EURATOM safeguards. See D. Fischer and P. Szasz, *Safeguarding the Atom. A Critical Appraisal* (ed. J. Goldblat) SIPRI, Sweden 1985, pp. 70, 79 (hereafter Fischer and Szasz). It has been alleged that the UK is considering the purchase of unsafeguarded Namibian uranium to fuel Trident, as other potential sources require safeguards against possible military use. *The Guardian*, 18 May 1985 (letters).

57 For discussion of the possible motives behind the interpretation adopted by the US and USSR, see Willrich, op. cit., p. 1478. The safeguards required under Article III.2 (discussed below) would not have satisfied the UAR's concern since those safeguards are applicable to nuclear materials and equipment provided for peaceful purposes only.

58 See generally, Edwards, op. cit.; D. Fischer, *International Safeguards 1979*, The Rockefeller Foundation/The Royal Institute of International Affairs, 1979; D. Fischer and P. Szasz, *Safeguarding the Atom: A Critical Appraisal*. SIPRI 1985. Part I. The special features of NPT safeguards are dealt with separately below.

59 Article III.1 (emphasis added). More specifically, safeguards follow such material at every stage of its production, processing or use within a principal nuclear facility or when it is located outside that facility.

60 Full-scope safeguards depend, in the first instance, on information supplied to the IAEA by each state identifying all nuclear material located there. This amounts to an 'act of faith' in a state's initial report. See Fischer and Szasz, op. cit., pp. 35-6.

61 The expression is not defined in the NPT but may be taken to have the same meaning as in the IAEA, Art. XX. This refers to both plutonium and enriched uranium.

62 This is the so-called 'right of pursuit' whereby 'substances produced by transmutations of safeguarded materials must in turn be themselves subjected to safeguards'. Goldschmidt, op. cit., p. 387.

63 For the position where the transfer is for non-peaceful use see note 54 above.

64 Willrich, op. cit., p. 1481.

65 'Building Confidence', 26 *IAEA Bulletin*, September 1984, p. 3.

66 'Safeguards and Non-Proliferation', 27 *IAEA Bulletin*, Summer 1985, p. 3 at pp. 5-6.

67 Ibid., p. 4.

68 Strict time limits for concluding the agreements are laid down for states ratifying or acceding to the Treaty (Art. III.4).

69　Herron, 'A lawyer's view of safeguards and non-proliferation', 24 *IAEA Bulletin*, September 1982, p. 32, who points out that 'it is only when the safeguard agreement is concluded that the question of the effectiveness of Agency safeguards can arise in the NPT context.'

70　i.e. Agency document, INFCIRC/66.

71　i.e. Agency document INFCIRC/153. Text reproduced in 10 ILM (1971) p. 855. For a comparison of this system with that contained in INFCIRC/66 see Edwards, op. cit., p. 12; Fischer and Szasz, op. cit., Ch. 11.

72　Edwards, op. cit.

73　INFCIRC 153, paras 28-29. For an account of the technical features of these measures, see Fischer and Szasz, op. cit., Ch. 4.

74　Ibid., para. 7 and Pt. II. There are currently 170 IAEA inspectors; the cost of operating the safeguards system is approximately $30 million per annum. Most of the inspection effort is concentrated on facilities which handle large amounts of sensitive material, in other words, in states that already have a firm political commitment to non-proliferation. See Grumm, 'Potential and limitations of international safeguards', *IAEA Bulletin*, 1982, Supplement pp. 40-3. For discussion of defects in the inspection system see Fischer and Szasz, op. cit., pp. 61-6.

75　Ibid., para. 5.

76　Para. (C).

77　Ibid.

78　Failure to remedy the non-compliance may also result in suspension of the privileges and rights of membership of the IAEA and in curtailment of assistance given by the Agency to the state (Article XII (C)). For a comprehensive discussion of sanctions for violations of safeguard agreements, see Fischer and Szasz, op. cit., Part II.

79　See Woodliffe, 'The Non-Proliferation Treaty Revisited', XXVII *Netherlands International Law Review*, (1980) p. 39, at 52-5.

80　This 'policy of denial' is seen by many developing states as an infringement of Article IV of the NPT which affirms the right of all states to further the peaceful uses of nuclear energy.

81　The guidelines for nuclear transfers were made public in 1978. Text reproduced in 17 *ILM* (1978) pp. 220-34. The guidelines are not, of course, legally binding. Among the member states is France – a non-party to the NPT – who is a leading exporter of nuclear technology.

82　The list includes fissionable material, and reactors and equipment therefor. (Annex A, Part A).

83　Defined as 'technical data in physical form designated by the supplying country as important to the design, construction, operation or maintenance of enrichment or reprocessing, or heavy water production facilities or major critical components thereof, but excluding data available to the public. For example, in published books and periodicals' (Annex A, Part B). The guidelines do not, of course, make the acceptance of full-scope safeguards by the recipient state a condition of supply.

84　This is known as a 'replication' clause.

85　It was an important factor preventing an agreed final declaration at the second NPT Review Conference in 1980.

86　Text in *Digest of US Practice in International Law 1975*, p. 849.

87　See Edwards, op. cit., p. 17. He points out that the US Nuclear Non-Proliferation Act 1978, one of whose main aims is stated to be the deferment, worldwide, of the reprocessing of nuclear fuel, may well produce a similar counterproductive effect.

88 See Greenhalgh, 'Atoms for Peace', *Atom* (1985), No. 346, 7 July, p. 9, who suggests that interdependence of states in the field of nuclear power reinforces non-proliferation goals for the reason that a state reliant on electricity generated by civil nuclear reactors would suffer severe economic disruption in the probable event of supplier states withdrawing essential materials or services by way of sanctions.

89 When measured against the NSG guidelines, their record as supplier states is far from reassuring. See below as regards China.

90 See discussion in *The United States and the Future of the Non-Proliferation Regime*. Report of a conference sponsored by the Stanley Foundation, 1984, pp. 24, 35-6; *contra*, Walker and Lönnroth, 'Proliferation and Nuclear Trade: a look ahead', 40 *Bulletin of the Atomic Scientists* (1984), April, p. 29.

91 This applies to industrialized and developing countries alike. It has been predicted that nuclear power will expand in only ten or so developing countries that have already surmounted the 'first formidable hurdles of its introduction'; for the remaining countries it remains out of reach for the foreseeable future: Fischer and Szasz, op. cit., p. 120, who also attribute the downturn in projected expansion to the rising capital costs of nuclear power plants, fears about safety after the Three Mile Island disaster, and mounting foreign debts. Presently, nuclear plants are in operation or under construction in 32 countries.

92 See *Financial Times*, 15 August 1985. China is now reported to have deferred the start of its civil nuclear programme until the 1990s. *The Guardian*, 15 March 1986.

93 Text in 24 *ILM* (1985) September, p. 1393. The agreement had been signed 15 months previously. On 16 December 1985 President Reagan signed into law the Joint Resolution relating to the approval and implementation of the agreement S.J. Res. 238, reproduced in 25 *ILM* (1986) March, p. 410.

94 The Presidential message asserted that this approval had given the assurance 'official status', ibid.

95 Presumably a veiled reference to the NSG guidelines.

96 There have been reports that China has sold unsafeguarded material to Argentina, Pakistan and South Africa. See Spector, 'Nuclear Proliferation – the Pace Quickens', 41 *Bulletin of the Atomic Scientists*, 1985 (January), p.11; Walker and Lönnroth, op. cit.

97 Article 5(2). By para. 3 of the same Article the parties undertake not to use any transferred material or facilities for any nuclear explosive device, for research specifically connected therewith, or for any military purpose; however an Agreed Minute states that Article 5(3) in no way affects the freedom of either party as a nuclear weapon state from pursuing military research that does not involve the use of material transferred under the agreement.

98 Article 8.

99 Willrich, op. cit., p. 1482.

100 Statement of President Johnson, 2 December 1967, 57 *Dept. of State Bull.* (1967), pp. 862-3; H.C. Deb., Vol. 775 col. 963-6 (4 December 1967).

101 In the sense that they do not result from binding multinational or bilateral undertakings.

102 Agreement between the UK, EAEC and IAEA for the application of safeguards in the UK in connection with the Treaty on the non-proliferation of nuclear weapons (with Protocol) Vienna, 6 September 1976, Cmnd. 7388. It entered into force in September 1978. The involvement of the European Community arises from the UK's membership of EURATOM which has its own system of safeguards and from the Soviet Union's refusal to accept these regional safeguards as adequate substitutes for IAEA safeguards. The agreement between the US and

the IAEA was submitted to the IAEA Board of Governors in September 1976 and entered into force in December 1978. For a review of the agreement's history and subsequent implementation see Houck, 27 *IAEA Bulletin* (1985), Summer, pp. 13-18.

103   The agreement was approved by the IAEA Board of Governors in February 1978 and entered into force in Sept. 1981. France, although consistently refusing to accede to the NPT, stated in 1968 that it 'will behave in the future in this field exactly like states which do decide to adhere'. Cited by Willrich, op. cit., p. 1493.

104   The agreement was approved by the IAEA Board of Governors in February 1985 and entered into force in June 1985. The text is reproduced in 24 *ILM* (1985), p. 1411.

105   e.g. UK agreement, op. cit., Articles 1, 14.

106   Goldschmidt, op. cit., p. 199.

107   Blix, op. cit., p. 7. In 1983, the IAEA inspection effort in the three NWS amounted to 6 per cent of the total inspection effort. Tempus, 'Progress in Safeguards: 1983 Implementation', 26 *IAEA Bulletin* (1984) September, pp. 7-12.

108   7 *IAEA Bulletin* (1985) Winter, p. 59.

109   Willrich, op. cit., p. 1481.

110   Under the cruise and MX missile programmes.

111   There is clearly no bar on plutonium derived from *military* reactors.

112   See note 37 above.

113   This was needed for the British nuclear warheads and for its nuclear submarine fleet.

114   See H.C. Deb., Vol. 63, col. 36 (2 July 1984). Clearly, any exchange or transfer of plutonium between the UK and US intended for *civil* purposes is now subject to safeguards by virtue of the 'voluntary offer' agreements. See e.g. Articles 12, 91, UK–EAEC–IAEA Agreement, see note 102 above.

115   H.R. 5048, Sec. 214. The Bill, sponsored by Congressman Richard Ottinger, was in part prompted by US government statements that did not rule out the eventual use of UK civil material for US weapons purposes. *The Guardian*, 4 May 1984.

116   H.C. Deb., Vol. 70, col. 82 (18 December 1984).

117   See note 102 above. The preamble reads: 'whereas . . . the Community has in particular the task of ensuring, through appropriate safeguards, that civil nuclear materials are not diverted to uses other than those for which they were intended.' Euratom is currently considering an inspection regime for the mixed civil-military reprocessing plants at Springfields and Sellafield. All other civil nuclear facilities in the UK are subject to regular inspection. H.C. Deb., Vol. 70, col. 26, (17 December 1984).

118   Text of news conference cited in Firmage, op. cit., p. 711.

119   In the sense of unambiguously convincing the world that it has become such.

120   27 *IAEA Bulletin* (1985) Autumn, p. 50. This figure includes three NWS and Taiwan, whose participation in the regimes remains uncertain since its expulsion from the IAEA in 1971. The figure also includes several parties who are not members of the United Nations (membership currently 159). They include: Republic of Korea, Liechtenstein, Nauru, San Marino, Switzerland and Tonga.

121   Agreements were in force with 78 of these states and awaiting entry into force with a further 6; the remaining 40 NNWS parties to the NPT had still not complied with Article III.4 which stipulates a deadline for concluding a safeguards agreement with the IAEA. However, none of the states 'overdue' have significant nuclear activities and the absence of an agreement has thus been of no practical consequence; however, the obligation to conclude an agreement within the time limit is a legal obligation and should not lightly be disregarded. See Fischer, 23 *IAEA Bulletin* (1981) no. 4, p.7.

122   In practice all but one of these agreements have been made pursuant to the NPT; the exception is Columbia. The safeguards are 'full-scope'.
123   i.e. the safeguards are 'non-full-scope'.
124   The six states are: Argentina, Brazil, Chile, Cuba, Democratic People's Republic of Korea and Spain.
125   Fischer, op. cit., p. 32.
126   *IAEA Bulletin* (1982), Supplement, p.4. By the end of 1984 a total of 163 safeguards agreements were in force with 85 states. 27 *IAEA Bulletin* (1985), Autumn, p. 64.
127   See summary in 26 *IAEA Bulletin* (1984), Autumn, p. 64; it was 'reasonable to conclude that the nuclear material under Agency safeguards in 1984 remained in peaceful nuclear activities or was otherwise adequately accounted for.'
128   India, Israel, Pakistan and South Africa.
129   Fischer, op. cit., p. 3. The current position concerning the development of a nuclear weapons capability in so-called 'threshold' states is documented in *Nuclear Proliferation Today*, an annual report on the spread of nuclear weapons compiled by Leonard S. Spector and published by the Carnegie Endowment for International Peace. The first report covers 1984 and is summarised in 41 *Bulletin of the Atomic Scientists* (1985), p. 11. It is alarming to find listed there states such as Libya and Iraq whom it is claimed have nuclear weapons ambitions even though they are parties to the NPT.
130   Fischer, op. cit., pp. 8-9.
131   Spain's membership of the European Community with effect from 1 January 1986, contrary to expectation, does not appear to have brought its accession to the NPT any nearer. Spain is, of course, obliged to accede to EURATOM. See Article I of the Treaty of Accession 1985, Cmnd. 9634. The Final Act contains a Declaration which reads:

> The Kingdom of Spain, not having acceded to the Treaty on Non-Proliferation of Nuclear Weapons, undertakes to seek actively and as rapidly as possible in close co-operation with the Commission and Council, the most appropriate solution calculated, whilst taking into account the Community's international commitments, to observe the obligations flowing from the EAEC in particular with respect to nuclear supplies and to movements of nuclear materials within the Community.

132   Fischer, op. cit., p. 22.
133   For an account of attempts by the US to persuade South Africa to accede to the NPT see, *Digest of US Practice in International Law 1978*, p. 471. See also resolution adopted by the IAEA General Conference in September 1985 calling on South Africa to submit immediately all its nuclear installations and facilities to Agency safeguards. 27 *IAEA Bulletin* (1985), Winter, p. 60.
134   See the instances of South Korea in 1974 and Taiwan in 1976 who deferred plans to build nuclear reprocessing plants ostensibly on pain of receiving cuts in US economic and military assistance, recorded by G. Hufbauer and J. Schott, *Economic Sanctions Reconsidered: History and Current Policy*, 1983.
135   Pakistan and South Africa provide clear examples of this tendency. In 1985, fresh bans on nuclear cooperation with, and on exports of nuclear technology to, South Africa were imposed by the European Community (text in 24 *ILM* (1985), 1479; by the US government, ibid., p. 1488; and by the IAEA General Conference, op. cit.
136   The International Fuel Cycle Evaluation (INFCE) initiated by President Carter in 1977 showed that there are no technical fixes that can produce a proliferation resistant fuel cycle.

137   e.g. the use of laser isotopic separation for fuel enrichment. See *Stanley Foundation Conference Report*, op. cit., p. 25.
138   Ibid., p. 18. For a discussion of possible nuclear weapons routes for a state determined to cheat, see Fischer and Szasz, op. cit., Ch. 6.
139   The joint statement of 21 November 1985 is reproduced in 25 *ILM* (1986), p. 102.
140   Article X.2.
141   Review of Operation of the Treaty and Recommendations on Art. VI, Doc. NPT/CONF/II64/Geneva 1985, Annex 1, pp. 10-14.
142   See note 139 above.
143   Goldschmidt, 22 *IAEA Bulletin* (1980), 73, p. 80.

6 Anti-ballistic missile systems and international law

Iain Cameron

On 23 March 1983, President Reagan signalled a highly significant change in United States strategic defence policy by announcing a massive research programme to devise means by which 'to intercept and destroy strategic ballistic missiles before they reach our own soil or that of our allies'.[1] In instituting this research programme, the Strategic Defence Initiative (SDI), the President put US defence policy on a collision course with the 1972 US–USSR Treaty on the Limitation of Anti-Ballistic Missile Systems (the ABM Treaty).[2] This chapter will examine the compatibility of SDI with the ABM Treaty and other relevant rules of international law and consider the strategic and political implications of the research programme.[3]

Background to the ABM Treaty

To understand the subject of ballistic missile defence it is necessary to examine briefly the military, technical and political reasons for the conclusion of the ABM Treaty in 1972. During the 1950s the US had constructed a large air defence network of radars, surface-to-air missiles (SAMs) and interceptor planes to deal with the perceived Soviet long-range bomber threat. With the deployment of Soviet inter-continental ballistic missiles (ICBMs) beginning in 1960, it became evident that an elaborate air defence network was largely a waste of money, and it was dismantled.[4] Soviet deployment of ICBMs had been anticipated, and research into effective means of defence had begun in the mid-1950s. Intercepting a missile is, however, a very different matter from intercepting a bomber. An ICBM in the final phase of its flight trajectory travels at some 7000 metres per second.[5] A conventionally armed (high-explosive) ABM would have to detonate in very close proximity to destroy the ICBM. A nuclear-armed missile can afford to miss by a much larger margin, but to guide even a nuclear missile within range of such a fast-moving target requires sophisticated radar for early warning and guidance, and the very short reaction-time available necessitates extremely complicated computers for target acquisition, tracking, aiming and guidance functions. The problems multiply with each target.[6] The success of ABM systems developed by the US during the later 1960s depended totally upon the radars, but these were extremely vulnerable to 'blinding' by nearby nuclear detonations – 'friendly' or enemy.[7] Even if steps could be taken to minimise the effect of radar blinding, it was clear that counter-measures – such as increasing the number of ICBMs, or providing missiles with multi-independently targetable vehicles (MIRVs) and radar distorting 'chaff' – could easily be taken. These would negate the effect of a defensive capability at much less cost. These considerations applied equally to 'point' defence of 'hardened' sites (missile silos and command control and communications posts) as to area defence of cities. Despite this, a decision was eventually taken to provide a limited deployment of the 'Safeguard' ABM system of nuclear-tipped interceptors on the grounds of the growth in the Soviet and Chinese offensive arsenals and the deployment of an (allegedly) working ABM system around Moscow.[8]

As well as the technical and economic arguments against this deployment, there were criticisms on strategic grounds. The vulnerability of the US land-based ICBMs was a long way from being proven.[9] Even if the ICBMs were vulnerable there were more effective ways of ensuring the survivability of the US deterrent – for example, increasing the sizes of the other two legs of the US strategic defence triad: missile submarines and long-range bombers. Finally, it was argued that uncertainty over the level of effectiveness of ABM systems deployed would force an intensified arms race on both offensive and defensive systems. Faced with such a potentially disastrous and economically and militarily pointless arms race both sides agreed to discuss the limitation of strategic arms. The US took the position that agreement had to be reached on limiting both offensive and defensive arms, as the two were inextricably linked, and that such limitations must be verifiable.[10] Agreement on limiting ABM systems was reached relatively speedily but negotiations on offensive systems were deadlocked until it was agreed to fix an interim (five-year) limit on the number and type of such systems for both sides pending the conclusion of a long-term comprehensive agreement. The ABM Treaty and the Interim Agreement and Protocol on the Limitation of Strategic Offensive Arms was signed in Moscow on 26 May 1972.[11]

Terms of the ABM Treaty

The preamble to the Treaty states, *inter alia*, the parties' view that 'effective measures to limit anti-ballistic missile systems would be a substantial factor in curbing the race in strategic offensive arms and would lead to a decrease in the risk of outbreak of war involving nuclear weapons'. To this end the parties undertake in Article I, not to deploy ABM systems for the purpose of nationwide defence, nor to provide a base for such a defence, and not to deploy a localised ABM defence except in accordance with the Treaty. Article II defines an ABM system as 'a system to counter strategic ballistic missiles or their elements in flight trajectory', such systems currently being composed of 'interceptor missiles constructed and deployed for an ABM role, or of a type tested in an ABM mode', ABM missile launchers and 'radars constructed and deployed for an ABM role, or of a type tested in an ABM mode'.

The phrase 'currently consisting of' is qualified by one of the interpretations agreed by the parties that 'in the event ABM systems based on other physical principles and including components capable of substituting for ABM interceptor missiles, ABM launchers, or ABM radars are created in the future, specific limitations on such systems and their components would be subject to discussion and agreement.'[12]

Article III limits the deployment of ABM systems to two sites for each party. This was later amended to one site by a Protocol in 1974.[13] The number of permitted launchers and missiles is restricted to 100 for each party and there are equivalent limits on ABM radars. The USSR has chosen to deploy its permitted system around Moscow, while the permited US system in Grand Forks, North Dakota was deployed to protect the nearby Minuteman ICBM silos.

Article VII expressly permits continuing research into fixed land-based ABM systems and Article IV specifically allows the development and testing of ABM systems and components at 'current or additionally agreed' test ranges, although the number of ABM launchers at test ranges is restricted to 15. This provision prevents either side from constructing the basis for an ABM system around a city or ICBM field supposedly as a 'test range'. The US delegation to the SALT I talks stated that the 'current' US test ranges were in White Sands, New Mexico and Kwajalein Atoll in the Pacific Trust Territories and that the Soviet test range was near Sary Shagan in the Kazakhastan SSR; new ranges could not be introduced without prior agreement. The USSR refused to discuss the location of present test ranges but stated that national technical means[14] permitted their identification, and the reference to 'additionally agreed' ranges was sufficiently clear.[15]

Under Article V each party undertakes 'not to develop, test or deploy ABM systems or components which are sea-based, air-based, space-based, or mobile land-based', and not to develop, test or deploy ABM launchers capable of firing more than one missile at a time or rapidly reloadable launchers. Agreement on these basic prohibitions was reached early on at the SALT I talks, partly because neither side had any such systems but also because of the greatly increased verification problems that would result if any sort of mobile system, space, air, sea or land-based, was deployed.[16] The prohibition applies to components as well as complete systems, thus a space-based missile that was capable of substituting for a current land-based missile would not be permitted whether or not the other components of the system remained fixed land-based. 'Mobile' was agreed by the parties to include transportable as well as mobile components and it accordingly precludes the development, testing or deployment of any system or component which is not (permanently) fixed and land-based.[17] The reason for the prohibition on rapidly reloadable launchers is obvious; the theoretical limit of 100 missiles and launchers could otherwise be easily circumvented. This effect of the limit could also be avoided if an ABM interceptor had more than one independently targetable warhead, and so both sides agreed not to develop, test or deploy such missiles.[18]

Article VI prohibits the upgrading of air defence radars, launchers and missiles to give them the 'capabilities to counter strategic ballistic missiles[19] or their elements in flight trajectory' and prohibits their testing 'in an ABM mode'. Article VI(b) prohibits the future deployment of radars to give early warning of strategic missile attack 'except at locations along the periphery of its national territory and oriented outward'. As shown later, there have been a considerable number of disagreements concerning the precise meanings of the terms used in this Article and this lack of shared understandings has led both sides to allege violations on the part of the other. These disagreements are the inevitable result of the versatility of missiles and radars. The continually improving range, speed and accuracy of surface-to-air missiles (SAMs) will progressively bring their performance closer to the level of an ABM interceptor. The USSR was none the less reluctant to avoid this future problem by defining precisely the meaning of 'tested in an ABM mode' in case the definition constrained projected improvements to its large force of SAMs which are designed to deal with US long-range bombers. The US eventually issued a unilateral statement giving its understanding of the term.[20]

Similar problems of versatility afflict radars. An ABM system needs both short range missile guidance radars and long range tracking radars. For the latter to be done effectively large-phased array radars (LPARs) are necessary. These are computer-directed radars which can track thousands of rapidly moving objects simultaneously. By requiring the location of early warning radars on the periphery of national territory and oriented outwards the Treaty seeks to reduce the capability of such radars for 'battle management'. If a radar is situated far away from the ABM launchers, which are further inland, and if it is pointing in the wrong direction, then although it will still be able to give early warning of missile numbers and trajectories, its ability to track accurately the missiles after they have crossed the border will be reduced. As the majority of ICBMs are aimed at targets in the heartland of the USA and USSR, LPARs located on national borders will not be able to hand over to the short-range radars that will accurately guide 'terminal' interceptor missiles onto their targets because they will not have complete radar coverage of the ICBMs' trajectories.

ABM radars need to be very large. Air defence radars, whose targets are smaller in number and much slower moving, need not be so large and powerful. The parties accordingly agreed that there should be no limits on air defence-phased array radars with a potential of less than 3 million watt/square metres, but that no LPARs with a larger potential could be deployed except for the one permitted ABM site, for early warning, for space tracking and for use as 'national technical means of verification' (that is, to monitor the other side's compliance with the Treaty).[21]

As previously mentioned, Article VII allows continued research into fixed land-based ABMs and modernisation and deployment of improved systems in accordance with Articles I, III, IV, V and VI and the agreed interpretations.

Article VIII provided that ABM systems and components in excess of permitted numbers or of a type prohibited by the Treaty were to be destroyed or dismantled under agreed procedures.

Under Article IX as supplemented by Agreed Statement G, the parties undertake not to transfer ABM systems and components, or technical descriptions and blueprints of such systems and components, to other states, and not to deploy ABM systems and components outside of its national territory. Such a prohibition does not apply to a missile that may be in the future designed to intercept a tactical (short- or intermediate-range) ballistic missile (an ATBM). As most tactical ballistic missiles are deployed in the European theatre then the ATBMs would also need to be deployed there.

Article X provides that each party undertakes not to assume any international obligations which would conflict with the Treaty, and Article XI stresses the parties awareness of the link between offensive and defensive systems by stating their joint commitment to continue active negotiations to achieve limitations on strategic offensive arms.

Article XII relates to verification. Clearly this is essential to ensure the integrity of the Treaty, but both sides were reluctant to allow on-site investigation. Accordingly, it was agreed that 'national technical means' should be used to monitor compliance. These means were not defined, but they are understood to mean 'information collection systems in operation outside the territory of the other side . . . e.g. satellites carrying photographic or other equipment, radars in third countries or radars on ships or aircraft operating outside territorial waters or national airspace.'[22] These means are to be exercised 'in a manner consistent with generally recognised principles of international law', and both parties undertake not to interfere with national technical means complying with international law. This provision could cause problems for some satellites, as agreement has still to be reached between the US and the USSR on where air space ends and outer space begins. In theory, space vehicles in low earth orbit could be seen as infringing air space. Some western commentators consider that a consensus is emerging that the lowest altitude at which an earth orbit can be made (around 90 km) marks the end of air space.[23] The USSR favours a higher boundary, 110 km, and has reserved its position on the legality of unrestricted satellite surveillance even above that altitude.[24] In any event, no instances of interference with satellites in orbit have yet occurred.[25] Whatever dubious legal grounds could be adduced to justify interference with a satellite, the reliance both states place on satellites for early warning, communications and reconnaissance would make such an act an extremely dangerous provocation. As well as refraining from 'active' measures of interference, the parties pledge themselves not to use deliberate concealment measures to impede verification, although this obligation does not extend to changing current construction and maintenance practices.

Article XIII establishes a Standing Consultative Commission to discuss issues that arise over the interpretation and application of the provisions of the treaty and related matters.[26] The Commission consists of a US and a Soviet component, each headed by a Commissioner, and it has been meeting twice a year for six weeks at a time since 1972. Proceedings are private and discussions may only be made public with mutual consent. Under Article XIV the parties may propose amendments to the Treaty at any time. In addition, Review Conferences are to be held at five-year intervals. The next of these is due in 1987.

Article XV confirms the parties' statement in the Preamble that the achievement and maintenance of limitations in defensive arms is a substantial factor in curbing the strategic arms race by expressly providing that the Treaty shall be of unlimited duration. The same Article does, however, provide for a right of withdrawal on six months' notice if a party 'decides that extraordinary events relating to the subject matter of this Treaty have jeopardised its supreme interests'. The reason for the express incorporation of a modified version of the *rebus sic stantibus* rule[27] is the overwhelming danger that would be posed to the national security of one party by a breakthrough in ABM technology by one side or a massive build-up in offensive weaponry, altering the delicate strategic balance. During the negotiations, the US delegation made it clear that it would regard a failure to negotiate more complete limitations on strategic offensive arms within a period of five years as grounds for withdrawal from the Treaty.[28] The goal of agreed limits on strategic offensive systems was achieved in 1979 with the signing of the SALT II agreement which limits each side to 2250 launchers.[29] This Treaty was not ratified by the US Senate and so never formally entered into force. The US announced in May 1986 that it no longer considered itself bound by the Treaty and breached it in November 1986 by commissioning its 131st B52 bomber.[30]

The ABM Treaty as a whole rests on the concept of deterrence. By limiting defences, both sides are kept vulnerable to a second (retaliatory) strike. Both sides are thereby able to inflict mutually assured destruction (MAD)[31] on each other whichever side attacks first. Limiting defence is, however, only one part of the concept of deterrence. Massive improvements in the quality of offensive and permitted defensive systems by one side could, in theory, make a pre-emptive (first) strike against one side's offensive capability so successful that the minimal retaliatory capability remaining could be absorbed. Some US commentators argue that the USSR never really accepted the MAD concept which underlies the Treaty and that it is still striving for not only 'strategic superiority',[32] but a first-strike capability.[33] Persistent allegations have also been made that the USSR will be (or at least, *intends* to be) in a position to 'break out' of the Treaty – that is, deploy a network of working, localised ABM systems that would tip the offensive/defensive balance.[34] These allegations were behind the announcement of the Strategic Defence Initiative in 1983. Before examining whether effective ballistic missile defence is now feasible and scrutinising the compatibility of the SDI research programme with the Treaty it is necessary to examine Soviet and US compliance with the Treaty, and the effect of changes that have occurred in the strategic balance since 1972.

It is important to stress here that both sides' actions can be classed as either (relatively) innocent or extremely sinister depending on one's perspective, and on whether it is believed that the possession of a first strike capability is both possible and desirable.[35]

Soviet compliance 1972–86

In relation to permitted research, the independent authors of a report on the impact of US and Soviet missile defence programmes on the Treaty conclude that the USSR has pursued and is pursuing a large research programme into improving its fixed land-based ABMs but that it still lags considerably behind the US. The present upgraded system around Moscow is considered to be inferior to the US Grand Forks system that was shut down in 1976 on the grounds of cost-effectiveness.[36] The continued deployment of the Moscow system can probably be put down to bureaucratic and military inertia and inter-service rivalry.[37] The USSR is also considered to be engaged in research into the use of lasers for ballistic missile defence. Although the present US administration has taken the view that the USSR could begin testing components for a large-scale deployment in the early 1990s,[38] a working system would also need greatly improved tracking and guidance capabilities, so whatever the precise stage of laser development in the USSR deployment of an effective regional, let alone national, system is a long way off in the future.

Soviet upgrading of air defence radars and SAMs in an attempt to give them an ATBM capability has been criticised as a possible violation of Article VI of the Treaty. The problem here concerns the meaning to be given to the terms 'capability to counter' and 'tested in an ABM mode'. A short-range ballistic missile does not have the same trajectory and flight characteristics as a strategic ballistic missile but an intermediate ballistic missile, such as the Soviet SS-20 or the US Pershing II does possess similar characteristics to an ICBM. Given bad faith, an ABM test could be carried out under the guise of an ATBM test. No official allegations that Soviet air defence radars and SAMs have been successfully tested in this way have been made, but the controversy over the compatibility of these programmes with Article VI, particularly the new SA-X-12 SAM system, will certainly continue.[39]

It is with regard to ABM radars, however, that the most serious US allegations have been made. First, it is argued that the USSR has developed and deployed a transportable air defence radar which is sophisticated and powerful enough to function as an ABM radar. If true, this would violate both Article V and Article VI(a).[40] Second, and more important, the US has expressed concern over the network of LPARs that the USSR has been constructing since the late 1970s to upgrade its early warning.

Because of their size and complexity, LPARs take years to construct. ABM interceptors and launchers in contrast, can be deployed relatively quickly. LPARs therefore, are the longest 'lead-time' item for an ABM system,[41] and are thus crucial to determining whether a 'break-out' of the Treaty is being planned.

The sixth of the new Soviet radars is located in Krasnoyarak, central Siberia, some 750 km from the nearest border (Mongolia). The LPARs active face is not directed outwards towards that border but north-east, across some 4000 km of the USSR. The US first raised the question of this radar in 1983 in the Standing Consultative Commission. The USSR has claimed that the radar is for space tracking and therefore not a violation of Article VI(a). It does not appear that this radar is well oriented for space tracking.[42] While it would appear that this radar is a violation of Article VI(a), Rhinelander and other experts consider that it is ill-suited for a 'battle management' role and it is not, accordingly, an ABM radar within the meaning of Article III.[43]

US compliance 1972–83

Allegations of non-compliance have not all been one-sided. Regarding permitted US research, although the missiles and launchers in the Grand Forks base were mothballed in 1972, testing and upgrading of the Safeguard (later Sentinel and now called Sentry) ABM system has continued.[44] As previously mentioned, experts have concluded that the improved system now deployed around Moscow is of comparable quality to the Sentinel System deployed in 1972. The US has also been engaged in research into beam and kinetic (impact) weapons, and space sensors,[45] and has pursued a large research programme into anti-satellite weapons (ASATs) since 1974. Some ASAT research has applications to ABM research.[46]

In relation to upgrading of SAMs and ATBMs, the US has deployed a sophisticated air defence system, in West Germany and the US itself. This does not possess an ATBM capability, but it is the opinion of some experts that improvements in the system's radars, battle management computers and missiles could give it such a capability by the late 1980s.[47]

However, it is again in relation to LPARs that the most serious allegations have been made of non-compliance with the Treaty. The US deployed two LPARs in Massachusetts and California for early warning of submarine-launched ballistic missiles (SLBMs) and space tracking purposes in the 1970s. In 1978 the USSR questioned in the Standing Consultative Commission whether these radars were in violation of the requirement in Article I not to provide a base for national territorial defence. Other LPARs are being constructed as replacements for older early warning radars in Thule in Greenland in Alaska and in Fylingdale Moors in England.

Arguably this upgrading is permitted by Article VI(b) which only states that in *future* early warning radars must be on the borders of national territory and oriented outwards, although as already mentioned, Agreed Statement F appears to prohibit the construction of *any*

LPARs for early warning except those on US borders and oriented outwards. The USSR has offered to halt construction of its LPAR in Krasnoyarsk if the US forgoes upgrading of its Thule and Fylingdale radars, but this has been rejected.[48] Two further LPARs under construction in the US in Georgia and Texas, have caused the USSR concern. Although these are pointed outwards, they are quite far inland and they have an 'over-the-shoulder' coverage of 240 degrees, thereby including a large proportion of the continental United States. As such, they could have some ABM battle management capability.[49]

Strategic changes post-1972

The ABM Treaty was based upon the idea that both superpowers were, and should continue to be, vulnerable to destruction, whichever side initiated a strategic exchange. On warning of an attack, a retaliatory strike would immediately be launched by the other side at enemy cities. This strategy has, however, undergone significant changes. The USSR never adopted a 'counter-value' strategy in which an Armageddon assault is aimed directly at cities, but retains a 'war fighting' or 'counter-force' strategy aimed at US nuclear and conventional forces, command centres and military/industrial capacity (which, however, will include many cities).[50] The US has also formally adopted a 'war fighting' strategy.[51]

There are, however certain problems involved in a 'war fighting' strategy that includes strategic exchanges. The overwhelming majority of Soviet nuclear warheads are on ICBMs. US strategic forces, however, are split more or less evenly between submarines, missiles and bombers. Some sections of opinion in the US military consider that the US may become vulnerable to a pre-emptive counter-force strike. The 'vulnerability' scenario proceeds on a number of assumptions.

SLBMs are not yet considered accurate enough to serve as 'counter-force' weapons. So, although submarines possess significant considerable advantages in terms of survivability (barring quantum jumps in the technology of anti-submarine warfare) they are not regarded as 'silo busters'. The other legs of the US strategic 'triad' – ICBMs and bombers – are so regarded, but proponents of the 'vulnerability' scenario consider that many existing ICBMs and tactical nuclear forces in Europe could be destroyed before they could be readied to fire.[52] It is acknowledged that the bomber wings, or some of them, may have sufficient time in which to escape ICBM attack, but the risk exists that they could be destroyed by Soviet SLBMs fired at a depressed trajectory[53] from submarines close to the US coasts. Even if some bomber wings survived, doubts might reasonably exist as to whether the bombers or the cruise missiles they carry will be able to penetrate improved Soviet air defences. If some of the bombers, and a few US ICBMs manage to penetrate they may not be in sufficient number to disrupt the Soviet attack, bearing in mind the extensive Soviet civil defence preparations which provide for speedy and effective dispersal of forces, leadership, essential workers and industries. Those casualties that do result could afford to be absorbed by a country that lost 20 million people in World War II. The surviving US leadership will thus be placed in the position of having to decide whether to launch a SLBM attack on Soviet cities and therefore precipitate the destruction of all US cities from the remaining Soviet ICBM force, or to capitulate.

There are three military policies which the US could adopt to avoid this nightmare scenario, and insure the survivability of the US deterrent well into the 21st century. The first is to abandon land-based ICBMs altogether, and improve the accuracy of SLBMs and the penetration of the bombers and their stand-off missiles. The influence of the ICBM lobby (military/political/industrial) would make this option difficult to push through, but apart from this it has the disadvantage of putting too great an emphasis on bombers and submarines with the danger that future improvements in air defence and anti-submarine warfare will gravely reduce their deterrent effect. The second option would be to base US ICBMs in such a way as to enhance their survivability – either to hide them somewhere along a vast tunnel or railway network, or to put them so close together that incoming Soviet ICBMs are able to destroy no more than a few of them because of the 'fratricide' effect; the first nuclear warhead that detonates will destroy or fling off course the warheads arriving immediately after it. These basing modes have both been rejected by Congress on the grounds of cost and effectiveness. This leaves the third option; deploy an ABM system to provide a degree of protection for the ICBM fields.

This third option was being mooted long before the President's speech in March 1983.[54] The technological lead that the US possesses over the USSR has always meant that it would be the US that would be faced with the decision of whether to breach the ABM Treaty. Given an acceptance of the premises of US ICBM vulnerability and Soviet intentions to achieve a first-strike capability, it is a logical step. Both these premises, however, are highly dubious to say the least.

The first and most fundamental assumption that is made is that the USSR is attempting to secure a first-strike capability. The objective evidence for this consists of the fact of the Soviet ICBM build-up and extensive civil and air defence preparations. Combined with this is more speculative evidence of Soviet intentions, gleaned from Soviet military sources. The Soviet ICBM build-up can, however, be viewed as a logical and reasonable attempt to achieve parity with the US strategic forces. While Soviet military sources write in terms of winning a nuclear war, western military sources do the same.[55] The politicians of both sides have frequently made clear their views that a nuclear war is unwinnable. Although Soviet ICBMs are larger, more numerous and carry more warheads than their American counterparts, the total number of US warheads available (bombers, submarines and ICBMs) outnumbers Soviet warheads, and the US strategic forces are certainly more survivable, because of the much larger percentage of submarine launchers.[56] Regarding accuracy, commentators from both sides have credited each others' missiles with 'silo-busting' accuracy.[57] The accuracy of a missile is measured in terms of the 'circular error probable' (CEP) in nautical miles. The CEP is the radius of a circle in which half the projectiles fired at a particular target will land – that is, it is the grouping that is measured, not the actual proximity to the target. As Soviet warheads have a large megatonnage they can afford to be less accurate and still destroy a silo that is 'hardened' to withstand the pressure from a nearby blast. Achieving a 'silo-busting' capability is, however, extremely difficult. Every stage in the process must work with clockwork precision, as the slightest error will throw the warhead completely off course. Even if every component functions perfectly, the inertial guidance system of the missile can be thrown off by gravitational anomalies or unpredictable weather – factors which cannot ever be fully programmed into the guidance system. To destroy *all* the US silos, a very large percentage of Soviet missiles would have to be working perfectly, even if two warheads were assigned to each target.[58] It is difficult to come to any definite conclusion regarding the accuracy and reliability of Soviet ICBMs, save that they have been consistently over-estimated by the US military establishment for their own purposes. Regarding Soviet SLBMs, there is little doubt that they are both very unreliable and nowhere near accurate enough to serve as counterforce weapons.[59] Regarding civil defence precautions, although these may look impressive on paper, some commentators conclude that the centralised inefficient bureaucratic control and industrial production and the limited communications network of the USSR in fact make it more vulnerable to a nuclear strike than the USA.[60] Similarly the Soviet air defence network, although vast, is not considered, by the US Air Force, at any rate, to be capable of preventing US bombers from reaching their targets.[61]

The present author considers that there are no grounds for believing that the USSR has now, or will possess in the foreseeable future, a first-strike capability. It is the case, however, that such a capability is, in theory, attainable, so long as the US takes absolutely no countermeasures. It is also fair to say that in the absence of conclusive proof of the (relative) innocence of Soviet intentions the US is bound to give simple Soviet capability greater weight than any protestations of peaceful purposes. None the less even if a Soviet first strike will become feasible in the 21st century it has been pointed out that this in no way guarantees 'victory' in any conflict. The US SLBMs will remain intact and these could totally devastate all Soviet cities. The dilemma that the US President would be placed in by the decimation of his ICBMs – surrender or precipitate mutual annihilation – *already exists* without the need for a first strike.[62] The USSR could not ever take the risk of even a controlled response from SLBMs.

Bearing in mind these considerations, the feasibility of some form of nationwide ABM system, and the military and political advantages and disadvantages of SDI can now be studied.

Feasibility of ballistic missile defence

As already mentioned, the main drawbacks with the Sentinel ABM system were the inability of command and control computers and radars to handle a large attack or to function efficiently after nuclear detonations had occured. It is argued that with the vast improvements that have taken place in the technologies of sensing, microelectronics and data processing these technical issues can now be solved. A variety of different means of interception have been proposed, but common to all is the concept of 'layered' defence, that is, different forms of interception at different stages of the flight of the ICBM. The bulk of intercepting, practically speaking, should occur at the 'boost' phase of the missile (2–5 minutes) when the rocket booster is sending the ballistic missile through the atmosphere. The heat produced by the ICBM is easily detected during this phase. If the missile is not destroyed at this stage it will manoeuvre for another 2–5 minutes in space before discharging its MIRVs, its decoys and radar 'chaff'. The next (mid-course) phase lasts 15–20 minutes (7–10 for SLBMs). The terminal phase, lasting 30–60 seconds is when the warheads drop toward their targets. Distinguishing warheads from lighter decoys is easier in this stage because of the effect of gravity. Possible methods of interception are numerous. Lasers, chemical, excimer[63] or X-ray[64] powered, could be based permanently in space or 'popped-up' from land-based silos, aircraft or submarines when a launch is first detected. Chemical lasers could also be land- or air-based and used in conjunction with space-based mirrors to direct the beams to the targets. Particle beams[65] and kinetic weapons could be used in all flight phases, the latter being launched either by rocket or space-based 'railguns'.[66] In the terminal phase land-based explosive or impact rockets and particle beams would perform intercepts. If each of the four layers of defence (boost, post-boost, mid-course and terminal) allowed for 10 per cent 'leakage', then the overall 'leakage' of the whole system would be only 0.01 per cent. Each of these methods of interception has, however, particular deficiencies and particular susceptibilities to counter-measures. The whole system would require a massive and extremely advanced network of space sensors to provide early warning which would themselves be highly vulnerable to attack, as would any orbiting battle station or space mirror. 'Pop-up' systems on the other hand would not be as vulnerable, but these would have to be launched automatically at the first signs of an attack if they were to be in position in time. The longer these systems spent in orbit, the more vulnerable they would be to attack by 'killer' satellites. Regarding the mechanics of interception, particle beams bend in the earth's magnetic field making tracking and targeting extremely difficult, and lasers do not work well in the atmosphere. Both types of beam would need to be in contact with the missile long enough to destroy or disrupt it. Kinetic energy weapons guided onto their target by infra-red sensors would be blinded by heat friction in the atmosphere. Nuclear-powered lasers would create an electromagnetic pulse which would disrupt US command and control facilities. The system as a whole would demand detection-tracking, target-acquisition, aiming and guidance systems of unimaginable swiftness and complexity.[67]

None the less, given huge funding, these technical difficulties might be solved. The US Secretary of State for Defense, Casper Weinberger, has attacked sceptics by arguing that they underestimate American inventiveness; some people, he stated, thought that a moon landing was impossible.[68] The inappropriateness of such an analogy was underlined by critics who pointed out that 'The effort to get to the moon was not complicated by an adversary. A platoon of hostile moon-men with axes could have made it a disaster.'[69] Just as the original Sentinel ABM system was vulnerable to MIRVed missiles, so too is any conceivable space-based system vulnerable to Soviet counter-measures which the USSR would have had 20 years to develop while the US system was being developed and deployed. As well as the constant vulnerability of satellites to attack, the time in which the system has to destroy the ICBMs could be minimised by shortening the boost phase, the missile could be hardened against laser attack or made less easy to detect, the system could be overwhelmed by launching more missiles, better decoys could be made and so on. Nor could any ABM system protect against bombers, cruise missiles or, for that matter, nuclear bombs planted in the US by saboteurs. Why then is any such system being seriously considered?

Military and political advantages and disadvantages of SDI

What military advantages are there to a massive research programme into the feasibility of an ABM system? The first and most obvious is that, while area or nationwide defence will almost certainly be found to be technically impossible, given Soviet counter-measures, some form of point defence of hardened targets with land-based lasers, particle beams or missiles and space sensors may well turn out to be both technically feasible and cost-effective (that is, cheaper than deploying increased numbers of offensive weapons).[70] In the event that this turns out not to be the case, the research will have made possible vastly improved space-based command, control and communications systems as well as sophisticated anti-satellite weapons (ASATs). Laser and particle beam research may also turn out to have applications in other military fields. US research in these fields will also, it is argued, serve as a 'hedge' against a Soviet breakthrough in such technologies, allowing them to 'breakout' of the ABM Treaty.[71]

Strategically speaking, two contrary arguments are made; that an ABM system will do away with deterrence by making nuclear weapons obsolete, and that it will enhance it, by making the USSR less confident of its ability to launch a successful first strike.

Politically speaking, SDI will force the USSR to make the choice between a ruinously expensive arms race in outer space,[72] or negotiating deep cuts in offensive arms with the US. SDI was also designed to have an effect on both US and world public opinion. The psychological impact of the balance of terror has produced a large peace movement in the US and Western Europe. A war strategy ostensibly based upon defence seems both less threatening and morally superior.[73]

SDI has, in fact, produced a flurry of offers of arms reductions on the part of the USSR, on condition that the research programme is shelved, but the present US administration has made it clear that SDI is non-negotiable.[74] A variant of the old 'zero-sum' game appears to be being played; whatever frightens the Russians must be good for America. The USSR for its part has stated unequivocally that it will match any improvements in US defensive capability.[75]

Military and political disadvantages

The major military disadvantage is that the deployment of any defensive system is likely to have an extremely destabilising effect on the strategic balance. Defensive and offensive systems are inextricably linked. The USSR would not be able to estimate how effective the defences were and so would be forced greatly to increase its ICBMs to be certain that a proportion would get through. The USSR views a 'defensive' system as part of an attempt by the US to achieve a first-strike capability, and it points to parallel improvements in US offensive capability such as the deployment of very accurate cruise and Pershing II missiles in Europe, the BI bomber programme and Trident D11 submarines.[76] The USSR argues that US counter-force weapons could destroy the vulnerable Soviet ICBMs and the layered defence would then be used to destroy the disorganised Soviet SLBM response. In such a situation, the USSR might move towards adopting a 'launch on warning' strategy, controlled by computers linked to sensors, with consequent increased danger of accidental launch.

SDI will also have the military disadvantage of diverting money from other defence spending, and the political disadvantage of possibly alienating US allies.[77]

Compliance of SDI with the ABM Treaty

There is no doubt that deployment of an ABM system with space-based[78] components would violate the prohibitions contained in Articles III and V. A nationwide ABM system would also violate Article I.[79]

A very tenuous series of arguments can be made that space deployment is not unlawful. They proceed from the basis that Article II which defines an ABM system narrowly to mean only missiles, launchers and radars, qualifies Article V, which prohibits basing modes other than that of a fixed land base. The prohibition on development and deployment in Article V accordingly applies only to 'traditional' technologies. It is clear, however, that the parties envisaged the possibility of a different kind of ABM system because Agreed Statement D provides that 'In order to insure fulfilment of the obligation not to deploy ABM systems and their components except as provided in Article III' the parties agree that if any such systems or components 'based on other physical principles' are 'created' in the future, then specific limits upon them would be subject to discussion and agreement. Supposedly, space development and deployment are not limited by this provision because it does not refer expressly to Article V, but only to Article III, and thus the prohibition on systems based on other physical principles only applies to fixed land-based systems. Alternatively, as Agreed Statement D is the only provision that expressly refers to new technologies, then it should be read independently of the other provisions, and it prohibits only unilateral deployment, not development. This interpretation accordingly reads the statement to apply to all future systems, not simply land-based systems, despite the reference to Article III.[80]

These dubious propositions can be countered. The enumeration of ABM components in Article II should not be regarded as exhaustive, as the enumeration is preceded by the words 'currently consisting of. . .'. Development and deployment of all types of ABM systems other than a fixed land-based system in accordance with Article III is therefore prohibited. Such an interpretation accords with the purpose of the Treaty which, as stated in the preamble, is to 'limit ABM systems' this being 'a substantial factor in curbing the arms race'.[81] Mobile systems of whatever type pose greatly increased verification problems and will therefore undermine confidence that the Treaty is being complied with, leading to a reduction in mutual interest in maintaining the Treaty. In addition, to read Agreed Statement D so as not to qualify Article V is totally to negate the object and purpose of that Article which is to prohibit development and deployment of any kind of ABM system or component that is not fixed land-based. The Agreed Statement is an interpretation or elaboration of treaty obligations, not an anulment of them.

At the time of writing, it is still not clear if the present US Administration has abandoned the last of its 're-interpretatons' of the Treaty – that development is permitted. The reason is obvious; it will be difficult, if not impossible, to justify the test programme to be carried out after 1988 on the basis that this is 'research'.[82]

The original US position on the distinction between research and development was made clear in a statement by the head of the SALT I delegation, Ambassador Smith, to the US Senate in 1972. Smith said: 'it was understood by both sides that the prohibition on "development" applies to activities involved after a component moves from the laboratory development and testing stage to the full testing stage wherever performed.'[83]

The Soviet understanding of the distinction between the two terms is considered to be the same. Although the Soviet text of the Treaty, which is equally authentic, uses the term *sozdavat* ('create') and although this can be interpreted to include theoretical work, the better interpretation (and the one that appears to be followed by the USSR) is that 'development' begins when field-testing commences. This is also the stage at which 'national technical means' can detect tests; insistence on an earlier prohibition would be pointless.[84]

More serious is the question of 'sub-components' of an ABM system. Clearly, an ABM component will be composed of many separate items, the overwhelming majority of which have other military and civilian uses. This being the case, the Treaty did not attempt to grapple with the intractable problem of defining what sub-systems should not be developed, but confined itself to regulating the development and testing of only integrated ABM components and systems. The prohibition of testing of components 'in an ABM mode' could mean prohibiting the testing of all components which are capable of being used as ABM components, or simply those components which are incapable of being used for anything other than ballistic missile defence. If the latter interpretation is followed, then the only legal limitation on the testing of ABM sub-components intended for use in a prohibited mobile system is the customary international law rule that provides that treaty obligations are to be interpreted in good faith.[85] It is difficult, though, to prove bad faith in the absence of an authoritative and impartial interpretative body. The US has stated that it will not be held to a higher standard of compliance than the USSR and it has expressly reserved its position on appropriate responses including (counter) breach, to alleged Soviet violations.[86]

The only practical limitations are that, eventually, field-testing of integrated systems will be necessary in order to determine their performance as a whole, and at that point Article V, and possibly Articles IV and VI (depending on what is being tested and where) will have been breached.

There may even be ways in which to circumvent most of these practical limitations. The Treaty does not limit the testing of anti-satellite weapons (ASATs). Both the USSR and the USA now have working ASATs. The former has what has been described as 'an old blunderbuss';[87] an orbiting satellite containing high explosives which manoeuvres close to the target and then detonates. The latter has a more sophisticated 'direct ascent' missile (the Miniature Homing Vehicle or MHV) which is carried to high altitudes by an F15 fighter plane where it is fired. It then homes into the satellite and destroys it by direct impact. Both ASATs are at present only capable of destroying satellites in low earth orbit. Neither is of any use against ICBMs. Satellites are very much easier to destroy than ICBMs because the former have predictable orbits and are much more fragile. None the less, some ASAT research has ABM implications. This is particularly true for directed energy weapons. Once the problems of tracking, target acquisition, aiming, fire control and beam 'jitter' have been solved for laser ASATs, then much of the work will also have been done in developing a working laser ABM – although the power (destructive) levels and targetting speed of the latter will have to be much greater.[88]

The other way in which the limitations on testing prohibited ABM components may be circumvented is to test these components in a fixed land-based mode at one of the permitted test sites. As previously stated, Article VII expressly preserved the parties' freedom to engage in continued development and testing of fixed land based ABMs. Ground-based lasers and kinetic weapons ultimately intended for space deployment can be tested in ways compatible with the Treaty, while testing of the components of the final layer of any projected ABM defence can proceed almost unrestricted by the Treaty, whether involving existing or exotic technologies, so long as the components are tested in a fixed land-based mode.

The present programme of SDI experiments as set out in unclassified SDI Report in 1985 exploits these weaknesses in the Treaty. Some programmes are categorized as laboratory experiments,[89] or as non-ABM components because of reduced power levels[90] or because they are subcomponents or adjuncts or components of ASAT systems.[91] Other experiments are to be carried out in a fixed land-based mode.[92] As one of the negotiators of the Treaty, John Rhinelander, comments 'if the Administration's policy is in fact to prevent the "erosion of the ABM Treaty" then [this programme] demonstrates what should *not* be done as a matter of US national policy.'[93]

Rhinelander and the other authors of the Report on the Impact of SDI on the Treaty concluded that the administration's position that none of the experiments through to the early 1990s should be considered to be advanced development or testing of ABM components was 'factually suspect and legally questionable'.[94] The Report considered that while the tests scheduled until 1988 were compatible with the Treaty, thereafter the Treaty would have to be either abrogated or amended to delete all or some of the prohibitions on space testing and development (Article V), upgrading of ATBMs to ABMs (Article VIa) and deployment of them outside of the USA (Article IX), transfer of technology (Article IX) and providing a base for national ABM defence (Article I (2)). If a decision was eventually made to deploy any system or component that was not fixed land-based point defence, then the Treaty would have to be radically altered or scrapped.[95] If the USSR refused to agree to amendments the USA could exercise its option to withdraw under Article XV, presumably citing a Soviet missile build-up as the 'extraordinary events'. It is unlikely that such an excuse will have to be manufactured; if the USA does go ahead with development of prohibited ABMs, the USSR will probably feel bound to increase its offensive capabilities in either strategic weapons (which would violate SALT II) or tactical weapons.

Although the SDI programme is supposed to be limited to simple research into the feasibility of the various defence technologies, the expenditures involved are so vast ($1.4 billion for FY 1985, $2.7 billion for FY 1986 and a projected $4.9 billion for 1987)[96] that the programme will undoubtedly generate its own momentum. Should any of the technologies turn out to be feasible, survivable and reasonably cost-effective[97] then the pressure to go ahead and deploy a system will be almost unstoppable.[98]

Compatibility of SDI with other relevant rules of international law

Development and deployment of space-based ABMs will violate the ABM Treaty, but it may also violate the Outer Space Treaty of 1967.[99]

Article IV of this Treaty prohibits the placing 'in orbit around the earth of any objects carrying nuclear weapons or any other kinds of weapons of mass destruction', and states that military activities on the moon and other celestial bodies are prohibited and that these bodies shall be used exclusively for peaceful purposes.[100] The Treaty, however, deliberately does not provide for a total demilitarization of outer space; spacecraft in earth orbit can still be used for military purposes. The large majority of satellite launches, in fact, are for military purposes.[101] However, as Article 2(4) of the UN Charter extends to outer space[102] it is prohibited to threaten the territorial integrity or political independence of any state from space. It is almost certainly a violation of Article 2(4) to attack any satellite[103] although, as mentioned, the USSR has claimed that satellites in low earth orbit may be regarded as infringing Soviet air space, and satellites in any orbit that are engaged in 'illegal military purposes' may be subject to attack.[104] Western states reject this destabilizing view, although they would presumably feel bound to concede the USSR a right of anticipatory self-defence.[105] This being the case, it is submitted that the main issue as far as ABM defences are concerned is whether any of the weapon systems or components thereof, that it is suggested might be deployed in space, are weapons of mass destruction and so prohibited under Article IV of the Outer Space Treaty. Western states, including the USA, have considered since 1948 that the phrase should be defined 'to include atomic explosive weapons, radioactive material weapons, lethal chemical and biological weapons and any weapons developed in the future which have characteristics comparable in destructive effect to those of the atomic bomb or other weapons mentioned above'.[106] Although the USSR has never expressly agreed to this definition, it has been argued that the USSR accepted the western definition in 1977 when it supported a General Assembly resolution calling for a convention banning 'weapons of mass destruction', these weapons being limited to those in the 1948 definition.[107]

The USSR has called high-energy lasers and particle beams 'space strike weapons', and has argued that if they were deployed in space they would be capable of hitting targets on earth as well as satellites and ICBMs, and that their destructive power is no less than that of nuclear arms.[108] None the less, the fact that the USSR has felt the need to introduce proposals for conventions specifically banning such weapons indicates that it considers that they are not already prohibited by Article IV.[109] Only one of the proposed beam weapons – the X-ray laser

– is fairly clearly a weapon of mass destruction, as it would utilize an atomic explosion to accomplish its purpose.[110] Such a weapon would also violate the prohibition on nuclear explosions in space in Article 1(1)(a) of the Partial Test Ban Treaty of 1963.[111] Conceivably, it could still be argued that an ABM which intercepted a ICBM and caused its *detonation* would be a 'weapon of mass destruction' because although the ABM was defensive, its use would still result in an explosion on the 'mass destruction' scale and, possibly, depending on at what stage the interception took place, massive casualties. It would, however, be difficult to argue this because it would seem to be the characteristics of the weapon itself which place it in the category of 'mass destruction' rather than the consequences of its use.[112] In any event, some ABMs will not cause a warhead to detonate, and with others it would be impossible to say without actually testing them. Several proposals have been made, from the USSR and other states, to forestall an arms race in outer space and prevent the deployment of ASATs.[113] Some of these proposals would also have the effect of banning any type of ABM. The USA will undoubtedly continue to reject any proposals which it sees as reducing its flexibility so far as an eventual deployment of space ABMs is concerned.

Conclusion

The SDI programme goes to the heart of the concept of arms control; why should the side with the technological lead have to accept any restrictions when it might be in a position to establish a decisive strategic advantage? The answer – an extremely obvious one – appears to have eluded influential sections of the present US administration. It is that restraint by the US will enhance both its own security and that of the world as a whole. The political and strategic factors underpinning the Treaty have not changed, however great the advances in technology have been. Recent history has shown that whatever weapons the US develops the USSR will attempt to follow suit. If US defensive technology cannot be duplicated, then Soviet offensive nuclear weapons – ICBMs, bombers, cruise missiles – can be expected to proliferate. Deployment of some sort of point ABM defence could indeed go ahead, while maintaining mutual security, but only if corresponding decreases in US missiles, or increases in Soviet offensive capabilities were accepted. It is most unlikely, however, that the USA would ever be prepared to allow this. Why should it, when it is well able to keep pace with Soviet production of offensive systems *and* deploy point defences? SDI is supposedly designed to enhance strategic stability, but it appears instead to be another pursuit after the chimera of strategic superiority.

The best case analysis is that SDI will not produce a cost effective ABM point defence and that those informed sections of US public opinion that want value for money in defence manage to halt the momentum of the programme before it leads to deployment. The worst-case analysis is that SDI will lead to some form of point ABM defence, the abrogation of the Treaty and a consequent arms race in ASATs and offensive and defensive weapons.

Notes

1   *The Times*, 24 March 1983.
2   23 *UST* 3435; 11 *ILM* (1972) 785.
3   In studying ABM systems it is necessary to understand the strategic reasons for such systems. This in turn requires a very brief examination of the current state of US and Soviet offensive forces and strategic doctrine. A chapter of this length cannot, however, deal fully with such an issue. The reader is accordingly referred to the works listed at notes 50-52 below.
4   It would appear that the threat posed to the US by Soviet long-range bombers and ICBM's in the 1950s and 1960s was greatly overestimated. See Cockburn, 1983, pp. 191, 220-5. The USSR still maintains a large air defence network to counter US long-range bombers.
5   Tsipis, p. 108.
6   Ibid., pp. 169-76.
7   Ibid., National Academy of Sciences, 1985, p. 141.
8   This deployment was also defended on the grounds that it would provide a limited defence against an accidental launch of an ICBM, and that it would be necessary as a bargaining counter in projected US – USSR ABM negotiations. See Willrich and Rhinelander, 1974, p.64.
9   See below notes 57 and 58 and accompanying text.
10 National Academy of Sciences, 1985, p. 143.
11 The Interim Agreement, together with a Protocol, froze construction of fixed land-based ICBMs and of SLBM launchers (except for replacement of older missiles), for a period of five years. This agreement was replaced by the SALT II Treaty in 1979. (See below, note 29.)
12 Agreed Interpretation D. Seven 'agreed Statements' and five 'common understandings' were reached during the SALT I talks. The former were initialled, the latter were oral or written replies to US understandings communicated to the Soviet delegation. The head of the US delegation to the talks, Ambassador Smith, considers that the initialled interpretations reached by the parties are as binding as the Treaty itself. Smith, 1980, p.344. The interpretations can be viewed as an integral party of the Treaty, or as a separate bilateral treaty or as simply forming part of the context of interpretation; i.e. as definitively indicating what the 'ordinary meaning' of the relevant term is taken to be, and what is its 'object and purpose' (Article 31(2) of the Vienna Convention on the Law of Treaties, 1969, Misc 19 (1971), Cmnd. 4818). Whichever way the initialled statements are regarded, a subsequent unilateral attempt by one party to revise its interpretation of what the terms of the Treaty demands that runs counter to an initialled agreed interpretation or understanding would probably be estopped.

The 'common understandings' should be seen as part of the context of interpretation.

13 27 *UST* 1645; 13 *ILM* (1974) 904.

14 See below note 22.

15 The USSR later began using a new test range in Kamchatka, arguing that there was already a test radar in the locality at the time of the conclusion of the Treaty, and that they were not bound to seek prior US approval before activating a different test site. See Levitt, 1981, pp.382-3.

16 Willich and Rhinelander, 1974, p.134.

17 Common Understanding D.

18 Agreed Statement E.

19 The parties did not agree on the precise meaning of this phrase. The USSR argued that a missile was 'strategic' if it could hit targets in the territory of the other side from its operational deployment, while the US considered 'strategic' weapons to be those whose longer range capabilities, greater nuclear payload and other characteristics distinguished them from 'theatre' or 'tactical' missiles. Jones, 1983, p.61.

20 Noted at 11 *ILM* (1972), p. 802. The US delegation stated that 'we would consider a launcher, missile or radar to be "tested in an ABM mode" if, for example, any of the following events occur (1) a launcher is used to launch an ABM interceptor missile (2) an interceptor missile is flight tested against a target vehicle which has a flight trajectory with characteristics of a strategic ballistic missile flight trajectory, or is flight tested in conjunction with the test of an ABM interceptor missile or an ABM rader at the same test range, or is flight tested to an altitude inconsistent with interception of targets against which air defences are deployed (3) a radar makes measurements on a cooperative target vehicle of the kind referred to in item (2) during the re-entry portion of its trajectory or makes measurements in conjunction with the test of an ABM interceptor missile or an ABM radar at the same test range. Radars used for purposes such as range safety or instrumentation would be exempt from application of these criteria.' Partial agreement on what the phrase meant was reached in the S.C.C. (see below) in 1978, but the text of this has not been made public.

21 Agreed Statement F. This has not solved the problem. See below notes 40-43 and accompanying text.

22 Willich and Rhinelander, 1974, p. 139. The parties are not limited to these means; public sources and information, lawfully gathered by embassy staff can be used. The US is placed at a disadvantage here as information on those of its activities which may infringe the Treaty is much more freely available in the form of congressional hearings, executive releases and US and foreign press sources. Soviet interference with US 'national technical means' is therefore a more serious matter than US interference with Soviet N.T.M.

23 Meredith, 1984, p. 423.

24 Russell, 1984, p.179.

25 Ibid., p.159.

26 The S.C.C. is also the forum for discussion of issues arising out of the SALT II agreement on the limitation of offensive systems (Article XVII). 18 *ILM* (1979), p.1112.

27 The International Law Commission considered that under customary international law, an unforeseen fundamental change of circumstances could be invoked by one party to a treaty as a ground for terminating or withdrawing from the treaty where the continued existence of those circumstances was an essential basis of that Party's consent to be bound by the treaty. *YBILC*, 1966, vol. II, p.257. The rule is incorporated in Article 62 of the Vienna Convention on the

Law of Treaties. See above, note 12. Article XV is not so strict as Article 62 in that the events, although 'extraordinary' need not be unforeseen, and the determination that 'supreme interests' are in jeopardy is wholly subjective.

28 Unilateral Statement A. 11 *ILM* (1972), p.801.
29 Article III. Of this number only 1320 can be bombers carrying cruise missiles, or 'MIRVed' missiles (that is, with multiple independently targetable re-entry vehicles). Of these 1320 only 1200 can be MIRVed strategic missiles and not more than 820 of these can be (land-based) ICBMs (Article V).
30 See *The Guardian*, 10 and 28 November 1986.
31 This was defined by the Pentagon in 1965 as the capacity to destroy 25-33 per cent of the Soviet population and 75 per cent of Soviet industry. The estimate of 'unacceptable' losses from the Soviet point of view was later reduced in 1968 to 20-25 per cent of population and 50 per cent of industrial capacity. See Meredith, 1984, p. 419.
32 Meaning clear superiority in warheads and megatonnage for political purposes, i.e. to create a perception of a massive Soviet war machine to cow American and western public opinion, clip the wings of western 'containment' policies and so expand its spheres of influence. See Davis *et al.*, 1980, p.VII. Again, this theory makes a number of dubious assumptions, not the least of which is that western and Third World states will be so overawed by Soviet weapons statistics that they will permit themselves to be 'Finlandized'.
33 Ibid., pp.3-4 and Nitze, 1976, p.207 *et seq*. Cf. Lodal, 1976, p.462 *et seq*.
34 See US State and Defense Depts, 1985.
35 Miko, 1978, pp.4-7 splits American 'Sovietologists' into three schools of thought; Those who believe in (a) the 'continuity' of Soviet policy since World War II (i.e. intent to dominate the world); (b) 'qualified continuity' (not bent on world domination but opportunistic); and (c) the 'transformation' of Soviet policy goals into a simple desire for peaceful coexistence. He considers that 'all the schools are internally consistent, if their basic assumptions are accepted' (p.8).
36 Longstreth *et al.*, 1985, p. 48. $5.7 billion had been spent on constructing the site.
37 Cockburn, 1983, pp.223-5.
38 The UK Ministry of Defence takes the view that while Soviet research into beam weapons is extensive, the USSR still has serious deficiencies in the essential electronic components of an ABM system (early warning, computer-controlled target-acquisition and guidance). See Statement on Defence Estimates I, Cmnd. 9763-1 (1986).
39 Longstreth and Pike, 1985, p.13. The US unilateral statement on 'tested in an ABM mode' (note 20) does not bind the USSR.
40 US State and Defense Departments, 1985, p. 12.
41 Longstreth and Pike, 1985, p. 13.
42 *Washington Post*, 7 August 1985. One explanation advanced for the location of the new radar is that the existing ABM radar in Siberia was too difficult to maintain, while Krasnoyarsk is much closer to the Siberian railway. See *Observer*, 27 October 1985.
43 Rhinelander, 1985, p. 8 Cf. US State and Defense Departments, 1985, p. 10.
44 See Jones, 1983, pp.66-72. Aldrich, 1983 pp.197-206. Viewed in the light of the major research programmes in the 1970s and early 1980s into early warning, exo-atmospheric non-nuclear impact missiles and endo-atmospheric low-yield nuclear interceptors and systems, SDI does not, in fact, constitute a radical shift in US strategic thinking.
45 Jones, 1983, pp. 55-6.
46 See below, notes 87 and 88 and accompanying text.
47 Longstreth and Pike, 1985, p. 12. The desire to continue development of this

system, called Patriot, is apparently the reason why the US is reluctant to brand the SA-X-12 as a definite violation of Article VI (a).

48 *The Guardian*, 30 October 1985.
49 Longstreth and Pike, 1985, p. 14. National Academy of Sciences, 1985, p. 158.
50 Burt, 1981, pp. 158-9, 165.
51 Cockburn, 1983, p. 194.
52 Davis *et al.*, 1980, p. V.
53 Missiles fired at a low trajectory will not register as quickly on radar screens, and so less warning can be given of attack.
54 Kerr, 1984, p. 109. Aldrich, 1983, p. 202, refers to a research programme in 1977 to detect and destroy SLBMs in boost phase.
55 Cockburn, 1983, pp. 192-4. Gartoff, 1981, pp. 92-124.
56 USSR deliverable capability was 5835 Megatons (Mt) in December 1983 as compared to 3886 Mt US. The total number of USSR warheads was 8800 as compared to 9665 US warheads. Approximately 70 per cent of the former are land-based as against approximately 21 per cent of US warheads (*c.*53 per cent being on SLBMs) *SIPRI Yearbook 1984*, p. 96.
57 See *'Star Wars' Delusions and Dangers*, 1985, p. 28-34. Davis *et al.*, 1980, pp. 3-4.
58 See Tsipis, Chapter 5 and Appendix H.
59 Ibid.
60 Miko, 1978, pp. 44-5.
61 Cockburn, 1983, pp. 226-8.
62 Ibid., p. 194.
63 In this type of laser, the input energy is produced by the bonding of an atom in its ground state with another atom in an excited state (the excimer). Input/output efficiency levels are higher than those yet obtained with chemical lasers. See Jasani, 1985, p. 173.
64 This laser would direct the X-rays generated by a nuclear explosion onto targets, damaging internal components and throwing it off course. Ibid., p. 174.
65 If streams of atoms are accelerated to nearly the speed of light by a particle accelerator, they can penetrate material targets without leaving a hole and destroy the electronics and guidance system of a missile. See Bethe *et al.*, 1985, p.62.
66 A railgun accelerates a projectile to very high velocities by means of the repulsion force generated by extremely powerful electromagnets. See Jasani, 1985, pp. 166-71 for an explanation of the principle of the railgun and its feasibility for use as a space weapon.
67 It is outwith the scope of this chapter to attempt to analyse the feasibility of a space-based ABM system. There is now copious material published on the subject. The reader is referred in particular to Bethe *et al.*, 1984 and 1985, and Carter, 1984. A simplified analysis, which draws interesting parallels between SDI and the furore over the deployment of the abortive Safeguard system can be found in Burrows, 1984, pp. 850-6.
68 See *The Times*, 21 December 1984. Weinberger has declared himself to be 'dismayed by the absolute assurance with which, some distinguished American scientists and others declare the President's dream to be impossible'. Weinberger, 1985, p.112.
69 Bundy *et al.*, 1984, p. 264.
70 It would appear that point defence is now the main focus of the research programme. See National Academy of Sciences, 1985, p. 145. As well as having to cover a much smaller area, defence of hardened targets need not be quite so 'leak-proof'.
71 The USSR has pointed out that this particular argument was put forward some

time after the President's speech in March 1983, and that the main thrust of that speech was that SDI would put the USA in a position of strategic superiority. *Star Wars*, op. cit., note 57, p. 39.

72   The hawks in the US administration would probably be happy with such an outcome; massive Soviet investment in ABM research would divert resources from other military programmes and from the civilian sector of the economy (stimulating discontent) and provide a convenient justification for yet more US investment in SDI.

73   The historian E.P. Thompson has argued that SDI strikes a deep psychological cord in the minds of Americans, who (reasonably enough) long for a return to the pre-World War II days of safety from external threats. He also points out that a more sinister motive can be found for SDI; if an impermeable shield could be deployed, the USA could threaten other states with impunity, and so impose its will on the world. See E.P. Thompson, 1985, Chapter 5.

74   Secretary of State for Defense Weinburger repeated this most recently in March 1986. See *International Herald Tribune*, 22/23 March 1986.

75   *Star Wars*, 1985, p. 54.

76   Ibid., p. 30. The USSR is particularly worried about the accurate Pershing II missile which can reach targets in European Russia in 7 minutes from its operational deployment.

77   The United Kingdom, France, Germany and Canada at present all support SDI as a research programme, but US deployment of an ABM system would have vitally important consequences for these countries' defence and foreign policies that would almost certainly not be welcomed.

78   An argument can be made that a 'pop-up' system is not 'space-based' (see Jones, 1983, p. 56) but it is not persuasive. Although an ICBM is not 'space-based' because it simply passes through space, a pop-up system would be operationally deployed in space and thus prohibited by Article V.

79   The USSR has argued that 'the very announcement of the programme is at variance with the provisions of the Treaty' (*Star Wars*, p. 36). Rhinelander, op. cit., p. 6 draws the analogy from municipal law of an anticipatory breach of contract. It is submitted that the simple announcement of a research programme which, if successful, would give one party the practical option of withdrawing from the treaty is not *per se* a 'repudiation' of the Treaty. The Treaty is intended to be permanent, but it was also intended to be a living accord; continuing research is expressly permitted.

80   See Sofaer, 1986. Cf. Chayes and Chayes, 1986.

81   Ibid. Resort to the preamble to interpret the object and purpose of a treaty provision is permitted by Article 31(2) of the Vienna Convention on the Law of Treaties, op. cit., note 12. Although this mode of interpretation is not binding on the parties the principle of *effectiveness*, of which it forms a part, was considered to be part of customary international law by the International Law Commission. *YBILC*, 1966, Vol. II, p. 219.

82   *The Guardian*, 23 February 1987 and see Chayes and Chayes, above note 80. For the programme see below, p. 129.

83   Quoted in *SDI Report*, 1985, p. B. 4.

84   The chief Soviet space weapons negotiator at the Geneva talks, Mr Kvitsinsky, explicitly stated that the USSR was not seeking to ban pure research and that scientific technical means would be used to verify compliance, although other Soviet spokesmen have claimed that even laboratory research into prohibited systems is forbidden. See *The Times*, 26 July 1985, *The Guardian*, 24 1986.

85   See the ILC Commentary on Articles 26 and 31 of the Vienna Convention, op. cit. *YBILC*, 1966, Vol. II, pp. 211, 219.

86 US Defense Department, 1985, Appendix B. p. 2 ('We do reserve the right to respond to those violations in appropriate ways, some of which may eventually bear on the Treaty constraints as they apply to the United States'). The Treaty does not contain express provisions governing breach and counter-breach. Under customary international law, a material breach of a provision essential to the accomplishment of the object and purpose of the treaty gives the injured state the right to invoke this as a ground for suspending the operation to the treaty in whole or in part. (*YBILC*, 1966, Vol. II, pp. 253-5). The reciprocal obligations contained in the Treaty, however, are to a large extent interdependent. It is difficult to see how one side, regardless of how justifiable its actions might be, could openly and deliberately breach one set of obligations, without destroying the entire treaty regime.

87 See *The Times*, 6 September 1985.

88 See Kerr, 1985, pp. 113-24.

89 i.e. the ALPHA ground-based laser designed to 'explore the potential of chemical lasers for space-based applications', the Large Optics Demonstration Experiment (LODE) and LODE Advanced Mirror Programme (LAMP) designed, respectively, to demonstrate 'critical beam control and optics technologies' – these later to be integrated with a high power chemical laser and an Acquisition, Tracking and Pointing (ATP) series of experiments, designed to demonstrate the technologies required for ground and space based weapons and sensors. US State and Defense Department, 1985, Appendix B, 6.

90 e.g. the laser and optical tests against ground-based static targets at White Sands Missile Base. Ibid., p. 7, one of which has already been carried out (see *Observer*, 29 December 1985).

91 e.g. the proposed demonstration of a rocket-propelled impact vehicle, the 'performance of the demonstration hardware [being] limited to the Satellite defence mission'. Ibid., p. 8.

92 e.g. the launch of a sensor, the Long Wavelength Infrared Probe, into space will be carried out from a fixed land-based launcher at an agreed test site. Ibid., p. 6.

93 Rhinelander, 1985, p. 9 (my emphasis).

94 Ibid.

95 Ibid., pp. 4-6. Ambassador Smith in evidence to the House of Representatives that amending the Treaty to allow SDI would be like amending the Volstead Act to permit the sale of liquor. Arms Control in Outer Space: Hearings before the Sub-Committee on International Security and Scientific Affairs of the Committee on Foreign Affairs, House of Representatives, 98th Cong, 10 November 1983, at p.117. US withdrawal from the Treaty would require Senate approval.

96 See *Keesing's Contemporary Archives* 33915 1985. *Guardian*, 31 January 1986. Congress attached the provisos to the Fy 1985 appropriation that the funds may not be used 'in a manner inconsistent with' the US's international obligations (including the Treaty) and that should the research lead to deployment, the President must certify before deployment that the ABM system will function despite Soviet counter-measures and that it will be cost-effective. (See *The Guardian*, 26 September 1985.)

97 Rhinelander, 1985, p. 5 considers that SDI will never be able to be survivable and cost-effective, although some form of point ABM system may be technically feasible.

98 The Foreign Secretary, Sir Geoffrey Howe, expressed this opinion at a Royal United Services Institute seminar in 1985. See *The Times*, 16 March 1985.

99 Treaty on Principles Governing the Activities of States in the Exploration and Use of Outer Space, including the Moon and other Celestial Bodies. *1967 UKTS* 10 (1968), Cmnd. 3519. It is beyond the scope of this chapter to examine the

broader issues of the growing militarization of outer space. The reader is referred to Rosas, 1983, p. 357, Danielsson, 1984(1), pp. 1-11, and the *Proceedings of the American Society of Int. Law*, 1982.

100　Danielsson, 1984(2) p. 161 points out that Article 3 of the Agreement Governing the Activities of States on the Moon and Other Celestial Bodies, 1979, 18 *ILM* 1434 (1979) purports to confirm and expand the provisions of Article IV to orbits around, and trajectories to, all other celestial bodies (i.e. all of space except earth orbits). The US and the USSR are not parties.

101　See Jansani, 1984, Appendix 1.

102　By virtue of Article 1 of the Outer Space Treaty.

103　Danielsson, 1984(2), pp. 160-2 lists the other multilateral and bilateral treaty provisions prohibiting interference with particular early warning, communications and surveillance satellites.

104　Above notes 22–24 and accompanying text.

105　On the right of self-defence in international law, see I. Pogany, 'Nuclear Weapons and Self-Defence in International Law', Chapter 4, this volume.

106　This was the definition agreed by the UN Security Council Commission on Conventional Armaments in that year. Quoted in Jones, 1983, p. 75.

107　Ibid., p. 76.

108　*Star Wars*, pp. 5, 9.

109　For a discussion of the relative merits of the proposals made, see Russell, 1984, pp. 189-93. An examination of the issues to be dealt with by an ASAT treaty can be found in Slocombe, 1984, pp. 145-55. For the text of the Soviet proposals in 1981 and 1983 (and the Italian proposals in 1979), see Jasani, 1984.

110　Russell, 1984, writes that nuclear weapons are generally thought to include 'all arms which utilize atomic energy in accomplishing their intended purpose, irrespective of size of destructive force' (p. 160). X-ray lasers would probably require a high-yield explosion because of the inefficient input/output energy conversion.

111　Treaty Banning Nuclear Weapon Tests in the Atmosphere, in Outer Space and Under Water (1963), *UKTS* 3 (1964), Cmnd. 2245.

112　Cf. Article 35(3) of the 1977 Protocol I to the 1949 Geneva Conventions 16 *ILM* 1391 (1977) which prohibits all 'methods or means of warfare which are intended, or may be expected, to cause widespread, long-term and severe damage to the natural environment'. Both the USA and the USSR have signed but not yet ratified the treaty.

113　See note 109. See also *UN GA* Res. 39/59 of 12 December 1984 on the prevention of an arms race in outer space (A/39/744).

Bibliography

Aldrich, R.C. *First Strike*, Pluto Press, London, 1983.

American Society of International Law Proceedings, 'Arms Control in Outer Space', 1982, vol 76, pp. 284-97.

Barnaby, C.F. and Boserup, A. (eds) *Implications of Anti-Ballistic Missile Systems*, Pugwash Symposium, London, 1969.

Bethe, H. *et al.* 'Space-Based Ballistic Missile Defence', *Scientific American*, 1984, vol. 25, October.

Bethe, H. *et al.* 'BMD Technologies and Concepts in the 1980's', *Daedalus*, 1985, vol. 114, no. 2, p.53-71.

Bundy, M. *et al.* 'The President's Choice: Star Wars or Arms Control', *Foreign Affairs*, 1984, no.4, pp. 264-79.

Burrows, W.E. 'Ballistic Missile Defence: The Illusion of Security', *Foreign Affairs*, 1984, vol. 62, pp. 843-56.

Burt, R. 'Arms Control and Soviet Strategic Forces: The Risks of asking SALT to do too much', in J. Erikson and E.J. Feuchtwanger, *Soviet Military Power and Performance*, Macmillan, London, 1979.

Carter, A. *Directed Energy Missile Defence in Space*, Office of Technology Assessment, Washington, D.C., 1984.

Chayes, A. and Chayes A.H. 'Testing and Development of Exotic Systems under the ABM Treaty', *Harv. L.R.*, 1986, vol. 99, pp. 1956-71.

Cockburn, A. *The Threat: Inside the Soviet Military Machine*, Allen and Unwin, London, 1983.

Danielsson, S. 'An Examination of Proposals Relating to the Prevention of an Arms Race in Outer Space', *Journal of Space Law*, 1984, Vol. 12, pp. 1-11.

——'Approaches to Prevent an Arms Race in Outer Space', in B. Jasani, *Space Weapons: The Arms Control Dilemma*, Taylor and Francis, London, 1984.

Davis *et al. The Soviet Union and BMD*, Special Report from the Institute for Foreign Policy Analysis Inc., Washington D.C., 1980.

Ericson, J. and Feuchtwanger, E.J. (eds) *Soviet Military Power and Performance*, Macmillan, London, 1981.

Gartoff, R.L. 'Mutual Deterrence, Party and Strategic Arms Limitation in Soviet Policy', in D. Leebaert, *Soviet Military Thinking*, Allen & Unwin, London, 1981.

Jasani, B. (ed.) *Space Weapons: The Arms Control Dilemma*, Taylor and Francis, London, 1984.

Jasani, B. 'Space Weapons', *Space Policy*, May 1985, pp.164-78.

Jones, A.M. 'Implications of Arms Control Agreements and Negotiations for Space-Based BMD Lasers', in K.B. Payne, *Laser Weapons in Space: Policy and Doctrine*, Bowker, Epping, 1983.

Kaldor, M. *The Baroque Arsenal*, André Deutsch, London, 1982.

Kerr, D. 'Implications of anti-satellite weapons for ABM issues', in B. Jasani, *Space Weapons, The Arms Control Dilemma*, Taylor and Francis, London, 1984.

Levitt, J. 'Problems in the verification and enforcement of SALT agreements in the light of the record of Soviet compliance with SALT 1', *Harv. Int. L.J.*, 1981, vol. 22, pp. 380-404.

Lodal, J.M. 'Assuring Strategic Stability: An Alternative View', *Foreign Affairs*, 1975-76, vol. 54, no. 4, p. 472.

Longstreth, T.K. and Pike, J.E. 'U.S., Soviet Programmes threaten ABM Treaty', *Bulletin of the Atomic Scientists*, April 1985, pp.11-15.

Longstreth T.K. *et al. A Report on the Impact of U.S. and Soviet Ballistic Missile Defence Programmes on the ABM Treaty*, 1984, National Campaign to Save the ABM Treaty, Washington D.C.

Meredith, P.O. 'The Legality of a High-Technology Missile Defence System: The ABM and Outer Space Treaties', *A.J.I.L.*, 1984, vol. 78, no. 2, pp. 419-25.

Miko, F.T. *Soviet Strategic Objectives and SALT II: American Perceptions*, Cong. Records Service, Rept. 78-119 F, Washington D.C., 1978.

National Academy of Sciences. *Nuclear Arms Control*, National Academy Press, Washington D.C., 1985.

Nitze. P. 'Assuring Strategic Stability in an Era of Détente', *Foreign Affairs*, 1975-76, vol. 54, no. 2, p. 207.

Piradov A.S. (ed) *International Space Law*, Progress Publishers, Moscow, 1976.

President's Strategic Defence Initiative, US Government Printing Office, Washington D.C., 1985.

Rhinelander, J.B. 'How to Save the ABM Treaty', *Arms Control Today*, 1985, vol. 15, no. 4, May, pp. 1-12.

Rosas, J. 'The Militarization of Outer Space and International Law', *J. Peace Research*, 1983, vol. 20, pp. 357-70.

Russell, M. 'Military Activities in Outer Space. Soviet Legal Views', *Harv Int. L.J.*, 1984, vol. 25, Winter, pp. 153-93.

Slocombe, W. 'Approaches to an ASAT Treaty', in B. Jasani, *Space Weapons: The Arms Control Dilemma*, Taylor and Francis, London, 1984.

Smith, G. *Doubletalk: The Story of SALT I*, Doubleday, New York, 1980.

Sofaer, A. 'The ABM Treaty and SDI' *Harv. L.R.*, 1986, vol. 99, pp. 1972-85.

Star Wars; Delusions and Dangers, Progress Publishers, Moscow, 1985.

Stockholm International Peace Research Institute (SIPRI) Yearbook 1984.

Thompson, E.P. (ed.) *Star Wars*, Penguin, London, 1985.

Tsipis, K. *Arsenal: Understanding Weapons in the Nuclear Age*, Simon and Schuster, N.Y., 1984.

United States Congress House of Representatives, Committee on Foreign Affairs. Subcommittee on International Security and Scientific Affairs, Arms Control in Outer Space, 98th Cong. 10 November 1983.

United States State and Defense Departments, *Soviet Strategic Defense Programmes*, US Government Printing Office, Washington D.C., 1985.

United States Defense Department, *SDI Report*, US Government Printing Office, Washington D.C., 1985.

Weinberger, C. 'U.S. Defence Policy', *Foreign Affairs*, 1986, vol. 84, no. 4, p. 683.

Willrich, R. and Rhinelander, J. *SALT: The Moscow Agreements and Beyond*, Free Press, New York, 1984.

Year Book of the International Law Commission, 1966, UN Pub., London.

7 Law of the Sea and nuclear weapons: Legal aspects

Patricia Birnie

Introduction

It has become something of a cliché for works on any aspect of the Law of the Sea to start by pointing out that about 71 percent of the earth's surface consists of the sea and that over two-thirds of the world's population resides within about 188 miles of the coast, but in the case of nuclear weapons it is salutary to recall these facts since the seas are now both the main hiding place and main launching site of such weapons. Despite the fact that the Law of the Sea has imposed various restrictions on their use and deployment, it is also at present the vehicle for approval of the freedom of movement and deployment of nuclear weapons in certain areas and circumstances.

The term 'Law of the Sea' in this context has to be given a wide interpretation because provisions relevant to nuclear weapons in the seas are contained not only in the UN's 1958[1] and 1982 Conventions[2] on the Law of the Sea (LOSC) and in the customary Law of the Sea,[3] but also in several treaties which deal with arms control questions in a broader context. Such instruments include the Antarctic Treaty 1959;[4] Treaty Banning Nuclear Weapon Tests in the Atmosphere, in Outer Space and Underwater (Test Ban Treaty) 1963;[5] Treaty for the Prohibition of Nuclear Weapons in Latin America (Treaty of Tlatelolco) 1967;[6] Treaty on the Limitation of Anti-Ballistic Missile Systems (ABM Treaty) and the SALT I and SALT II Agreements 1972 and 1979, respectively.[7] Moreover there is one treaty, other than the UN Law of the Sea Conventions already referred to, which relates specifically to control of the use of nuclear weapons in the sea, namely the Treaty on the Prohibition of the Emplacement of Nuclear Weapons and Other Weapons of Mass Destruction on the Sea-Bed and the Ocean Floor and in the Sub-soil Thereof 1971 (hereafter referred to as the Sea-Bed Treaty or SBT).[8] As the broader treaties are the subject of other chapters of this work, as also is the concept of nuclear-free zones, they will be referred to here only in passing, to set the scene; attention will be concentrated on the UN Law of the Sea Conventions, especially the 1982 Law of the Sea Convention (hereafter referred to as the LOSC), and on the SBT, i.e. the one convention specifically relating to nuclear weapons and the sea.

In the recent UN report *Study of the Naval Arms Race*[9] presented by the UN Secretary-General and executed by a group of qualified experts appointed by him, the whole range of both conventional and nuclear maritime weapons is surveyed, as well as the political and legal framework within which they now operate. It is remarked that nuclear energy and weapons systems, *inter alia*, have improved the capabilities of navies to levels inconceivable even 30 years ago, those linked to nuclear energy being the most significant of all since it is used for propulsion of the nuclear-armed submarines that carry nuclear intercontinental ballistic missiles (ICBMs) and even for some of the surface vessels that carry tactical nuclear weapons. Missiles are also carried by aircraft and helicopters, some launched from aircraft carriers at sea, but it is the nuclear submarines that are the most dangerous weapon because they can evade detection and pursuit by diving to great depths and staying at sea for months at a time. This ability has provoked the development and use of revolutionary counter-measures, anti-submarine warning systems (ASW): radar for use on the surface, sonar for detection in the ocean deeps and electronic counter-measures (ECM), by means of which submarines try to avoid detection, hide their location or confuse attacking missiles. In response the weapons themselves are always developing both quantitatively and qualitatively, as are the vessels that carry them. New technology is having a profound effect which will require further development of the law of the sea if the stability and balance that are necessary to provide and maintain international peace and security, as required by the UN Charter, are to be secured.

Five states have ballistic missile-carrying submarines: USA, USSR, France, UK and China. The last three have only 6, 4 and 2 respectively, but the USA has 37 and the USSR 62 of different classes within the scope of the SALT Agreements. The numbers of submarine-launched missiles (SLBMs) carried are: USA, 640; USSR, 928; France, 96; UK, 64; China, 24. Most modern USA and USSR SLBMs have multiple independently targetable re-entry vehicle capabilities (MIRV).[10] Quality, rather than quantity, of missiles is thus the main consideration in developing arms control and disarmament today. There are many other nuclear weapons that can be used at or from the sea: short-range ballistic missiles; cruise missiles, short-range non-ballistic missiles, bombs, depth-charges, mines. Estimates suggest that there are 5900 tactical nuclear warheads for use by naval forces for various purposes. Sea-launched cruise missiles, the latest major development, have caused particular concern. Nor must the existence of conventional non-nuclear naval weapons be forgotten. It is against this situation that such legal developments as the 1971 SBT and the 1982 LOSC are evaluated by the international community, particularly by the approximately 160 states which do not have nuclear submarines or SLBMs. It is not surprising that, especially following the Falkland Islands campaign, more medium-range states with urgent defence problems are now reported to be seeking to acquire at least cruise missiles.

Developing states are particularly concerned at the pace of technological change since they can seldom afford to manufacture or purchase the more sophisticated modern weapons, let alone operate nuclear submarines or deploy ASW; they see them as a threat to international peace and security over which they have little control in the absence of agreements based on verification and enforcement at an international level. The spread of nuclear weapons in the oceans is also generally perceived as a threat to the marine environment, which both treaty and custom now require to be protected from pollution from all sources. Once radioactive materials enter the seas they may be dispersed but can never be removed, thus at some point the level of radioactivity in the oceans could become critical in relation to the levels advised by the International Atomic Energy Authority to be safe or at least acceptably so.

Legal background to the LOSC and SBT

The Secretary-General's Report referred to above gives a brief summary of the law of the sea relevant to use and deployment of naval arms and the use of the sea for peaceful purposes. A much more detailed analysis has been made recently by Professor Treves in the course of considering the emplacement of military devices on the seabed.[11] It must be borne in mind that all discussion of this subject takes place within the context of the current international law concerning the permissible use of force, as laid down in Articles 2(4) and 51 of the UN Charter which permit states to use it only in self-defence, though they can exercise this right collectively. As the significance of this limitation is the subject of another chapter of this work, nothing further will be said about it here, except to point out the special limitations imposed by the law of the sea.

The four Geneva Conventions of 1958 were silent on this subject; this silence has generally been regarded as widely permissive of use and deployment of all weapons, on the seabeds, in the subsoil beneath, in the waters above and on their surfaces, subject to the qualification just referred to that the exercise can be justified as non-aggressive or defensive since Article 2(4) of the UN Charter forbids 'the threat or use of force against the territorial integrity or political independence of any State or in any other manner inconsistent with the purposes of the United Nations'.[12] As pointed out by Booth, the situation created by this silence is 'one of obscurity',[13] deliberately adopted to disguise areas of disagreement in relation to military issues. This perception explains much of the confusing ambiguity that will be pointed out in the ensuing sections relating to the various Law of the Sea Conventions and the Sea-Bed Treaty. Treves also adduces as reasons for the omissions and vague allusions in these treaties, a certain reluctance, especially on the part of the superpowers, to discuss the subject explicitly and the emphasis during the twenty years since the Law of the Sea debate reopened has been on economic issues and uses of the sea rather than military ones. It is the economic potential that has led to the phenomenon that some writers, such as Booth, call the increasing 'territorialization' of the seas and seabeds but which this writer prefers to call the 'zoning' of these areas. The difference in shades of meaning between these terms is especially important in the context of military uses of the seas since territorialization implies that the seas and seabeds are being reduced to the same legal status as the land territory of states, i.e. subject not merely to specific jurisdictional competences and controls of the coastal state, as laid down by custom and treaty law, but to its sovereignty and thus the exercise of exclusive rights. Booth and others consider that states will increasingly see the seas in this way. Zoning on the other hand is, it is submitted, nearer to the true position, with all its latent obscurity, namely that the seas and seabeds have been divided into a complex interconnecting and overlaying series of jurisdictional zones. Holding back 'territorialization' and structuring 'zoning' are what the UN's Law of the Sea Conferences have been about following unilateral declarations from the 1950s onwards of 200-mile Territorial Seas by some Latin American and other states, stimulated by the US unilateral declaration of sovereign rights over the continental shelf in the 1945 Truman Proclamation. Ascertainment of the rights and jurisdictions of coastal and flag states in each zone requires a detailed analysis of the state of customary law and of all the relevant treaties, not only those directly laying down the law of the sea as such but those impinging on the military uses of the sea such as the arms control and collective security agreements and declarations of nuclear free zones and zones of peace.[14] Thus scrutinized legal rights and duties will be seen to be subtly different in each zone, though some interrelationships are made specific. Such explicit analysis is beyond the scope of this chapter and in any case has been done elsewhere.[15] Here we can only refer briefly to the situation.

The law of the sea based on custom and the four Geneva Conventions is often called the 'old' law of the sea to distinguish it from the 'new' law, based on the provisions of the 1982 LOSC and the new customs codified in or evolving from it. This is useful shorthand but misleading as the 'old' law is still in force for many states pending the entry into force of the LOSC, and even when that event does occur, will still be regarded in some respects as the source of existing law by states that have not signed or become full parties to the LOSC. These include at the present all five nuclear weapon states though their precise position on the LOSC varies. The USA has adopted the hardest position, having rejected the LOSC and announced that it will never sign a convention that provides for a deep seabed regime in the form laid down in it.[16]

The Geneva Conventions on the Law of the Sea: Legal regime

In discussing both the 1958 Geneva and the 1982 LOSC it has to be borne in mind that *prima facie* treaties bind only the states party to them and then only when they enter into force. However, they may bind even non-parties to the extent that they codify existing customs or generate new ones, i.e. consistent state practice develops round certain provisions and leads to a sense of obligation. Customary law can also develop outside the comprehensive Geneva and Law of the Sea conventions, either stimulated by other, more specific treaties (e.g. the large number concerning prevention of marine pollution), the SBT and PTBT, or any unilateral declarations or other state acts (e.g. the 1946 Truman Proclamation on the Continental Shelf by the USA, the 1952 Santiago Declaration on the Maritime Zone by three Latin American States, the Canadian Arctic Waters (Pollution Prevention) Act 1970, the 1983 Reagan Proclamation of the US Exclusive Economic Zone).[17] The extent to which the Geneva and 1982 LOSC represent customary law has been considered in detail elsewhere. Much of these treaties can be so considered and in announcing its EEZ, the US indicated that most of the 1982 LOSC was acceptable to the US, which would like to see most of its provisions enter into customary law; it is mainly Part XI, instituting the deep seabed regime, that is rejected by the USA. As the LOSC was negotiated on the basis of consensus until the final session of UNCLOS (when it was put to the vote at the US request), it is likely that most states will put most provisions (other than those concerning the deep seabed) into practice though not necessarily in a form identical to the LOSC in respect of detail. Since the need for consensus led to many compromises, often reflected by ambiguous wording in the text many provisions are therefore open to interpretation, and since the opening for signature of the LOSC in 1982 several states have taken up the option of making interpretative declarations.[18]

The 1958 Geneva Conventions on the Law of the Sea made only indirect or implied reference to the military uses of the sea. The Territorial Sea Convention recognized that the coastal state's sovereignty extends beyond its land territory and internal waters to a belt of adjacent territorial sea and to the airspace above it, but it did not explicitly fix the limit of that belt. As the Convention, however, also acknowledged the possibility of asserting a further zone contiguous to the territorial sea, measured from its baselines, up to a distance of 12 miles from them, in which the coastal state could exercise certain controls to prevent infringement of customs and other regulations within its territorial sea and punish infringement of them, it was subsequently assumed by many states that they could legitimately claim territorial seas of up to 12 miles, even before that limit was accepted in the LOSC. By 1985 the majority of coastal states, including the USSR, claimed this limit or more, although several states still limit themselves to 3,4 or 6 miles, including the USA and UK.[19]

In their territorial sea, states have full sovereignty over both the water column and seabed, subject only to a right of innocent passage for foreign flag vessels, including warships. Only 46 states are party to this Convention, and some states, even amongst those party to it, insist that the passage of warships, including submarines, requires either notification or prior consent; some consider that passage can be denied if vessels are carrying nuclear weapons,[20] a policy that, in turn, has resulted in some nuclear weapon states refusing to say whether ships with the capacity to carry nuclear weapons actually have them on board. The 1958 Convention, however, clearly states that its rules are applicable to *all* ships and that ships of all states have the right of innocent passage through the territorial sea. It requires, though, that submarines navigate on the surface and show their flag. As it limits the right of passage through straits used for international navigation to non-suspendable innocent passage, submarines must similarly pass on the surface through such straits. Innocence is defined in terms of whether the passage is prejudicial to the peace, good order or security of the coastal state, i.e. by the mode of passage rather than the character of the ship, its cargo or crew. States, such as the USA, which accept only 3-mile territorial sea limits maintain that in straits more than 6 miles wide, unless agreement to the contrary is arrived at, there remains a right to high seas passage beyond each state's 3-mile limit. Straits states with 12-mile territorial seas, however, claim the right to reduce the whole 24-mile width of relevant straits to innocent passage, in the absence of accept- `

ance of the new LOSC, which, as we shall see, has different provisions covering both definition of innocent passage and transit passage through straits.

Subject to non-interference with innocent passage, the coastal state has the right to emplace, deploy or transport nuclear weapons in a territorial sea of up to 12 miles, since this limit coincides, as we shall see, with that permitted by the Seabed Treaty. Meanwhile, the status of claims to a territorial sea of more than 12 miles remains disputed by parties to the Territorial Sea Convention. The states that make more extensive claims will certainly have to reduce them to 12 miles if they become parties to the LOSC when that Convention enters into force; most states would in any event contend that a 12-mile limit for the territorial sea is now part of customary international law.

The waters lying within the baselines of the territorial sea are regarded as internal waters. In these the Territorial Sea Convention also recognizes that the coastal state has full sovereignty, but in this case without the need to concede any rights of innocent passage. Entry of foreign ships carrying nuclear weapons and employment of such weapons can clearly be denied here. Both this convention and the LOSC, which is almost identical in this respect, permit the coastal state to draw the baselines of its territorial sea in such a way that, where specified conditions exist such as deeply indented coastlines, fringing islands, certain low-tide elevations or so-called historic bays,[21] large areas of sea and seabed can be reduced to the status of internal waters. Since islands, under the 1958 Convention, have their own territorial sea much less than 71 percent of the earth's surface is thus subject to the SBTs and LOSC prohibitions that are discussed below.

The 1958 Continental Shelf Convention further extended the coastal states jurisdiction over the seabed, in so far as it can be claimed as continental shelf within the definition of that area in this convention, as subsequently interpreted.[22] In this case, however, a distinction was made between the physical shelf lying within the territorial sea, the bed and superjacent waters of which remained subject to coastal state sovereignty under the TSC, and the 'legal' shelf to which the CSC applied and which commenced beyond the territorial seas' outer limits, however drawn. Over this part of the shelf the coastal state explicitly exercised only sovereign rights limited to the purpose of exploring and exploiting its natural resources since the waters above remained high seas, and were thus open to the exercise of the freedom permitted under the High Seas Convention and customary law (see below). Some measures could be taken by the coastal state in relation to submarine cables and pipelines (laying of which is otherwise regarded as a high seas freedom), as reasonable to facilitate exercise of the right to exploit the seabed and subsoil of the shelf. In pursuit of this right the coastal state was recognized to be entitled to construct and maintain or operate on the shelf installations and other devices necessary for its exploration and the exploitation of its natural resources; these then fell under its jurisdiction.

These distinctions are deliberate and significant in relation to nuclear weapons, ASW and ECM generally. In the absence of any other treaty, since the coastal state rights are limited by the economic purposes for which they can exclusively be exercised, the rights of other states to carry out activities on the shelf for other purposes, such as emplanting nuclear or other weapons or ASW devices of all kinds are preserved, as long as they do not unduly interfere with the coastal states' shelf rights. The point is reinforced by the fact that the CSC requires that the coastal state's exploration and exploitation of the shelf must not result in any unjustifiable interference with navigation, fishing, conservation of the living resources of the sea, nor with fundamental oceanographic or other scientific research which is to be openly published. Though this convention did not specially refer to emplantation of military devices, it did recognize the existence of rights exercised by others than the coastal state and the silence on military activities was part of the deliberate obscurity that permitted conclusion of the convention, since until the assertion of shelf rights these areas had been freely used for military purposes by all states with the necessary capabilities.

As we shall see, the present position is complicated by the fact that, even before the entry into force of the LOSC which now permits EEZs, a large number of coastal states unilaterally have asserted rights in Exclusive Economic or Fisheries Zones (hereafter EEZs or EFZs)[23] and the International Court of Justice has acknowledged that the EEZ provision, at least to the extent that it accords to coastal states rights to exploit the resources of the seabed within 200 miles of their baselines as part of the legal 'continental shelf', whether or not a physical continental shelf exists, is now part of customary international law.[24] Moreover, the LOSC provision concerning the rights of the coastal state and others to place installations and devices on the shelf differs from that in the CSC and introduces further ambiguities: these are compounded by the fact that only 44 states are party to the CSC and only 32 to the LOSC at the time of writing.

The High Seas Convention, which purports to codify the rules of international law relating to the high seas, defines them as all parts of the sea that are not included in the territorial sea or internal waters. It will be appreciated that the advent of EEZs and EFZs complicates this position since the LOSC, in its section dealing with the High Seas (Part VII) states that it applies, *inter alia,* only beyond the limits of the EEZ, although subsequently some of the provisions of the section are specifically applied to the EEZ (Part V). For states that are not party to the

Seabed Treaty, emplacement of nuclear weapons in the high seas is governed by the provisions of the HSC, since in the relevant respects it codifies the customary law. It is not clear whether the HSC applies to the seabed beneath the high seas, and, of course, in relation to exploration and exploitation of its mineral resources the UN has declared that the area beyond national jurisdiction (viz beyond the continental shelves) is the common heritage of mankind to be exploited only under an international regime to be established, on a generally acceptable basis, with appropriate international machinery.[25] A regime has been established in the LOSC, which also confirms the common heritage status of the seabed, but it has not as yet proved generally acceptable to two of the nuclear weapon states (USA, UK); the LOSC has been signed, but not ratified, by the other three (USSR, France, China). The first two, supported by another non-signatory (Federal Republic of Germany), maintain that in the absence of their acceptance of the LOSC the status of the deep seabed is governed by the doctrine of the freedom of the high seas, codified in the HSC. What remains unclear is the extent to which these high seas freedoms endure within the EEZs, either under the LOSC or existing practice, as evidenced by the unilateral declarations.

What then are the high seas freedoms under the HSC? The HSC refers to four freedoms, *inter alia,* thus implying that there may be others. This view is reinforced by the fact that though it goes on to list four specific freedoms – of navigation; of fishing (now limited by the coastal EEZs and EFZs); to lay submarine cables and pipelines (to the extent that this is not restricted by the provision of the CSC referred to above); of overflight – it adds that these 'and others which are recognized by the general principles of international law' must be exercised by all states with reasonable regard to the interests of other states in the exercise of the freedom of the high seas (Article 2). It has generally been assumed that these others include freedom of scientific research, disposal of waste, conduct of military exercises and manoeuvres, deployment and emplacement of nuclear weapons (now subject to the SBT), and testing of nuclear weapons (now only by states not party to the SBT). Not all states accept this view and these freedoms too have been much restricted by the concession in the LOSC that coastal states have, within their EEZs, jurisdiction (subject to other provisions in the Convention) over scientific research and preservation of the marine environment, a jurisdiction which some states, even before the entry into force of the LOSC, are already seeking to exercise. The alleged freedom to test nuclear weapons in and over the seas has been disputed in the Nuclear Test Cases that are the subject of Chapter 9 and would certainly seem likely to run counter to the recently established principle of customary law, codified in the LOSC (Part XII), which requires states to protect and preserve the marine environment.[26]

These limitations apart, it would appear that, for states which are not party to the LOSC or implementing it on the ground that it is, or is now becoming, customary law, the position in relation to nuclear weapons is that they *could* place nuclear weapons on the seabed (if not party to the SBT), arguing that in the absence of a specific prohibition accepted by them, the doctrine of freedom applies to the seabed of the high seas.[27] They could also assert the freedom to deploy nuclear weapons or navigate vessels with nuclear weapons on board (including submarines) in and on the surface of the high seas to the extent that this does not cause damaging pollution and the freedom to conduct temporary manoeuvres or exercises on the high seas or in the air-space above with nuclear weapons either individually or collectively. Whether these activities are desirable is another matter; we are only concerned here with their legitimacy under the present law of the sea. In addition it seems clear that such states could certainly establish or deploy anti-submarine warning or other monitoring detection devices in the high seas on or under the seabeds of the high seas. Problems arise here, however, in relation to the location of the outer limits of the continental shelf, since some states argue that this freedom does not exist on the shelf, as explained earlier, and the new LOSC appears to treat the 200 mile shelf differently in this respect from the naturally prolonging shelf beyond that limit, as we shall see.

Not all states accept this view of the Geneva Convention or of the customary regime outside the LOSC. Some equate, in their national legislation, rights over the continental shelf with rights over the territorial sea and characterize them as sovereignty; they thus purport to exclude all foreign activity at least on the seabed, whether or not it interferes with the exercise of the economic rights of exploration and exploitation of their continental shelf. Latin American states, in particular, take this view, and not all are parties to the relevant treaties (e.g. TBT, NPT, Tlatelolco Treaty, Seabed Treaty). Such views have been emphasized, as we shall see, during the two Review Conferences that have taken place under the SBT.

Under the Geneva Conventions, unlike the LOSC, there is no specific provision concerning archipelagic waters; this problem is dealt with, therefore, only in connection with the LOSC below. The 1958 Convention on Fishing has no immediate relevance to nuclear weapons, except that it prescribes that all states have the duty to adopt, or to cooperate with other states in adopting, such measures for their nationals as may be necessary for the conservation of the living resources of the high seas; using or deploying nuclear weapons in a way that interfered with conservation might be construed as a breach of this conservatory obligation.

UNCLOS III: The legal regime established under the UN Law of the Sea Convention 1982

The question of reservation of the seabed for peaceful purposes

The military aspects of the Law of the Sea have been characterized as one of the issues neglected by the UNCLOS III,[28] and there is still a dearth of writing on this subject.[29] Especially is this true of the use of nuclear weapons in the seas and their emplacement on the seabeds. Very little has been written about the 1971 Seabed Treaty, concluded before the opening of the UNCLOS III. It seems to have been regarded for many years as ending the problem of nuclear weapons in the sea and its very conclusion served to prevent this issue being regarded as an important one to be included in the 'package deal' of the LOSC provisions. Instead, faced with the threat of territorialization of the seas referred to earlier, the major powers that possessed these weapons were more anxious to ensure that the new treaty provided for the continued freedom of movement of their fleets, especially their naval vessels, through the world's oceans and international straits and across the seabeds. The increasing number of unilateral declarations in the 1970s of 200-mile EEZs, EFZs and of archipelagic waters based on baselines constructed round the perimeters of the outermost islands of archipelagic states to enclose vast areas as internal waters through which there would not even be a right of innocent passage, as well as the rapid increase in the number of states claiming a territorial sea of 12 miles or more drawn from baselines ever more distant from the natural coastline, resulted in the concentration of the naval and nuclear states' attention on navigational issues. Protection of freedom of movement for nuclear submarines in Arctic waters was a particular and shared objective of both the USSR and the USA in order to preserve the strategic balances vital to their security interests.[30] Their interests coincided on most defence aspects of negotiations at UNCLOS III, although seldom allowed to surface in the few sessions that are reported in the official records of the conference.

In the light of these developments it is often forgotten that the catalyst precipitating the UNCLOS III was an item put on the agenda of the United Nations General Assembly at its 22nd meeting in 1967 by Ambassador Arvid Pardo of Malta, who is better remembered for his proposal, made at the same time, that the seabed beyond national jurisdiction should be declared the Common Heritage of Mankind, to be exploited only under some form of international regime or the UN itself. But Ambassador Pardo linked this proposal to a request that the seabeds should be reserved exclusively for peaceful purposes and he introduced the item in the following terms:

Declaration and treaty concerning the reservation exclusively for peaceful purposes of the seabed and of the ocean floor, underlying the seas beyond the limits of present national jurisdiction, and use of their resources in the interests of mankind.[31]

Actions by the UN General Assembly

The General Assembly remitted to its First Committee (its Political Committee) following debate on the item, the more modest task of conducting:

Examination of the question of reservation exclusively for peaceful purposes of the seabed and ocean floor, and the subsoil thereof, underlying the high seas beyond the limits of present national jurisdiction and the use of their resources in the interests of mankind. (emphasis added)

The major powers, particularly the USA and USSR, were not at that stage at all anxious to enter into negotiation of a treaty of such broad scope which in their view might prejudice the existing freedoms of the high seas, especially since the term 'peaceful uses' is inherently ambiguous in relation to nuclear weapons, a problem that will be discussed further below. The First Committee, however, recommended further study.

Establishment of the Ad Hoc Committee

After considering the First Committee's report in 1968, the Assembly decided to establish an *Ad Hoc* Committee merely 'to study the peaceful uses of the seabed and the ocean floor beyond the limits of national jurisdiction'.[32] The military aspects of Pardo's original proposal were thus played down from the outset, though an accompanying Memorandum suggested that the seabed area 'shall be reserved exclusively for peaceful purposes in perpetuity', as originally intended by Pardo.[33] The Preamble of the relevant Resolution referred to the need to ensure that the area's exploration and use should be consistent with the UN Charter and in the interests of maintaining international peace and security, to the importance of preserving it from actions and uses which might be detrimental to the common interests of mankind, and to the fact that developing technology was making the area accessible and exploitable for military purposes. In fact Pardo feared that the superpowers might be about to emplace nuclear weapons on the deep seabeds but the item referred to the *Ad Hoc* Committee made no express mention of this concern and, significantly, the UN Secretariat, after conducting a requested study on the UN's Eighteen Nation Disarmament Committee's (ENDC) work in this field found that even the ENDC had never discussed it.

This development begged a number of questions which remain largely unsolved in the Law of the Sea even today. First, what is meant by peaceful purposes; secondly, where does the international area of the seabed begin; thirdly, what is the legal position of the areas inside as well as outside the international area, i.e. in the Territorial Seas; on the Continental Shelves and the High Seas above the seabed? Did existing custom and treaty law reserve them to peaceful purposes, whatever that term might mean, or were states free to engage in non-peaceful activities in such areas, subject only to the obligations imposed by custom and the UN Charter concerning use of force, both of which expressed these duties in somewhat vague and general terms,[34] which required them to maintain international peace and security, to settle disputes by peaceful means and to eschew use of force except in self-defence and did not clearly prevent them from acquiring or deploying nuclear weapons for this purpose, whether on land, in the air or in or over the sea, except in areas subject to the sovereignty of other states?

This position had, as we have seen, prevailed since Grotius's time, when the doctrine of the freedom of the seas became established, up to the present day, having been codified in the 1958 Geneva Convention on the High Seas.[35] The nuclear weapons states had assumed that this freedom, as interpreted in state practice, covered not only deployment of such weapons in the sea on ships and submarines but also on the seabed although, as far as is known, the last option had not been taken up by 1968. At this date also, the majority of states still retained territorial seas of less than 12 miles, limited fisheries zones to 12 miles and claimed continental shelves beyond a 200-metre depth only in terms of their exploitability; the international areas were therefore vast. Aware of the questions begged by its terms of reference and the existing law of the sea at that date, the *Ad Hoc* Committee saw the need to develop new principles for the international area, reserving its use exclusively for 'peaceful purposes for the benefit of and in the interest of mankind as a whole' but it found that further study was required before these could be elaborated. The General Assembly thereupon established a permanent Committee on the Peaceful Uses of the Seabed and Ocean Floor beyond the Limits of National Jurisdiction (PUSOF) and instructed it to study further, taking into account the studies and international negotiations being undertaken in the field of disarmament, the reservation exclusively for peaceful purposes of the deep seabed.

In 1968 the ENDC had at last begun to address the seabed area and had made provision for discussion of the question of prevention of an arms race on the seabed but neither in the course of the following discussions nor in the *Ad Hoc* Committee or in PUSOF was any agreement arrived at on the limits of the area, the meaning of 'peaceful uses', or the legal position outside national areas. The superpowers maintained their dual concerns. First, they were anxious to maintain the maximum freedom to deploy their nuclear weapons in the widest possible area. They thus wanted to ensure that any principles or rules developed for the international area were sufficiently flexible to allow the required freedom of operation. Secondly, they sought to ensure that the limits of exclusive coastal state control were kept as narrow as possible. Developing states, on the other hand, being without nuclear weapons and nuclear submarines, were interested in expanding their control over adjacent coastal areas and restricting the freedom of the superpowers, and other states that may in time obtain them, to position or use weapons and engage in manoeuvres involving them.

The confrontation of these interests and the need to reach some accommodation on them resulted in 1970 in the issues being addressed separately, viz. (i) the establishment of the limits of national jurisdiction, and (ii) the reservation exclusively for peaceful purposes of the areas beyond. The first question became one of the major issues on the agenda of the UNCLOS III which in 1970 the General Assembly decided to convene in 1973. The second was also put on the agenda but as a separate item. It was also decided, however, to proceed separately with negotiation of a convention to prohibit emplacement of nuclear weapons on the seabed in an area to be determined. The question of the limits to freedom of emplacement of nuclear weapons on the seabed was thus disengaged entirely from the new zonal limits under negotiation at UNCLOS and from the question of establishing an international regime for the international area and its boundaries. The specific question of emplacing nuclear weapons could, therefore, be left out of the UNCLOS negotiations though freedom of movement for submarines carrying nuclear missiles remained an important item related to its preservation in the variety of zones with which the proposed convention would be concerned. We too, therefore, will proceed to address these issues under separate heads, and will examine first the provisions developed by UNCLOS III, although, of course, there remains a close relationship between the two since a large part of the area covered by the SBT is also covered by the Deep-Sea Mining Regime established by the 1982 LOSC, which includes the institution of an International Seabed Authority to administer the area. No formal linkage of the two conventions has yet been made, however, and neither refers to the other, a matter which has caused some concern at Seabed Treaty Review Conferences.

The Declaration of Principles Governing the Deep Sea-Bed

In 1970 the General Assembly, however, also adopted a 15-point Declaration of Principles Governing the Exploration and Exploitation of the Sea-Bed and Ocean Floor, and the Subsoil thereof, beyond the Limits of National Jurisdiction.[36] It declared the seabed and ocean floor of this area, as well as its resources, to be the common heritage of mankind, not open to appropriation or claims of sovereignty by any state. All activities regarding exploration and exploitation of its resources were to be governed by the international regime to be established. Point 5 declared that:

> The area shall be open to use exclusively for peaceful purposes by all States whether coastal or land-locked, without discrimination, in accordance with the international regime to be established.

Point 6 added:

> The area shall be reserved exclusively for peaceful purposes, without prejudice to any measures which have been or may be agreed upon in the context of international negotiations undertaken in the field of disarmament and which may be applicable to a broader area.

The meaning of 'peaceful' was not elucidated but this time some indirect reference was made to nuclear weapons treaties since Point 6 added that:

> One or more agreements shall be concluded as soon as possible in order to implement effectively this principle and to constitute a step toward the exclusion of the sea-bed, the ocean floor and the sub-soil thereof from the arms race.

This remains the sole guidance on the relation of the LOSC and SBT: neither must prejudice the other. The Declaration forms the basis of the regime for the international area laid down in the 1982 LOSC and though the latter has been rejected by the USA, the Declaration, on which it and other major maritime states abstained, so that it can be said to have been adopted unanimously, has not.

Relevant provisions of the LOSC 1982

There are three categories of provisions in the LOSC that are relevant to nuclear weapons: those extending coastal states' control over specific maritime areas, either with regards to geographical area or to the range of powers to regulate activities; those affecting freedom of navigation; those relating to peaceful uses of the sea. The LOSC is innovative in all these respects, though it is only possible here to deal with particularly relevant provisions. Since the freedom of navigation is dealt with in the treaty specifically and differently in the provisions concerning each zone or area, the first two categories will be dealt with together.

Effects on freedom of navigation of extension or revision of coastal state jurisdiction

There are several ways in which the LOSC extends the geographical scope of coastal state jurisdiction. It continues the system of straight baselines introduced in the Geneva Convention on the Territorial Sea, equating them with other methods and no longer referring to them as the exception; it permits a 12-mile limit for the territorial sea itself and a 24-mile limit for the Contiguous Zone measured from the baselines. The coastal state retains full sovereignty in internal waters and the territorial sea and because the SBT relates only to the seabed beyond 12 miles from the baselines of the Territorial Sea, it can emplant weapons on the seabed of this area and prevent the placing there by foreign states not only of nuclear weapons but of ASW etc. devices.

The LOSC also introduces the concept of the 200-mile EEZ in which the coastal state can exercise a variety of jurisdictions—sovereign rights for purposes of exploring and exploiting, conserving and managing the living and non-living natural resources of the seabed and water column and other economic uses of the sea; jurisdiction (as separately provided in the convention) over establishment and use of artificial islands, installations and structures, over marine scientific research and protection and preservation of the marine environment.

The rights concerning the seabed and subsoil are exercised in accordance with the part of the convention (Part VI) relating to the continental shelf and though emplacement of nuclear weapons on the seabed of most of this area is banned by the SBT, as we shall see, these provisions throw into some doubt the rights of the coastal state to control the emplacement by foreign states on the seabed within its 200-mile EEZ, which is thus equated with and included in the definition of the continental shelf, of ASW and other devices which are an essential part of the strategic deterrence system associated with nuclear weapons. Article 56, concerning the EEZ, gives the coastal state control of 'installations and structures within it'; Article 60 (1) (which under Article 80 applies *mutatis mutandis* to similar structures on the continental shelf) says the coastal state:

shall have the exclusive right to construct and to authorize and regulate the construction, operation and use of: (a) artificial islands; (b) installations and structures for the purpose of Article 56 and other *economic* purposes; (emphasis added) (c) installations and structures which may interfere with the exercise of the rights of the coastal state in the zone.

This would appear to cover installation of such ASW and other installations as have that impeding effect although precisely what amounts to 'interference' is left unclear, presumably to be determined by the coastal state in good faith. Numerous specific requirements are laid down – due notice of construction of such structures and permanent warning of their presence must be given; safety zones can be established around them, and so on. These provisions appear to have in mind only structures established for economic purposes; not self-defence or security systems. Yet the EEZ provisions are drafted so as to limit the coastal state to exercise of sovereign rights and jurisdiction (it is not accorded sovereignty) which would imply that other states retain residual freedom and rights deriving from the area's previous status as high seas. Indeed Article 55 defining the EEZ, says that it is an area 'subject to the specific legal regime established in this Part (Part V), under which the rights and jurisdictions of the coastal state and the rights and freedoms of other states are governed by the relevant provisions of this Convention.' Furthermore, Article 59, laying down the basis for resolution of conflicts regarding the attribution of rights and jurisdiction in the zone, says that they should be resolved 'on the basis of equity and the light of the relevant circumstances, taking into account the respective importance of the interests involved to the parties as well as to the international community as a whole'. It is not surprising that controversy has arisen concerning the application of these articles to emplacement of ASW and similar devices on the shelves of other states. Opinion is divided: Treves takes the view that foreign states *can* undertake such activities;[37] Zedalis has argued the opposite[38] though Treves, in a reply, rejected Zedalis's arguments, contending that it was the clear intention of the negotiators and drafters that such activities should be permitted.[39] As the continental shelf is permitted under Article 76 of the LOSC to extend beyond 200 miles where there is a natural prolongation of the coastal states territory into and under the sea beyond that limit, up to the edge of the continental margin, and as Article 80 of the LOSC applies Article 60 to the whole of this area, the same arguments would apply to the shelf beyond 200 miles. This area, especially the continental slope, is the most likely area for emplanting the electronic, acoustical and magnetic anomaly detection devices which are vital to tracking strategic ballistic missile carrying submarines, especially in Arctic waters.[40]

Part XI of the LOSC establishes an International Area of the deep seabed beyond the continental margin. Theoretically, under Article 137, only the exploration and exploitation of the Area's resources should fall under the control of the International Seabed Authority (ISA) which the LOSC also establishes to act on behalf of mankind as a whole and in which it vests the rights to the resources. Thus both emplacement of nuclear weapons and of ASW and other devices could freely occur. However, as this area also comes within that covered by the SBT, emplanting of nuclear weapons is forbidden so far as parties to that convention are concerned. Though *prima facie* the ISA would not have any role in controlling ASW and similar devices, it could be that the ISA will try to justify some role in this respect. It appears that the Preparatory Commission (PrepCom), established to prepare for the operation of the ISA once the LOSC enters into force, and which is now therefore, drafting the preliminary rules and regulations for exploitation, is beginning to assume that, despite the provision in Articles 143 on Marine Scientific Research which permits parties to the LOSC to carry it out, though 'exclusively for peaceful purposes and for the benefit of mankind as a whole', the ISA will be able to regulate research if it is related to the seabed and affects exploration or exploitation activities there. It would thus be only a small step for the ISA to claim that it can require information on emplacement of ASW or even on movements of underwater vessels and vehicles that might interfere with such activities, with a view to regulating them. The expansion of coastal state control over scientific research on or directed to the continental shelves under both the 1958 and 1982 LOSC, and the view held by some states that they can prohibit placement of ASW on their shelves under these conventions, creates a climate in which such expansionist ideas could take root and flourish, although it was the clear intention of the negotiators that the ISA should not control research and that the area should remain free for activities other than resource exploitation. The common heritage concept, under Articles 1, 136 and 137, is confined to the seabed and does not relate to the waters above, which remain high seas and subject to the various freedoms of the high seas preserved under Part VII of the LOSC.

There are other provisions which states anxious to restrict the superpowers nuclear-related activities might similarly interpret broadly to achieve this restrictive end. Article 138 requires that 'The general conduct of states in relation to the Area shall be in accordance with the provisions of this Part, the principles embodied in the Charter of the United Nations and other rules of international law in the interests of maintaining peace and security and promoting international cooperation and understanding'; Article 141 states that 'The Area shall be open to use exclusively for peaceful purposes by all States'. Installations used for carrying out activities in the Area, are also required under Article 147 (2) (d) to be used 'exclusively for peaceful purposes', and its section 3 lays down that 'other activities in the marine environment shall be conducted with reasonable regard for activities in the Area'.

Navigation is one of the most important of these. Freedom of navigation is carefully preserved, subject to specific regimes, in both the old and new zones of jurisdiction. It does not exist in internal waters, but generally entry into ports and harbours is freely permitted, though whether there is a *right* of entry into them is controversial and has led to the dispute concerning entry of nuclear ships or ships carrying nuclear weapons into some foreign ports. The LOSC is silent on this question. In the Territorial Sea, however, Part III of the 1982 Convention is unequivocal in maintaining the right of innocent passage for *all* ships, but not for aircraft, as long as they do not present a threat to the peace, good order or security of the coastal state. It defines, in Article 19, much more circumspectly than hitherto, however, the circumstances in which passage will lose its innocence. The activities listed as occasioning this loss include:

(a) any threat or use of force against the sovereignty, territorial integrity or political independence of the coastal state, or in any other manner in violation of the principles of international law embodied in the Charter of the United Nations;
(b) any exercise or practice with weapons of any kind;
(c) any act aimed at collecting information to the prejudice of the defence or security of the coastal state;
(e) the launching, landing or taking on board of any aircraft;
(f) the launching, landing or taking on board of any military device;
(l) any other activity not having a direct bearing on passage.

The freedom is restricted in other ways relevant to nuclear weapons. Submarines and other underwater vehicles must navigate on the surface and show their flag (Article 20). There is no right of overflight whether or not aircraft carry nuclear weapons. Foreign ships can be required to use sea lanes and traffic separation schemes overviewed by the appropriate organization (such as the IMO). This Article (Article 22) particularly specifies that tankers, nuclear-powered ships and ships carrying nuclear materials, *inter alia,* must use such lanes, and Article 23 requires that they carry documents and observe special precautionary measures laid down in relevant international agreements, which are not identified. The coastal state can also regulate the safety of navigation and prevention of pollution; foreign ships must comply with such regulations (Article 21). Passage must be continuous and expeditious (Article 18) but it can be temporarily suspended (Article 25(3) in specified areas if essential for the coastal state's security 'including weapons exercises', i.e. *inter alia,* if it is exercising its nuclear weapons (subject to any other relevant treaty obligations).

The extension of the territorial sea to 12 miles affects the freedom of passage through many more international straits than hitherto since parts formerly regarded as high seas will fall within the territorial sea and passage through these will be restricted to innocent passage. The LOSC therefore provides, in Part III, a special regime for such straits, known as Transit Passage, under which both foreign ships *and* aircraft, including military ones, will, subject to meeting certain requirements, have a right of unimpedable passage, which can be conducted in their 'normal mode', a term taken to indicate that submarines can navigate under the surface and will not be required to surface as in innocent passage (Article 39). Passage must, however, be continuous and expeditious and not present any threat or use of force against the sovereignty or territorial integrity of the coastal state, or violate the principles of international law and the UN Charter; the coastal state's safety and pollution prevention regulations must be observed and activities *en route* must be confined to those incidental to normal transit. Sea lanes and traffic separation schemes can be prescribed for use and other permitted coastal state laws must be observed. Only straits defined for this purpose as 'international' in Article 37 are covered by this regime, i.e. those used for international navigation between one part of the high seas or an exclusive economic zone and another part of the high seas or an exclusive economic zone. Other straits are either left under the regime of non-suspendable innocent passage or are subject to specific regimes under other conventions, such as the Montreux Convention, which restricts the passage rights of certain classes of warships, including aircraft carriers, through the Bosphorous, Dardanelles and Sea of Marmara.

The acceptance of the drawing of straight baselines joining the outermost islands of archipelagos necessitated, as the *quid pro quo* for naval and maritime states, conclusion of a regime of sea lanes passage for ships and aircraft through and over the waters thus enclosed, which though recognised in the LOSC as now subject to the sovereignty of the coastal state are *sui generis* in status, a construct of the convention – neither clearly regarded as territorial or as internal waters in the LOSC. Article 49, recognizing the archipelagic state's sovereignty over these waters, also requires that it be 'exercised subject to this Part'. It permits the coastal state to designate sea lanes and air routes above suitable for continuous and expeditious passage and prescribes in Article 53 that

'All ships and aircraft enjoy the right of archipelagic sea lanes passage' therein, subject to safety and other measures and refraining from threat of or use of force, i.e. as required for transit passage through straits (Article 54). None the less some archipelagic states still appear to regard the waters enclosed as internal waters.[41]

In the EEZ, under Part V, states continue to enjoy freedoms of overflight, navigation, laying of submarine cables and pipelines (on terms referred to in the high seas provisions in Part VII) and 'other internationally lawful uses of the sea related to these freedoms, such as those associated with the operation of ships, aircraft and submarine cables and pipelines, and compatible with the other provisions of this Convention' (Article 58). Foreign states must have due regard to the rights and duties of the coastal state in exercising their EEZ rights and duties and comply with its laws, adopted in accordance with the Convention, to the extent that they are compatible with Part V. This contributes to the ambiguity which has encouraged some coastal states to argue that installation of ASW and other devices requires their consent. The problem is not reduced by the vagueness of the provision for resolution of conflicts concerning rights and duties in the EEZ not attributed by the LOSC. They should, under Article 59, 'be resolved on the basis of equity and in the light of all the relevant circumstances, taking into account the respective importance of the interests involved to the parties as well as to the international community as a whole'.

The redefinition of the coastal states' continental shelf in Article 76 in terms of distance and natural prolongation, not exploitability, to comprise:

> the seabed and sub-soil of the submarine areas that extend beyond its territorial sea throughout the natural prolongation of its land territory to the outer edge of the continental margin, or to a distance of 200 nautical miles from the baselines from which the breadth of the territorial sea is measured where the outer edge of the continental margin does not extend up to that distance

to a maximum of 350 miles from the territorial sea baselines or 100 miles from the 2500 metre isobath, has also already been remarked upon, as has the application to the EEZ of the shelf regime laid down. Unlike in the 1958 Convention on the Continental Shelf, the waters above are no longer specifically designated as high seas, even to the extent that they project beyond 200 miles. The Convention ambiguously states in Article 78 that 'The rights of the coastal State over the continental shelf do not affect the legal status of the superjacent waters or the air space above these waters.' The status of freedoms within the 200-mile limit has been dealt with above. Beyond that limit we have to refer to Part VII of the LOSC relating to the high seas. In any event, in either area, the exercise of coastal state rights over the shelf must not infringe on or cause unjustifiable interference with navigation and other freedoms provided in the Convention.

The high seas provisions *do not* apply to the parts of the sea included in the EEZ, territorial sea, archipelagic or internal waters (Article 86). They thus *do* apply to the areas over the continental shelf beyond 200 miles and over the deep seabed area, whether it begins at the outer limit of the territorial sea (whatever limit the coastal state so determines up to 12 miles), the 200-mile or extended continental shelf. The high seas, under Article 87, remain as before, open to all states, although the exercise of the six freedoms now listed in the Convention as appertaining *inter alia* is subject to the conditions laid down in the Convention. The freedoms include freedom of navigation, of overflight, of laying submarine cables and pipelines, of scientific research, and to construct such artificial islands and installations as are 'permitted under international law', subject to the continental shelf provisions referred to earlier (in Part VI). These, in Article 79 (4), preserve the coastal state's jurisdiction over activities on the shelf and activities related to exploration and exploitation of its resources but, unlike the EEZ provisions, do not require that conflicts over residual rights be resolved 'on the basis of equity' etc., as laid down in Article 59; on the outer shelf, if there is doubt, the residual rule is freedom of the high seas which clearly enhances the arguments in favour of freedom to install or deploy ASW and other electronic devices, a position that probably does not exist in customary law.[42] They must be exercised with due regard for the interests of other states exercising their freedoms and for the rights concerning the Area. One of the major conditions laid down is that in Article 88, namely that the high seas, like the Area, shall be reserved for 'peaceful purposes' but again without any indication being given of the meaning of this term. Nowhere in the LOSC is this term defined. As the same problem arises under the Seabed Treaty we must, before considering its significance, investigate the various interpretations states give to this term.

The debates on the meaning of 'peaceful purposes'[43]

This concept was introduced into the UN Law of the Sea debates by Ambassador Pardo, as we have seen, and included in the Declaration of Principles Governing the Seabed. It appears in the LOSC only in relation to the reservation of the Area and the high seas for such purposes and in connection with the objectives of marine scientific research.[44]

Pardo's action led to a dichotomy of views in the UN General Assembly. The USSR and others took the view that the term 'peaceful purposes' required complete demilitarization of the seabed; all military uses were assumed to be non-peaceful, following the precedent of prohibition of 'any measures of a military nature' in Article 1 of the Antarctic Treaty which reserves Antarctica for 'peaceful purposes'. The UK, USA, Canada and others, on the other hand, considered that the actual purpose of the military measures should be the first test since they could be differentiated: some might be aggressive or threatening to the peace but others might be purely defensive. The US then thought that the second consideration should be whether the measures conformed to the purposes and principles of the UN Charter.

The 1969 Outer Space Treaty provided a precedent for this view; it bans only specific activities in the context of 'peaceful purposes', such as placing nuclear weapons in orbit. The seabed debate was transferred to the UN Disarmament Committee when it was decided to proceed separately on negotiation of the Seabed Weapons Treaty. The conclusion of the SBT made the confrontation of views less acute and enabled the term 'peaceful purposes' to be included in the Declaration of Principles and to be discussed more moderately during UNCLOS III on the rare occasions the topic arose.[45] The LOSC, Article 298 (1)(b), allows states on ratifying to declare that they do not accept any one or more of the dispute settlement procedures provided under it, *inter alia*, for 'disputes concerning military activities, including military activities by government vessels engaged in non-commercial service' and impliedly accepts that some military activities will be conducted in areas reserved to peaceful purposes.

According to Brown, in the ENDC the US pressed its view that 'peaceful purposes' did not preclude military activities generally, specific limitation of specific military activities could be achieved by detailed arms control agreements.[46] Military activities not prohibited by these could continue under the doctrine of freedom of the seas, if for peaceful purposes. Clearly placing acoustic and other devices is less likely to be regarded as a 'military' activity than emplanting nuclear weapons. Tanzania proposed that any military purpose whatsoever should be banned, including specifically use of the treaty area by nuclear submarines, military fortifications and missile bases. The unacceptability of such proposals to some of the nuclear weapon states caused others to seek a more moderate solution. Though the USSR continued to press for a ban on use of the seabed beyond the territorial sea for military purposes, and also suggested that views should be exchanged on mutual limitation and subsequent reduction of delivery systems for nuclear weapons, the USA thought arms control measures should be considered in the context of the relation of this area to the marine environment as a whole. Proposals, drafts and counter-proposals were put forward in support of both lines of argument.

Use of the term, whether in the LOSC or SBT or other relevant instruments, does have legal consequences, as Treves points out,[47] since it makes illegal use for non-peaceful purposes; when the texts concerned do not define the term the precise effect depends on whether interpretation is left to whichever party has control of a particular situation or whether other principles or customary rules of law require that a particular interpretation be accorded to it and whether dispute settlement mechanisms are available. The option provided in Article 298(1)(b) of the LOSC, permitting the withdrawal of 'military activities' from the LOSC compulsory dispute settlement procedures, narrows the opportunities to resort to conciliation procedures under Article 284 and even this is subject to consent (Article 298(3)) of the state objecting to the activities. Doubt thus still surrounds the meaning of the term in the LOSC though the position may be clearer under the SBT for reasons explained below.

The Treaty on the Emplacement of Nuclear Weapons and Other Weapons of Mass Destruction on the Seabed and the Ocean Floor and in the Subsoil Thereof 1971[48]

This treaty was opened for signature on 11 February 1971, and entered into force on 18 May 1972. It provides for Review Conferences to appraise its operation. The first was held in August 1977; the second between 12-23 September 1983. By that date, 73 countries had become party to it, including three nuclear weapons states – the USSR, the USA and the UK – and several major maritime powers.

The treaty emerged from the ENDC negotiations begun in 1969 following the USSR's proposal that the ENDC should conclude an agreement to prohibit all military use of the seabed beyond national jurisdiction. Both the USSR and the USA submitted draft treaties. The Soviet one called for complete demilitarization of the seabed beyond 12 miles (the USSR's claimed limit of its territorial sea); the USA's for the proscription of the emplacement of nuclear and other weapons of mass destruction in the seabed area beyond a three-mile limit (the USA's territorial sea limit). Eventually, the USSR and USA were able to produce a common draft and to submit it jointly to the ENDC on 7 October 1969; after intensive debate, during which the draft was modified and revised several times,[49] the treaty was finally agreed on and adopted by the General Assembly at its 25th Session in 1970.[50] Briefly it provides as follows:

The Preamble   expresses, *inter alia*, the conviction that the treaty constitutes a step towards the exclusion of the seabed from the arms race.

Article I: The parties undertake not to emplace nuclear and other weapons of mass destruction and facilities specifically designed for storing, testing or using such weapons beyond the outer limit of a seabed zone.

The undertakings apply to the seabed zone, except that within it they do not apply to the coastal state's territory or the seabed beneath its territorial waters.

Article II   defines this zone as one coterminous with the 12-mile zone referred to in the 1958 Geneva Convention on the Territorial Sea and Contiguous Zone. It is to be measured 'in accordance with Part I, Section II of that Convention and in accordance with international law'.

It does not, it should be noted, equate the legal status of the seabed area in which nuclear weapons may be emplaced with that of the contiguous zone, only the method of delimitation.

Article III   concerns verification procedures. Each party has the right to verify, solely by observation, only the activities of other parties on the seabed *beyond* the zone defined in Articles I and III, provided that such observations do not interfere with those activities. It also provides the possibility for parties to consult and cooperate on such further verifications procedures as may be agreed to, including appropriate inspection of objects, structures, installations or other facilities that may reasonably be expected to be of a character forbidden under Article I.

Article IV   declares that nothing in the Treaty shall be interpreted as either supporting or prejudicing any party's position on issues or disputes concerning the law of the sea.

Article V: Parties undertake to continue negotiations in good faith concerning further measures in the field of disarmament to prevent an arms race on the seabed and ocean floor and their subsoils.

Article VI   lays down the amendment procedures; any party can propose them but they enter into force for those accepting them only if a majority of the parties has accepted them.

Article VII   requires the parties to hold a conference within five years of entry into force of the treaty to review its operation with a view to assuring that both the purposes of the Preamble and the Treaty provisions have been achieved. Any relevant technological developments are to be taken into account, a requirement that has given rise to most concern at Review Conferences.

Article VIII   provides for the right of withdrawal 'in extraordinary circumstances' and for the procedures to be followed, without defining these circumstances.

Article IX   disclaims any effect for the treaty on obligations assumed by the parties under international instruments establishing nuclear weapon-free zones.

The first Review Conference was held from 20 June – 1 July 1977; it was attended by 42 of the then 63 parties and 3 signatories; the second was held from 12-23 September 1983 and was attended by 45 of the 73 parties, 4 signatories, 2 observer states and 2 non-governmental organizations. The Second Conference followed important developments in the UN affecting the treaty. The General Assembly had held its First Special Session devoted exclusively to disarmament and, in paragraph 79 of its Final Document, had requested the UN Committee on Disarmament to proceed promptly with consideration of further measures for disarmament and prevention of an arms race on the seabed, ocean floor and subsoil, and of course, as already outlined, the UNCLOS III had in 1982 concluded and opened for signature the LOSC containing the provisions relating to peaceful uses of the Area and the high seas. The Committee on Disarmament had also, at the request of the Second Review Conference's Preparatory Committee, held an informal meeting to consider follow-up measures on the conclusions of the First Review Conference.

Before we consider the points arising from the two Review Conferences, however, we must first examine the inherent problems and weaknesses of the Treaty.

The most apparent problem is that of the treaty's scope, both as to weapons and to area. The treaty does not prevent emplacement of all weapons, only of nuclear ones and weapons of mass destruction. It does not define the latter but presumably they include those with the same destructive impact as the former, such as chemical, biological and radioactive weapons. Possibly some mines and anti-satellite weapons might have the same effect as nuclear weapons, as might environmental modification weapons, with or without use of nuclear materials. The treaty proscribes emplacing and emplanting, thus weapons or vehicles that can move on the seabed only by maintaining contact with it (the so-called 'creepy crawlies') would be prohibited but not vessels that can navigate above its surface, such as nuclear submarines. Also included probably are some dual-purpose installations and structures and facilities designed for storing and testing weapons *inter alia,* since the criterion is the purpose, not the capability, of such instruments, though any test of nuclear weapons would, for parties to it, have to conform to the

Test Ban Treaty, which bans underwater tests in the high seas or territorial sea or any other environment if it results in deposit of radioactive debris outside the Territorial Sea of the testing state (Article I).

Article II effectively limits the treaty's geographical scope to areas beyond 12 miles measured from the territorial sea baselines. The 1958 Geneva Convention's acceptance of straight baselines taking in fringing islands, bays and so-called 'historic bays' (a term which is neither defined nor qualified) means that the prohibited area in many cases will not begin until much more than 12 miles from the coasts. The reference to the 1958 Convention and to 'international law' in this Article deflects (and reflects) the controversy surrounding such extensive and disputed claims to bays as the USSR's to Peter the Great Bay, which has little historical basis.

It appears, taking Articles I and II together, that despite the opaqueness of language, the coastal state is not, within the 12-mile zone (or its internal waters behind its baselines), subject to the ban on emplacement even if it does not claim a full 12-mile territorial sea, i.e. when part of the 12-mile zone is subject to the continental shelf regime, though emplacement by other states would be banned. This, as explained earlier, is not necessarily the case either in customary law or in LOS Conventions. As Article III limits verification in this zone to the coastal state it is impossible for other states to ascertain whether or not the coastal state is emplacing weapons there. In this respect, the SBT is potentially more permissive than the Treaty of Tlatelolco, which prohibits emplacement of nuclear weapons and installations (though not weapons of mass destruction or structures, etc. designed for storage and other purposes) within the 'whole of the territory' of its parties (Articles 3 and 4), defining this to include 'the territorial sea, air space and any other space over which the state exercises sovereignty in accordance with its own legislation' (thus apparently applying the treaty obligations even in territorial seas in excess of 12 miles). Article 4, however, if certain conditions are fulfilled, will in due course extend its scope to a specifically defined larger zone which extends even further than the 200-mile territorial seas claimed by six Latin American states. The EEZs approved in the LOSC would not fulfil the first definition of area of application since Article 56 of the LOSC recognizes only the sovereign rights of the coastal states in such zones, not sovereignty; pending entry into force of the LOSC these six states still maintain their 200-mile territorial seas, however.[51]

Finally, verification procedures are weak under the SBT. They apply only beyond the 12-mile zone (Article III). If after observation reasonable doubt about the activity remains, the two states concerned must consult; if doubts still persist other parties must be notified and the parties concerned must cooperate on 'such further procedures for verification as may be agreed, including appropriate inspection of objects, structures, installations or other facilities that reasonably may be expected to be of a kind described in Article I'. Regional and other concerned parties may be brought in; eventually a report must be circulated to other parties by the party initiating the further procedures. Enquiries can be made of other parties if the responsible state cannot be identified; if, as a result, the suspect is identified, he must consult, as outlined above. If the suspect cannot be identified further verification procedures can be undertaken. If finally, the doubts are not removed and a serious question of fulfilment of obligations remains, the matter can be referred to the Security Council 'which *may* take action in accordance with the Charter' (emphasis added). The likelihood, given the divisions of the superpowers, is that that body will not be able to take action because the veto will be used. Moreover, though states can use their own means of verification they must not interfere with activities of other parties and must show due regard for rights recognized under international law, including freedom of the high seas and coastal states' rights to explore and exploit their continental shelves.

We must now ask whether the Review Conferences have been able to remedy any of these deficiencies. The answer is that they have not, though they have twice reviewed the Treaty article by article and formal suggestions for amendments have been proposed. The first, in 1977,[52] found that the treaty had been faithfully observed though participants regretted that not only were all states not party, but not all nuclear weapon states were parties (France and China have not become so). Its Final Declaration reaffirmed the need to proceed with further measures of disarmament, as called for in Article V, and the Committee on Disarmament was asked to proceed with this and to establish an *ad hoc* committee to keep technological developments under review, though no major developments were found to have occurred at that date.

By the Second Conference in 1983[53] the various developments already referred to had occurred – the UN's Special Session on Disarmament had asked for further measures on the seabed arms race to be prepared by the CCD; the LOSC had been concluded requiring reservation of the high seas and seabed for peaceful purposes; the CCD had informally discussed follow-up measures. But the final Declaration, arrived at by consensus after hard bargaining, showed little change. The call for further disarmament measures was repeated and it was noted that it had not been fulfilled; the request for a CCD *ad hoc* expert group on technological developments was abandoned and instead the Preparatory Commission for the next Review Conference was asked to ensure that relevant information was made available.

But this bland outcome concealed disquiet on the part of some participants. Faced with the increasing uses of the oceans, both military and civilian, they sought new confidence-building measures (CBMs) such as nuclear-free zones and regional and bilateral agreements. Sweden, which would prefer a broader treaty, thought that the rapid civilian technological developments concerning the continental shelf would be directly applicable for military purposes,[54] though the USA thought that such scientific advances as had occurred were not relevant to the treaty.[55] The USSR continued to press for complete demilitarization and maintained that speculation about hypothetical circumstances and attempts to define 'technological developments' more broadly than in terms of the technology relevant to emplacement of nuclear weapons on the seabed would be 'unproductive', disturbing the superpower balance.[56]

The general concerns of developing states about discrepancy in verification opportunities available to them compared to the nuclear weapons states was articulated by Argentina which called for more machinery for exchange of information on technical developments.[57]

Some states thought that the Article II limit should be raised to take account of the LOSC's new zones – archipelagoes (though Indonesia and the Philippines are not parties to the SBT), the EEZ and Common Heritage Area[58] and feared a weakening of the SBT if this were not done. For example, the LOSC extension of the Contiguous Zone to 24 miles could lead to demands to extend the zone excepted from the prohibition on emplacement of nuclear weapons on the seabed in view of Article II's reference to the 1958 Convention. This reference should be deleted. Better verification techniques should be developed on the lines of the Environmental Modification Treaty, with a body of experts established for fact-finding; at the very least states declaring that there were no relevant technological developments should make available the information on which they based that view,[59] to enable others to check their compliance with Article V. No party had exercised its rights of verification; thus no formal violations were reported. Universal verification by the UN would be preferable in the view of some.[60]

Conclusion

Despite the criticism voiced at the SBT Review Conference, one can agree with the USA that it has been 'a quiet success' of importance to the security of all nations because it served the superpowers collective interests and reflects the balance between the need to prevent an arms race on the seabed and the 'right' of the superpowers to control verification activities close to their own coasts.[61] It is, as the Mexican delegate concluded in 1971, 'better than no treaty at all'.[62] More than this cannot be hoped for at the present time, however desirable the 130 non-nuclear states might find a broader treaty.

Vigilance will be required, however, to ensure that the extensions of coastal state jurisdiction in the LOSC and the customary law developing in relation to it is not allowed to undermine the SBT, removing further areas from the prohibited zone under that treaty. It is not necessary to revise the SBT to achieve this, only for parties to agree on a harmonized interpretation of its terms which supports a strict application. It is also important to continuance of the SBT that the LOSC's Preparatory Commission should not attempt to extend the scope of the controls it is devising for seabed mining in such a way that the freedom of surveillance of nuclear submarine movements is disturbed.

The Study of the Naval Arms Race concluded that two basic objectives for further action remained.[63] The first includes the achievement by negotiation of effective measures of nuclear disarmament at sea to reverse the nuclear arms race until total elimination of nuclear weapons and their delivery systems has been achieved; further measures pursuant to Article V of the SBT are required to this end and application of the Antarctica Treaty's nuclear weapon-free regime to the seas within its area of application (south of 60° south). The second target relates to achieving more effective ocean management for peaceful use, aided by a more positive naval contribution. The challenge for UNCLOS IV will perhaps be to integrate a revised SBT and a revised LOSC within a more transparent system of verification in order to ensure that 'peaceful uses' are indeed those that any reasonable person would assume that term means and that the states' responsibility and liability for any damage arising for abuse of this term is more clearly spelt out.

Notes

1   The four Conventions, viz. the Convention on the Territorial Sea and Continguous Zone; Convention on the High Seas; Convention on Fishing and Conservation of the Living Resources of the High Seas; Convention on the Continental Shelf are in UN Doc.A/CONF. 13/L.52-L.55 and MISC. No.15 (1958), Cmnd. 584; see also I.Brownlie, Basic Documents in International Law (3rd edn) 1983.
2   United Nations Convention on the Law of the Sea 1982, UN Publication, Sales No. E83. v. 5 1984.
3   For a succinct account of the customary law of the sea in relation to the above conventions and others, see V. Lowe and R. Churchill, *The Law of the Sea* 1985, 2nd ed. Manchester University Press.
4   The Antarctic Treaty, 1 December 1959, 402 *UNTS* 71.
5   Treaty Banning Nuclear Weapons Tests in the Atmosphere, in Outer Space and Under Water, 8 August 1963, 480 *UNTS* 43.
6   Treaty for Prohibition of Nuclear Weapons in Latin America, 14 February 1967, 634 *UNTS* 364.

7   US-USSR Treaty on the Limitation of Anti-Ballistic Missile Systems 1972; US-USSR Interim Agreement on Certain Measures with Respect to the Limitation of Strategic Offensive Arms 1972 (Salt I). For texts and analysis see M. Willrich and J. Rhinelander, *SALT: The Moscow Agreements and Beyond*, 1984. US-USSR Treaty on the Limitation of Strategic Offensive Arms (with Protocol; Memorandum of Understanding and Joint Statement) 1979. (SALT II Treaty), in *ILM*, 18, 1979, pp.111-70.

8   Treaty on the Prohibition of the Emplacement of Nuclear Weapons and other Weapons of Mass Destruction on the Seabed and Ocean Floor, 11 February, 1971 (in force 18 May, 1972).

9   'General and Complete Disarmament: Study on the Naval Arms Race', Report by the Secretary-General, UN Doc A/40/535, 17 September, 1985; hereafter referred to as Naval Arms Race Study. The study gives a brief synopsis of the treaties and agreements referred to in notes 4-8 at pp.63-7. Their texts are in Status of Multilateral Arms Regulation and Disarmament Agreement (2nd edn). UN Pub., Sales No. E.83.IX.5.

10 Ibid., Existing Forces, pp.33-43; see also *Soviet Military Power 1986*, a US government publication obtainable from the Superintendent of Documents, US Government Printing Office, Washington, DC 20402, passim at pp. 8-9.

11 Tullio Treves, Military Installations, Structures and Devices on the Seabed, 74 *AJIL* (1980). pp.808-980. See also the general works in this field mentioned in his n.1. and J.Alford (ed). *Sea Power and Influence: Old Issues and New Challenges*, Institute for Strategic Studies, Adelphi Library 2 (1980); and Ken Booth, *Law, Force and Diplomacy at Sea*, George Allen & Unwin (1985) esp. Pt. II, Ch.6, pp. 120-36.

12 United Nations Charter, Article 2 (4); in Brownlie *Basic Docs,* op.cit.; reservation of the 'inherent right of self-defence if an armed attack occurs against a Member of the United Nations until the Security Council has taken measures necessary to maintain international peace and security' is contained in Article 51 thereof.

13 Ken Booth, 'Military Implications of the Changing Law of the Sea' in J. Gamble (ed.) *Law of the Sea: Neglected Issues,* Proceedings of the 12th Annual Conference of the Law of the Sea Institute, 1979, pp. 328-97, at p.340; cited by Treves, op. cit.

14 For a brief survey of these see Naval Arms Race Study; for collective security agreements at pp. 51-2; for conventions relevant to maritime arms control at pp. 63-7; for Declaration on denuclearization of particular areas, at pp. 67-70.

15 See in particular in this context Treves, op. cit.; but for a more general analysis of the status of each zone, Churchill and Lowe, op. cit.; D.P. O'Connell (ed. Shearer), *International Law of the Sea,* 2 vols. Oxford University Press, 1979 and 1984; D. Larson, 'Naval Weapons and the Law of the Sea', paper given at the 19th Conference of the Law of the Sea Institute, 24-27 July, 1985, Cardiff, UK; publication forthcoming; ibid; 'Security, Disarmament and the Law of the Sea', 3 *Marine Policy* (1979) pp. 40-58.

16 See the White House Office of the Press Secretary, Fact Sheet, United States Ocean Policy, 10 March, 1983 and Statement by the President, 10 March, 1983, 22 *ILM* (1983) pp. 461-5.

17 United States: Proclamation of an Exclusive Economic Zone, Proclamation 5030 of 10 March, 1983, 22 *ILM* (1983), p. 465.

18 See *Law of the Sea Bulletin,* Office of the Secretary-General's Special Representative for the Law of the Sea, UN, New York, 1-6 passim.

19 G. Moore, Limits of Territorial Seas, Fishing Zones and Exclusive Economic Zones, Fisheries and Advisory Programme Circular No. 4, FAO, Rome, 1985, FAO Legislative Series No. 21 (Rev2), FAO, Rome (1985).

20   See e.g. David Lane, 'New Zealand's Security Policy', 63 *Foreign Policy* (1985), p.55.

21   See V. Prescott, *The Maritime Political Boundaries of the World,* Methuen (1985), pp. 46-73, for the extent of claims based on these provisions.

22   See *North Sea Continental Shelf Cases, ICJ Rep.* 1967, p.l. The ICJ regarded both treaties and unilateral proclamations as superfluous to creation of continental shelf agreements; it said the coastal state's right to explore and exploit the continental shelf was an inherent right, existing *ipso facto* and deriving *ab initio,* from the fact that the shelf was the natural prolongation of the coastal state's land territory into and under the sea. Coastal states quickly acted upon this to expand the jurisdictional scope of their national legislation over the adjacent continental shelf to cover not only the continental plateau but also its shape and use, i.e. the whole continental margin as now permitted in the LOSC 1982.

23   About 100 states have done so in various forms; see Coastal State Legislation over Foreign Fishing, op. cit., n. 19.

24   *Case Concerning the Continental Shelf: Libyan-Arab Jamahariya - Malta* 1985, *ICJ Rep.*, 13.

25   Declaration of Principles governing the Exploration and Exploitation of the Seabed and Ocean Floor Beyond the Limits of National Jurisdiction.

26   See also the Declaration of Principles Governing the Human Environment, Report of the UN Conference on the Human Environment, Stockholm, 1972, UN Document A/Conference 48/14/Rou/.para.3. See also 1977 Protocol Additional to the Geneva Conventions of 12 August 1949 and relating to the Protection of Victims of International Armed Conflicts (Protocol I) which prohibits use of methods or means of warfare which are intended, or may be expected, to cause widespread, long-term and severe damage to the natural environment (Article 35), which does not yet cover the marine environment but could be extended to it. (Naval Arms Race Study, p.85, para.304 (d)). See also n.25 above.

27   Article 2 certainly applies to cables and pipelines on the seabed, some of which are no doubt partially buried in the subsoil; Article 24 refers to the exploitation and exploration of the seabed and its subsoil requiring states to draw up regulations to prevent pollution from such activities; Article 25 requires states to take measures to prevent pollution from dumping of radioactive waste in the seas and air space above, resulting from any activities with radioactive material or other harmful agents (which it does not define). Many states, especially those in the Group of 77, dispute that this is either a codification of the international law or sufficient to justify the application of the doctrine of freedom to all seabed activities.

28   In 1978 the US Law of the Sea Institute devoted the annual conference held in The Hague to such 'neglected issues'; see J.K. Gamble (ed.) *Law of the Sea: Neglected Issues* (Law of the Sea Institute, Honolulu, Hawaii) 1979. The proceedings included a paper by K. Booth on 'Military Implications of the Changing Law of the Sea'.

29   See Booth, op.cit., for a brief bibliography at pp. 223-7.

30   For a detailed analysis of these hidden aspects of the Law of the Sea Conference, see B.J. Theutenberg, *The Evolution of the Law of the Sea: A Study of Resources and Strategy with Special Regard to the Polar Areas,* Tycooly Int.Pub.Ltd., Dublin (1984).

31   UN Doc. A/6695, p.l; For the most detailed account of events at this period leading to conclusion of the SBT, see E.D. Brown, *Arms Control in Hydrospace, 1971,* Ocean Series 301, Woodrow Wilson International Center for Scholars.

32   GA Resolution 2340 (XXII).

33   UN Doc., op. cit., note 31, pp. 2-3.

34   UN Charter, Ch.1, Purposes and Principles; Article 1 requires members to maintain international peace and security; Article 2 obliges them to settle disputes by peaceful means and to refrain in their international relations from the threat or use of force, *inter alia,* in any manner inconsistent with the purposes of the UN; Article 51 preserves states' 'inherent right of self-defence if an armed attack occurs against a UN member', until such time as the Security Council has taken the necessary measures. See Ch.4 of the present work for further discussion of the problems presented by these provisions.

35   UN Doc. A/CONF., 13/L.52-L, reproduced in Brownlie's *Basic Documents,* op. cit. The USA, USSR, UK and France are amongst its parties. Though the treaty remains in force it will, on entry into force by the LOSC 1982 be superseded by the latter for parties to both conventions.

36   GA Resolution 2749 (XXV), adopted 17 December 1970 by 108 votes to O with 14 abstentions.

37   T. Treves, op.cit., 835-6, Treves also notes that some, such as Goldblat ('Law of the Sea and Security of the Coastal State', in Christy *et al.* (eds) *Law of the Sea: Caracas and Beyond,* p.301 at p.306) consider that excessive 'transparency' of the oceans is undesirable and that security systems should be limited.

38   R. Zedalis, 'Military Installations, Structures and Devices on the Seabed: A Response', 75 *AJIL* (1981), p.926.

39   T. Treves, 'A Reply', ibid., p.933.

40   Theutenberg, op.cit., note 30.

41   See declaration made on signature of the LOS Convention by the Philippines, *LOS Bulletin No.1,* p.14; and on ratification, *LOS Bulletin No.4,* p.20-1; see also the objections raised by the USSR, Czechoslovakia, Israel, Byelorussia and Ukraine to the Philippine declarations, *LOS Bulletin No.6,* pp. 9-13.

42   Treves, op.cit. note 11, p. 833. As the LOSC in Article 298 allows states on signing, ratifying or acceding to it to declare that they do not accept compulsory dispute settlement procedures for 'disputes concerning military activities' and does not define the term 'military', it seems unlikely that these disputes will be clearly resolved. Five states have already exercised this option: USSR, Byelorussian SSR, German Democratic Republic, Ukrainian SS. See *LOS Bulletin No.4, 1985,* and Tunisia. *(LOS Bulletin No.6,* 1985).

43   For a full analysis of the views of states on the meaning of this term and an account of the relevant debates in the UN Seabed Committee and Disarmament Committee, see: Brown, op.cit., pp. 46-9 and Treves, op.cit., pp. 815-19. The term is used in other treaties such as the 1969 Outer Space Treaty and the 1959 Antarctic Treaty.

44   See Articles 141, 155(2) concerning the Area; Article 88 for the high seas; Articles 143(1), 147(2)(d); 240(a), 242(1) and 246(3) for marine scientific research. Coastal states can refuse consent for research that is not in their view for 'peaceful purposes'.

45   See Treves, op.cit., p.817 for details of these debates.

46   Op.cit., n. 31, pp. 46-9 at p.47.

47   Op.cit., p.818.

48   The best account of the background to this treaty and analysis of its provisions remains Brown, op.cit., see also Treves, op.cit., pp. 821-7.

49   See Brown, op.cit., pp. 36-106, for comparative analysis of the drafts and the final treaty and Treves, op.cit., pp. 821-5 for a critique of its final provisions.

50   GA Resolution 2660 (XXV), 7 December 1970.

51   Viz. Argentine, Brazil, Ecuador, El Salvador, Panama, Uruguay; Limits of Territorial Seas, Fishing Zones and Exclusive Economic Zones, FAO Fisheries Law Advisory Programme, Circular No.4. FAO, Rome (1985).

52   The Sea-Bed Treaty: Results of the Second Review Conference of the States Par-
     ties, 12-23 September 1983, Disarmament Fact Sheet No. 32; GAR 38/188 B, 1983
     welcomed the Conference's positive assessment of the effectiveness of this treaty.
53   Final Document of the Review Conference of the Parties to the Treaty on the
     Prohibition of the Emplacement of Nuclear Weapons and other Weapons of Mass
     Destruction on the Sea-Bed and the Ocean Floor and the Subsoil Thereof, CCD/
     543, 17 August 1977, Geneva.
54   SBT CONF/II/3. Add I, 9 August 1983.
55   Ibid.
56   SBT CONF/II/SR3, 15 September 1983, paras 10-11.
57   Doc. cit., n.52.
58   Doc. cit., n.54.
59   E.g. Sweden, SBT CONF/II/SR4, para 4; Australia, ibid., para 35; SR.7, para 43.
60   Sweden, ibid., paras 5-7.
61   Ibid., para. 17.
62   AK.1/PU. 1763, p. 17, cited by Brown, op.cit., at p.106.
63   Op.cit., n.9, pp.90-1.

8 Nuclear weapon-free zones

David Freestone and Scott Davidson

Introduction

Although there are a multiplicity of both legal and political definitions seeking to explicate in detail the nature of a nuclear weapon-free zone (NWFZ),[1] the concept of such a zone is, in essence, one of deceptive simplicity. It consists, in theory, of the establishment of a geographical or spatial area within which states acting either unilaterally or, more commonly, in concert, undertake to renounce the holding, manufacture or use of nuclear weapons. In a sense the NWFZ is the intellectual legatee of the demilitarized zone, a much older concept, but one which extends beyond the notions of simple nuclear disarmament and embraces the idea of total disarmament within a defined geographical area.[2] Demilitarized zones have been notoriously unsuccessful and have frequently fallen prey to shifts in regional power structures, changes in weapons technology, covert breach and a failure of verification procedures. It is feared in some quarters that NWFZs may well fail for the same reasons.[3]

While the concept of NWFZs can be stated simply and cogently and their juridical existence established, at least in theory, with some facility, the *de facto* creation of such zones is beset by acute practical difficulties. Not only are there differences of opinion between the non-nuclear weapon states (NNWSs) and the nuclear weapon states (NWSs) over provision of the inappropriately named 'negative security' assurances[4] by which the NWSs would guarantee by treaty the integrity of any NWFZ, but also between NNWSs themselves, who are unable to agree about the meaning of peaceful uses of nuclear energy. Securing agreement on the distinction between 'atoms for peace' and 'atoms for war' has proved to be somewhat intractable.

The NWFZ concept has not been greeted with universal acclaim by statesmen for, as Platias and Rydell suggest, NWFZs have frequently been regarded by them 'as political responses to a particular disturbing event rather than as a studied analytical move aimed at the narrow objective of controlling proliferation.'[5] It is difficult to quarrel with this proposition since the linkage of cause and effect between international tension and proposals for the creation of NWFZs can be readily documented. The 1956 Gromyko proposal for the 'denuclearization' of Central Europe (elaborated upon by the Rapacki Plans of 1958 and 1962) can be seen primarily as a response to the NATO decisions to deploy American intermediate-range ballistic missiles (IRBMs) in West Germany.[6] The proposal for the establishment of a Latin American NWFZ, culminating in the actual adoption of the Treaty of Tlatelolco,[7] was generated by the Cuban missile crisis.[8] Of the 14 other NWFZ proposals which have been mooted since the Rapacki Plan of 1957, the majority can be seen as having a direct link with some international tension.[9] It is arguable, however, whether this 'tactical issue linkage', as Haas describes it,[10] should give rise to cynicism since most international initiatives are responses to practical problems or attempts to prevent the repetition of such problems. Thus, although initiatives for NWFZs might be seen as *ad hoc* responses to particular occurrences, nevertheless, the concept itself has an internal consistency and is directed at an identifiable problem. Furthermore, as Platias and Rydell argue, in comparison to other arms control and disarmament proposals NWFZs are one of the few concrete achievements to which reference can be made.[11]

Although this claim may be slightly overstated, it is, nevertheless, substantially true. The agreements not to nuclearize the uninhabited portions of the globe – the Antarctic and the seabed – were achieved without much dissent, possibly because of the shared community of interest which the NWSs had in maintaining the nuclear-free *status quo* in these areas. The agreement not to nuclearize outer-space, the moon and other celestial bodies by all the major NWSs may also be regarded as a substantial achievement, albeit based upon the narrow self-interest of the 'superpowers'. Critics of the NWFZ concept are likely to point to the ease with which the uninhabited regions of the earth – arguably regions of secondary interest – have become the subjects of NWFZ regimes, while, for the most part, the inhabited regions have not become subject to such regimes, despite the constant cajoling of the UN. Even where agreements for inhabited areas have been reached (to date,

Latin America and the South Pacific) the full participation of all regional states cannot be guaranteed nor can the NWSs be relied upon to provide the necessary negative security assurances which would render the zones entirely effective.

Despite the obvious difficulties associated with the creation of NWFZs and despite the tendency to cynicism concerning their origin and efficacy by some statesmen, it is nevertheless salutary to examine the themes and the objectives underlying NWFZ initiatives. As Calderon suggests,[12] NWFZs are the product of two major areas of concern: first, the desire to strengthen regional security by eliminating the existence of nuclear weapons within a particular geographical region and second, to secure regional nuclear non-armament by forestalling or preventing the horizontal proliferation of nuclear weapons.[13] Although the focus of NWFZs is therefore primarily upon the maintenance of a regional non-nuclear *status quo* it is also arguable that a permanent freeze on the horizontal dissemination of nuclear weapons is also the first step towards a broader programme for nuclear disarmament. Calderon argues that an NWFZ therefore implies: 'the creation of a [nuclear weapon-free] sanctuary in a geographical area as well as the promotion of an auspicious climate towards making total nuclear disarmament possible'.[14]

In a sense therefore, NWFZs are only part, albeit a distinctive part, of the nuclear non-proliferation regime. this view is buttressed by Article VII of the Non-Proliferation Treaty (NPT) itself which specifically recognizes the right of states to conclude regional treaties in order to ensure the absence of nuclear weapons from their territories.[15]

Furthermore, the UN Conference of the Committee on Disarmament (CCD) in a 1975 report on NWFZs declared that such zones were not to be seen as substitutes for the NPT but rather as a 'powerful supplement' to it.[16] Views among commentators differ, however, as to the efficacy of NWFZs in controlling proliferation of nuclear weapons. Platias and Rydell,[17] take a view which amounts to a modification of the CCD position, believing that in the quest for non-proliferation, NWFZs offer one mechanism for substantive issue linkage in the political bargaining process. Epstein,[18] however, argues that NWFZs offer a rather more tangible form of progress than the NPT treaty itself, whereas the Stockholm International Peace Research Institute (SIPRI) feels that arguments about NWFZs detract attention from the need to ensure the universality of the NPT.[19]

While, therefore, there is no general agreement on the utility of NWFZs *vis-à-vis* the general NPT regime, nevertheless, it cannot be denied that focusing attention on these zones has provided a way forward in preventing the spread of nuclear weapons to the uninhabited parts of the earth, thus reducing the likelihood of superpower nuclear confrontations in those areas, and to certain non-nuclear weapon regions. These measures may seem insignificant in comparison to the lack of progress made towards the establishment of NWFZ regimes in the inhabited regions, but they represent real though limited measures to combat horizontal proliferation of nuclear weapons.

Given that such progress has been made through certain multilateral instruments and through unilateral state action to secure NWFZs, the remainder of this chapter will be devoted to a consideration of the development and definition of the NWFZ concept and a detailed examination of existing and proposed NWFZ regimes.

NWFZs: Development and definition

The idea of creating a geographical zone in which the manufacture, holding or use of nuclear weapons would be prohibited was first mooted formally by the Soviet Foreign Minister, Andrei Gromyko, before the Sub-Committee of the UN Disarmament Commission in March 1956.[20] Although part of a comprehensive military reduction package for Central Europe, the impetus to the proposal had been generated by a NATO decision to deploy American IRBMs in West Germany.[21] The Central European NWFZ did not meet with the approval of the allies, and despite a refinement of the proposal by the Polish Foreign Minister, Adam Rapacki (the 'Rapacki Plan'), first in 1957 and subsequently in 1962, the proposal died a lingering death and was eventually abandoned in 1964.[22]

With the burgeoning of nuclear weapons and states possessing nuclear weapons capability in the 1960s and 1970s the concern with the problems of proliferation extended beyond purely European horizons and a number of proposals for the denuclearization of various geographical regions emanated from a variety of sources, but most particularly, the CCD. Such proposals have been transmitted to the General Assembly and that body, through its resolutions has called for the creation of NWFZs in various areas. Proposals and calls for NWFZs have been made for the Balkans, the Baltic, Asia, the Pacific, Africa, the Scandinavian countries, the Middle East, Southern Asia, Eastern Asia, the Indian Ocean and the South Pacific and Latin America, but only in the two latter regions has significant progress been made.[23]

In 1974, however, the General Assembly by Resolution 3261 (XXIX) decided to undertake a comprehensive study of NWFZs. The body charged with carrying out the study was an *ad hoc* group of qualified governmental experts acting under the auspices of the CCD.[24] The *ad hoc* group completed its study in August 1975 and submitted its report to the CCD for transmittal to the General Assembly. In its report the group attempted to elaborate the concept of NWFZs, to identify the principal issues involved in the creation and functioning of such zones and to analyse their implications for zonal and extra-zonal states. It also identified certain principles and desiderata which it had followed in the course of its deliberations.[25] These included the desire to secure the complete absence of nuclear weapons from certain parts of the world and to spare nations involved in NWFZs from nuclear attack or involvement in nuclear conflict. The group also observed that although the primary function of a NWFZ was to promote national and regional security, it also served, as noted above, the additional functions of diminishing nuclear weapon proliferation, slowing down the arms race and reducing the possibility of nuclear war.[26] Although most group members felt that NWFZs could not be seen as an alternative to the 1968 NPT but rather as a powerful supplement to it, a number of experts considered that the concept of the NWFZ went beyond the issue of non-proliferation since it envisaged a total absence of nuclear weapons in certain geographical areas.[27]

In creating NWFZs, the *ad hoc* group of experts recommended that certain guiding principles should be taken into account. These principles were expressed as follows:

—Obligations relating to the establishment of a nuclear weapon-free zone might be assumed not only by groups of states constituting entire continents, but also by smaller groups of states and even individual states.

—nuclear weapon-free zone arrangements must ensure that the zone remains effectively free of all nuclear weapons.

—the initiative for the creation of a nuclear weapon-free zone must come from the states in the region concerned and must be voluntary.

—whenever a zone is intended to embrace a region, all militarily significant states, and preferably all states, in that region would enhance the effectiveness of the zone.

—the zone should have an effective system for verification to ensure compliance with agreed obligations.

—the arrangements should promote the economic, scientific, and technical development of the members of the zone through international cooperation on all peaceful uses of nuclear energy.

—the treaty establishing the zone should be of unlimited duration.[28]

Since the basis of any NWFZ was to be territorial, the *ad hoc* group agreed that the boundaries should be clearly defined by international law.[29] Several experts pointed out that states should not be able to create NWFZs outside their territorial jurisdiction, or in international air space. The concept of safety zones extending beyond the conventionally defined geographical limits of the states comprising NWFZs was, however, mooted by some members of the group. In such safety zones, which might in certain circumstances embrace areas lying beyond the jurisdiction of the states comprising an NWFZ, obligations would be created for states to remove weapons which might be targeted at states lying within the NWFZ or weapons that had delivery ranges suitable for such targets. The experts admitted however that such safety zones would have to be negotiated and agreed by third states if they were not to violate international law.[30]

One of the principles which would clearly be affected by the development of the concept of safety zones would be that of the freedom of the high seas. The experts acknowledged the continuing importance of the freedom to navigate on the high seas, but they raised the question of whether this might be restricted in the case of vessels carrying nuclear weapons. The group also questioned whether the right of innocent passage in territorial waters adjacent to the NWFZ should be reviewed since the passage of warships carrying nuclear weapons in such an area might be incompatible with ensuring the total absence of nuclear weapons within the NWFZ.[31] Although there is little doubt that coastal states have the right to close international ports to vessels of another state save in circumstances of distress, some of the group of experts felt that any treaty establishing a NWFZ should contain an explicit provision giving the right to states within the zone to close their ports to vessels having nuclear weapons on board.[32]

It became clear to the group of experts that the creation of an NWFZ depended solely on the conclusion of a treaty by states, in particular nuclear weapon states.[33] Thus, although from a legal standpoint, the objective existence of an NWFZ did not depend upon either recognition or guarantees by nuclear weapon states, nevertheless such recognition and guarantees would enhance the effectiveness of NWFZs, by giving states within them security from nuclear attack.[34]

The report of the group of experts was broadly welcomed by the General Assembly, but there were differing views on the question of the negative security assurances and guarantees to be given to states within an NWFZ by extra-regional NWSs. The UK considered that assurances or guarantees could not be given in advance and that such matters should be determined by individual negotiation and agreement.[35] The USSR on the other hand maintained that assurances should be given by all NWSs in advance.[36] The French, however, were altogether more resistant to the idea of NWFZs, claiming somewhat cynically that since nuclear conflict knew no geographical limits, it was doubtful whether states belonging to an NWFZ would derive any protection from membership thereof.[37]

Coupled with the presentation of the report of the *ad hoc* group by the CCD to the UN General Assembly was a draft resolution sponsored by Mexico which purported to define the concept of an NWFZ and the principal obligations of NWSs towards such zones and the states included therein. Although there was little disagreement about the definition of an NWFZ in the draft resolution, the major NWSs could not agree on the limits of the principal obligations to be imposed upon them. Britain, France and the US voted against the resolution and the USSR abstained. General Assembly Resolution 3472B (XXX) provides:

> I. Definition of the concept of a nuclear-weapon free zone.
>
>   1. A nuclear weapon-free zone shall as a general rule be deemed to be any zone, recognized by the General Assembly of the United Nations, which any group of states in the free exercise of their sovereignty has established by virtue of a treaty or convention whereby:
>
>   a) The statute of total absence of nuclear weapons to which the zone shall be subject, including the procedure for the limitation of the zone, is defined;
>
>   b) An international system of verification and control is established to guarantee compliance with the obligations deriving from the statute.

Although the above definition of an NWFZ is so vague as to have made it generally acceptable to nearly all states, it fails to deal with crucial issues such as the proper territorial limits of such zones (i.e. whether they can extend over the contiguous zone, high seas, international straits and international air space), what constitutes a nuclear weapon, or whether nuclear explosions for peaceful purposes, such as those permitted by the Treaty of Tlatelolco, are compatible with the concept.

Calderon, however, suggests that two major problems arise from the definition itself.[38] First, he argues, it is not clear what recognition of a zone by a resolution of the General Assembly would achieve since once a treaty creating an NWFZ has entered into force it cannot be affected by a resolution to which it is juridically superior. Second, he maintains that there is a certain asymmetry or imbalance in the definition arising from its reference to the statute of the total absence of nuclear weapons. This, he argues, strikes at the rationality of the NWFZ concept for weapons in such zones are banned not just for the sake of banning them 'but to create a situation of privilege which is only achieved when the zone in question is excluded from an eventual nuclear war as a sort of compensation for the prohibition of the military atom'.[39]

To deal with the first point, it is arguable that recognition of an NWFZ by the General Assembly is capable of producing both legal and political effects. It is true that recognition by a General Assembly resolution of such a zone created by treaty cannot be understood as creating a condition precedent for the objective juridical existence of the zone, but it is, perhaps, arguable that those states which vote for such a resolution, especially the NWSs, may be estopped from subsequently denying the juridical effectiveness of the zone.[40] From a political perspective sanction of an NWFZ may give it a weight and notoriety which it would be difficult for states to gainsay.

As for Calderon's second point, this is rather difficult to understand. Certainly if paragraph I of Resolution 3472B is taken in isolation, it appears as if the obligation to secure the absence of nuclear weapons from the territories of the states parties is solely upon the states comprising the NWFZ. This fails, however, to take account of paragraph II of the resolution which seeks to establish not only the rights and obligations of states within an NWFZ towards each other, but also the obligations of extra-NWFZ NWSs; the so-called negative security assurances.[41] Paragraph II, which was for the NWSs in the General Assembly the most controversial aspect of the resolution, requires all NWSs to undertake or to reaffirm by way of treaty, convention or protocol, the following obligations:

> a) To respect in all its parts the statute of total absence of nuclear weapons defined in the treaty or convention which serves as the constituent document of the zone.
> b) To refrain from contributing in any way to the performance in the territories forming part of the zone of acts which involve a violation of the aforesaid treaty or convention.
> c) To refrain from using or threatening to use nuclear weapons against any states included in the zone.

The NWSs were clearly reluctant to give a *carte blanche* assurance that they would be willing to subscribe to these principles. The rationale for such reluctance may be traced to the deterrent effect which strategic nuclear weapons are claimed to possess. A statement by any nuclear weapon state that it would not use its strategic nuclear weapons in particular areas of the globe would clearly remove an element of uncertainty inherent in any theory of nuclear deterrence. Nevertheless, the corollary to the negative security assurances, the positive security assurances, would seem to discount this argument to some extent. Positive security assurances are guarantees given by NWSs to states within NWFZs that they will come to their assistance should they be threatened by any other extra-NWFZ NWS. By the granting of such guarantees, it is arguable that the theory of deterrence remains substantially intact, although one can foresee certain difficulties if the tactical nuclear weapons of a state providing positive security assurances had to be used against an aggressor's troops within an NWFZ!

The effect of Resolution 3472B is difficult to gauge. Clearly it has no legislative or even quasi-legislative effect,[42] but it does indicate the thinking of both nuclear and non-nuclear weapon states in relation to the creation, status, and guarantee of NWFZs. What emerges is that the majority of states consider NWFZs created by treaty to be both viable and desirable in terms of strengthening peace and security in the world and in stemming the proliferation of nuclear weapons. It is also plain that the nuclear weapon states, by giving their support to NWFZs in principle, but by refusing to give concrete guarantees and assurances to states parties to treaties creating such zones do not wish to have their hands tied when the use of nuclear weapons, or their threatened use, may be tactically desirable.

Although state practice of NWSs in relation to NWFZs is hard to find, the statements which do exist tend to confirm that although such states regard the creation of NWFZs as being compatible with international law, they are for other states rather than themselves and they should not affect their own security. That the creation of NWFZs is permitted by general international law is made apparent by Article VII of the NPT, 1968,[43] which provides: 'Nothing in this Treaty affects the right of any group of States to conclude regional treaties in order to ensure the total absence of nuclear weapons in their respective territories.'

Although this Article establishes that the NPT recognizes the right of states to conclude agreements creating NWFZs, it does not define the concept nor indicate the limitations which may be placed on their geographical scope.[44] Some evidence of this may however be gleaned from the discussions which took place in the General Assembly in 1967 concerning the creation of the Latin American and Caribbean NWFZ by the Treaty of Tlatelolco.[45] In the debate the US stated that four requirements had to be met before an NWFZ could be said to have been properly created. First, the initiative for an NWFZ had to originate within the area or region concerned. Second, the zone had to include all states deemed militarily important. Third, the creation of such a zone was not to disturb necessary security arrangements, and fourth, the treaty creating the NWFZ had to have provisions permitting follow-up of alleged violations, in order to give reasonable assurance of compliance. In the view of the US the Treaty of Tlatelolco met all these requirements.[46] It can be seen, however, that the US response did not make mention of the necessity for either assurances, or guarantees from nuclear weapon states in order to give the NWFZ and states therein the kind of security which would make it a realistic and viable proposition. It is also clear that the US failed to make any observations *de ratione territoriae* of such agreements. Article 3 of the Tlatelolco Treaty defines territory for the purposes of the Treaty as including 'the territorial sea, air space and any other space over which the State exercises sovereignty in accordance with its own legislation'. Although Article 4(1) states that the Treaty is to apply throughout 'the whole of the territories for which the Treaty is in force', Article 4(2) delimits the zone of application which embraces extensive high sea areas. The US clearly saw nothing to object to in this, but the USSR protested that Article 4 would encompass large areas of both the Atlantic and Pacific Oceans 'hundreds of kilometres beyond the territorial waters of the States signing the Treaty'.[47] The most recent treaty creating a NWFZ, the South Pacific Nuclear-Free Zone Treaty, also purports to extend beyond the conventionally defined limits of the contracting states' territories to include large portions of the high seas, but Article 2(2) of that treaty makes it clear that it does not 'prejudice or in any way affect the rights, or the exercise of the rights, of any State under international law with regard to freedom of the seas'.[48]

In spite of the limited amount of state practice available, it may nevertheless be possible to provide a working definition of an NWFZ, as it is presently understood. It is an area of territory, including internal, archipelagic and adjacent territorial waters, and superjacent air space, in which the manufacture, testing, emplacement or maybe even possession or control, of nuclear weapons is prohibited. It may also include prohibitions on the supply of material which may be used in the manufacture of nuclear weapons, and on the dumping of nuclear waste. The prohibitions do not usually extend to possession of radioactive material for peaceful means, for example under the authority of the IAEA.

The creation of nuclear weapon-free zones

The preceding discussion suggests that the normal method of creating nuclear weapon-free zones is by multilateral treaty. There is no legal reason however, why they may not be created unilaterally by a single state declaring itself such a zone, or even extended by a series of bilateral treaties. It is also theoretically possible for such zones to be created by customary law – perhaps through the means of some crystallizing medium such as a resolution or resolutions of the United Nations

General Assembly as discussed above. As the critics of the 1967 Outer Space Treaty (see below and Chapter 6) have pointed out such a customary law regime which would bind all states except those which explicitly object, and might have more wide-ranging consequences than a treaty regime binding only upon those states party to it. None the less, the desire to involve explicitly the nuclear weapon states in the establishment of such zones, either as parties or as signatories of 'negative security assurances' by Protocol, has meant that multilateral treaties have been seen as the primary method of creation. A number of the multilateral treaties have been analysed in detail in other chapters, but the following section examines the main multilateral treaties which have sought to establish nuclear weapon-free regimes, and then examines the legal problems involved in establishing national zones by unilateral action, concluding with a brief examination of the practice of two states, Japan and New Zealand: the former having an established nuclear weapon free policy, and the latter in the process of taking such a step.

The Antarctic Treaty, 1959[49]

When the parties to the Antarctic Treaty (namely Argentina, Australia, Belgium, France, Japan, New Zealand, Norway, South Africa, USSR, UK and USA) guaranteed in 1959 that Antarctica should be used for peaceful purposes only, they 'prohibited, *inter alia,* any measures of a military nature, such as the establishment of military bases and fortifications, the carrying out of military maneuvers [sic], as well as the testing of any type of weapon' Article I(1). In addition they specifically prohibited 'Any nuclear explosions in Antarctica and the disposal there of radio active waste material' (Article V), and provided that any future international agreements relating to the use of nuclear energy, including nuclear explosions and the disposal of radio active waste material, to which they all became parties, would also apply in Antarctica. In a sense therefore, Antarctica became the first guaranteed nuclear-free zone, and like the demilitarized status of the continent, it could be argued to have an objective status opposable to non parties, at least during the period of the validity of the 1959 Treaty.[50]

The Treaty on Principles Governing the Activities of States in the Exploration and Use of Outer Space, Including the Moon and Other Celestial Bodies, 1967.[51]

It would not be true to say that this treaty establishes a nuclear weapon-free zone in outer space; indeed, some of the problems associated with the use of nuclear weapons in space are dealt with in Chapter 6, however, the 1967 Treaty does seek to establish that the exploration and use of outer space ('including the moon and other celestial bodies') shall be 'carried out for the benefit and interest of all countries' (Article 1), and State Parties agree by Article 4 not to

> place in orbit around the Earth any object carrying nuclear weapons or any other kinds of weapons of mass destruction, install such weapons on celestial bodies, or station such weapons in outer space in any other manner.

Although the Treaty has some 84 parties, including the US, the UK and the USSR, it has received considerable criticism in that, as Fawcett has said, 'it does little or nothing to elaborate or secure the principles already set out in General Assembly Resolutions' and '[i]t may even be that this ill constructed and precarious instrument is a retrograde step.'[52] Others too have argued that a customary law regime based on the principles declared in the General Assembly Resolutions would have been a more satisfactory basis for an outer space legal regime. The obligations of Article 4 are in present-day terms only a partial form of nuclear weapon free regime and there are no satisfactory verification procedures built into the Treaty.

The Treaty on the Prohibition of the Emplacement of Nuclear Weapons and Other Weapons of Mass Destruction on the Seabed and Ocean Floor and in the Subsoil Thereof, 1971

The parties to this treaty, which has been ratified by some 73 states, undertake in Article I, not to 'emplant or emplace on the seabed and the ocean floor and in the subsoil thereof beyond the outer limit of a seabed zone . . . any nuclear weapons or other weapons of mass destruction' or any structures etc. for launching testing or storing such devices. Because the 'seabed zone' is defined in Article II as 'coterminous with the twelve-mile outer limit of the zone referred to in Part II of the Convention on the Territorial Sea and Contiguous Zone', and measured in accordance with that Convention 'and international law', there remains a twelve-mile fixed zone within which the emplantation of such weapons by the coastal state (but by no other state, Article I(2)) remains legal. However, the development since 1971 of the International Law of the Sea, which now recognizes 200-mile exclusive economic zone and even more extensive continental shelf claims, means that contracting states may well have limited their sovereignty in a manner perhaps not fully appreciated when the Treaty was signed. More fundamentally, it is debatable whether this treaty also creates a regime for the seabed which is opposable to non-parties. This treaty is considered in detail in Chapter 7.

The Treaty for the Prohibition of Nuclear Weapons in Latin America, 1967[53]

The impetus for the movement in Latin America for a nuclear weapon-free zone seems to have originated from the 1962 Cuban missile crisis, when it was feared that Cuba was intending to install nuclear weapons supplied by the USSR. In the following year a letter signed by the Presidents of Bolivia, Brazil, Chile, Ecuador and Mexico was sent to all Heads of State in the region proposing the establishment of such a zone, and in 1964 a preliminary meeting of representatives was held in Mexico which resulted in the establishment of COPREDAL – the Organization for Preventing the Presence of Nuclear Weapons in Latin America by means of a Treaty. A distinguished group of experts was then commissioned to draft what became the Treaty for the Prohibition of Nuclear Weapons in Latin America – or the Treaty of Tlatelolco.[54] It sought to establish the first nuclear weapon-free zone for an inhabited region of the world.

Under this treaty the contracting states undertake to use exclusively for peaceful means the nuclear material and facilities which are under their jurisdiction, and to prohibit and prevent in their territories:

> a) The testing, use, manufacture, production or acquisition by any means whatsoever of any nuclear weapons, by the Parties themselves, directly or indirectly, on behalf of anyone else or in any other way; and
> b) The receipt, storage, installation, deployment and any form of possession of any nuclear weapon, directly or indirectly, by the Parties themselves, by anyone on their behalf or in any other way. Article 1(1)).

In addition, parties undertake to 'refrain from engaging in, encouraging or authorizing, directly or indirectly, or in any way participating in the testing, use, manufacture, production, possession or control of any nuclear weapon' (Article 1(2)).

The mechanism for the implementation of these obligations however, is notably cautious. The Treaty will only enter into force in its entirety when a number of conditions have been satisfied.

First, when all the Latin American republics, and all other sovereign states situated in their entirety south of latitude 35° north in the western hemisphere in existence when the Treaty is opened for signature, have become parties (Article 25(1)(a)). Other states which become sover-

both Treaties, but where the state is only a party to the Tlatelolco Treaty, then OPANAL provides such assistance and advice as may be required. It is the OPANAL Council which verifies compliance with Article 13. Every six months, each Contracting State must submit a report to OPANAL (and to the IAEA) stating that no activity prohibited by the Treaty has occurred in its territory (Article 14). In addition, it must submit copies of any report it may make to the IAEA relating to any matter covered by the treaty or its safeguard provisions. Every 60 days these reports are analysed by a meeting of the OPANAL Council.

Should there be suspicions that a Contracting State is not honouring its obligations under the Treaty, two main procedures are available (neither of which has had to be used to date): a Special Report request and an Inspection. To obtain a Special Report, the Secretary General (with the authorization of the Council) may request a Contracting State to supply 'complementary or supplementary information regarding any event or circumstance connected with compliance with [the] Treaty, explaining his reasons'. State parties agree to cooperate 'promptly and fully' with such requests, and the request and reply are then circulated to all Contracting States and the OPANAL Council.

Special Inspections may be carried out by the IAEA (under the terms of a negotiated safeguard agreement), or by the OPANAL Council. The Council must immediately arrange an inspection if it receives a request (with reasons) from any party which suspects that 'some activity prohibited by [the] Treaty has been carried out, or is about to be carried out, either in the territory of any other Party or in any other place on that Party's behalf'. The Council is under the same obligation if it receives a request from any Party which is 'suspected or charged with having violated the Treaty'. Once such an inspection has been authorized, Contracting States have undertaken by Article 16(4) to:

> grant the inspectors carrying out such special inspections full and free access to all places and all information which may be necessary for the performance of their duties and which are directly and intimately connected with the suspicion of the violation of [the] Treaty.

The inspectors may, at the request of the Contracting State being inspected, be accompanied by its own representatives, 'provided that this does not in any way delay or hinder the work of the inspectors'. Once a report on the inspection has been submitted by the inspectors to the OPANAL Council, copies must immediately be sent to all the parties, the UN and the Organization of American States (OAS). A special meeting of the OPANAL General Conference may also be called to consider the report (Article 16 (7)); This Conference may make recommendations to the Contracting States and may itself submit a report to the UN.

In any case where the General Conference considers that a Contracting State is not 'complying fully with its obligations under [the] Treaty', it has the power to take note, and to 'draw the matter to the attention of the Party concerned, making such recommendations as it deems appropriate' (Article 20). If the Conference feels that the non-compliance constitutes a violation of the Treaty which might endanger peace and security, then it must report this to the UN, the OAS, and where relevant the IAEA.

The zone of application of the Treaty is also of some originality in international law. Under Article 4(1) it includes 'the whole of the territories for which the Treaty is in force'. This must include the land and air space, and the internal waters of all the State Parties. What is more controversial however, is whether the complete ban on nuclear weapons also extends to territorial waters. Two issues are involved here. The first, which is discussed in detail below, is whether it is permissible under international law to deny the right of innocent passage through territorial waters to foreign vessels carrying nuclear weapons. The Treaty, however, makes no reference to this issue although COPREDAL, before completing its preparatory work on the draft treaty, issued a declaration that decisions about transit of nuclear weapons should be left to individual states.[61] The second arises from the practice of many of the South American states of claiming 200-mile territorial sea zones. The exact status and the rights conferred by these zones are discussed in Chapter 7. Briefly, however, although some major maritime states still claim a territorial sea of only three miles,[62] the 1982 Law of the Sea Convention (LOSC) envisages a 12-mile territorial sea,[63] together with a 12-mile contiguous zone,[64] both measured from a coastal baseline from which the 200-mile exclusive economic zone may be measured.[65] A 200-mile territorial sea claim has not received the approval of the world community.[66] Thus, even if it were to be accepted that it was legitimate under international law for a coastal state to deny the right of innocent passage through territorial waters to a nuclear-armed foreign vessel, such a prohibition could only apply under general international law to that area generally recognized by the world community as territorial waters: namely the 12-mile zone.

However, the Tlatelolco Treaty ultimately envisages a far more extensive ambit than territorial waters. Once all the conditions outlined above have been satisfied and the Treaty has come fully into force, then the zone of application of the Treaty will be as defined in Article 4(2). As Map 1 indicates this covers an area larger than the territories of the Contracting Parties and in general terms runs from 35° north latitude to 60° south latitude and from 20° west longitude to 115° west longitude (with a westerly angle from 5° north latitude) so that it follows the general direction of the Central American landmass. The outward limit of this zone reaches in places more than 200-miles from the coast, and Dr Martinez Cobo, of OPANAL has been at pains to point out that this is envisaged as a protection zone 'of a special nature, the scope of which is required in order to confer adequate nuclear protection on the region' and that the Treaty 'does not confer sovereignty over this zone upon the States of Latin America, and does not extend or justify the extension of their territorial waters'.[67] As the nuclear weapon states have already undertaken to respect this zone, it would not require policing in a traditional sense involving the exercise of coastal state enforcement jurisdiction. Such violations as were detected would have to be dealt with at an inter-state level and settled by normal legal and political means, including reference to the International Court of Justice, as envisaged by Article 24, if the parties so agree.

The complex implementation process of the Tlatelolco Treaty points out well the advantages and disadvantages of collaborating with the nuclear states in the construction of such a regime. The Tlatelolco Treaty proves that such collaboration is possible, although Latin America, unlike Europe, is not an area of past superpower rivalry and so far as it was possible to determine such things, there were no nuclear weapons in the region at the time the Treaty was promulgated. The system of waivers, and the Protocols requiring ratification by non-Latin American states with territorial interests in the region as well as by the nuclear powers (providing the so called 'negative security assurances'), mean that when the treaty does enter fully into force it will have a truly objective status, recognized by all interested states. These mechanisms also reflect the rather cautious atmosphere in which the Treaty seems to have been negotiated. It is noteworthy that nine of the 31 Articles (Articles 7-16) are in one way or another concerned with control and verification. It should perhaps also be remembered that unlike later treaties, the Tlatelolco Treaty specifically permits nuclear explosions for peaceful purposes, (Articles 17-18).

As the means by which the first nuclear weapon-free zone has been instituted in an inhabited area, the Tlatelolco Treaty is unique. It has, however, provided a stimulus and a model for similar developments in other regions. Its staged implementation process provide an ingenious method of bringing the Treaty into force, while at the same time retaining the clear aim of, and the pressure for, unanimous adherence. When, or perhaps if, it attains the full adherence for which it aims, the geographical scope of the nuclear weapon-free regime which it brings into force will be truly enormous, joining the Antarctic regime to the South, and possibly the South Pacific Nuclear Free Zone to the West.

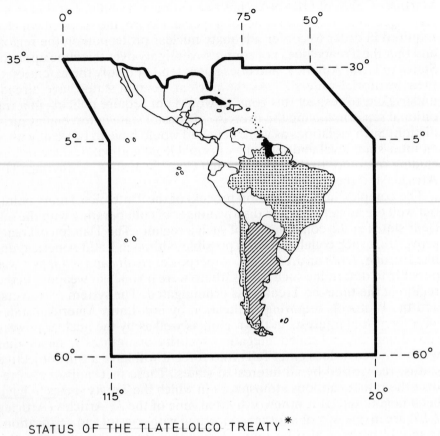

STATUS OF THE TLATELOLCO TREATY *

▭ States party to Treaty

▨ States that have signed but not ratified Treaty

▦ States that have signed and ratified Treaty, but have not
    availed themselves of waiver under Article 28 (2)

■ Latin American States not associated with the Treaty

* *Officially entitled the Treaty for the Prohibition
   of Nuclear Weapons in Latin America*

Map 1   Zone of Application of the Tlatelolco Treaty

The South Pacific Nuclear-Free Zone Treaty, 1985

On 6 August 1985, at Rarotonga in the Cook Islands the members of the South Pacific Forum concluded the South Pacific Nuclear-Free Zone Treaty (SPNFZT).[68] The origins of this treaty are broader than those of the Treaty of Tlatelolco, discussed above, even though in many respects the SPNFZT is modelled upon it. With the growth in the number of independent states in the region, the strength of opposition to the continuation of nuclear testing, started by Australian and New Zealand protests at the French tests in Mururoa in the 1970s[69] was, as Sutherland comments, 'broadened to take in wider issues relating to the international nuclear industry and superpower rivalry in the region.'[70] The SPNFZT reflects this wider concern, for unlike many of the treaties considered above it is not simply a nuclear weapon-free zone treaty, it seeks to prohibit a very wide spectrum of nuclear activity in the South Pacific: including the disposal of nuclear waste, the supply of materials for the nuclear weapons industry, as well as the testing, possession, control and presence of nuclear weapons. Unlike the Tlatelolco Treaty it does not permit explosions for 'peaceful purposes'.

The first steps towards the conclusion of the SPNFZT were taken at the 15th session of the South Pacific Forum held in Fanafuti, Tuvalu in August 1984, which endorsed an Australian proposal for the establishment of such a zone. A similar proposal by New Zealand had been supported by the Forum in 1975, but changes of government in Australia and New Zealand had resulted in the project being shelved.[71] The August 1984 meeting established a working group of officials to examine the legal and other issues involved, with a view to producing a draft treaty for the 1985 Forum Meeting. The working group held six meetings and in June 1985 submitted its report. The draft treaty was then adopted at the 16th Forum Session at Rarotonga in August of that year. Eight states signed the Treaty at that time: Australia, Cook Islands, Fiji, Kiribati, New Zealand, Niue, Tuvalu and Western Samoa. A further four states, Nauru, Papua New Guinea, Tonga and the Solomon Islands expressed support for the Treaty, but only Papua New Guinea has since signed. Only two states have so far ratified the Treaty, Fiji and the Cook Islands.[72]

The basic obligation of the Treaty is set out in Article 3, where each Contracting State undertakes:

a) not to manufacture or otherwise acquire, possess or have control over any nuclear explosive device by any means anywhere inside or outside the South Pacific Nuclear Free Zone;
b) not to seek or receive assistance in the manufacture or acquisition of any nuclear explosive device;

c) not to take any action to assist or encourage the manufacture or acquisition of any nuclear explosive device by any State.

In addition, states parties undertake to respect the NPT and IAEA systems and not to 'provide source or special fissionable material, or equipment or material especially designed or prepared for the processing, use or production of special fissionable material for peaceful purposes' either to non-nuclear weapon states unless subject to the safeguards of the NPT,(Article 4(a)(i)), or to nuclear weapon states unless subject to the IAEA safeguards, (Article 4(b)(ii)). They also agree to prevent the stationing or testing of any 'nuclear exploding device' in their territory, and not to assist in or encourage the testing of such devices by any other state (Articles 5 and 6). Parties also undertake themselves not to dump nuclear or radioactive waste within the SPNFZ area, or to assist or encourage any other state to do so, or to permit such dumping within their own territorial sea (Article 7).

The Treaty has clearly been influenced by the model of the 1967 Treaty of Tlatelolco, although it goes further than that treaty in a number of important respects. It seeks to prevent its parties from participating in any way in the manufacture, acquisition, possession or control of nuclear weapons. In doing so the Treaty links in with the NPT and IAEA systems. While the peaceful uses of nuclear energy are not prohibited, unlike the Tlateloloco Treaty, it does not permit nuclear tests for peaceful purposes, and the Contracting States agree to prevent the testing or stationing of any 'nuclear exploding device' in their territory,[73] and indeed undertake not even to assist in or encourage the testing of such devices by any other state (whether party to the SPNFZ or not).[74] The prohibition on dumping of nuclear or radioactive waste within the SPNFZ area, and on assisting or encouraging any other state to do so, adds a dimension of contemporary significance not covered by the 1967 Treaty.

The drafters of the Treaty have obviously been conscious of the framework of international law principles within which the SPNFZ Treaty would operate. The specific obligations that it imposes are only binding upon contracting states, and it seeks to operate by restricting contracting states from giving aid or comfort to non-contracting states. There are nevertheless, as Sutherland has pointed out,[75] certain tensions within the Treaty itself. The South Pacific Nuclear-Free Zone is defined (in Article 1(a)) as an area covering virtually the whole South Pacific Region (see Map 2).[76] However, the Treaty does not require the consent of all the states covered by this area; it enters into force after only eight states have ratified. It is therefore feasible, maybe even probable, that when the Treaty comes into effect the definition of the Nuclear-Free Zone will include the territory of states which are not par-

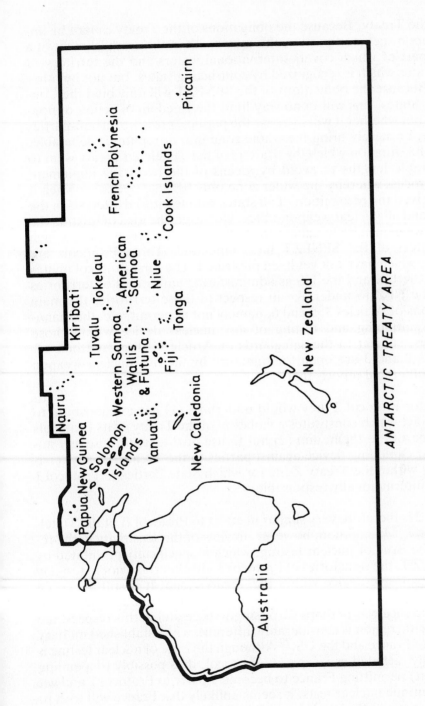

Map 2   Zone of Application of the South Pacific Nuclear-Free Zone

Source: South Pacific Nuclear-Free Zone Treaty, Rarotonga, 6 August 1985

ties to the Treaty. Because the obligations of the Treaty cannot be imposed upon such non-parties, this may result in the establishment of a Zone, part of which covers international waters and the territory of other states which is recognized by contracting states, but not by other states. Because the obligations of the SPNFZT will only bind the Contracting States, this will in no way limit the freedom of action of non-parties, but whether it will increase the political pressure on non-parties to ratify, or merely bring the whole zone into disrepute, is debatable. This is the situation which the drafters of the Tlatelolco Treaty went to considerable lengths to avoid by means of the two-stage implementation process whereby the wider zone only became operative when it had received the recognition of all states with territorial interests in the region, and all nuclear weapon states. However, the idea of inviting the nuclear weapon state to adhere to Protocols to the Treaty is one which the drafters of the SPNFZT have emulated. Three Protocols are planned, which have not yet been published. The First Protocol invites France, the UK and the US as administering authorities of territories within the NFZ to undertake in respect of those territories the main obligations of Articles 3, 5 and 6, namely not to permit, etc. the manufacture, stationing and testing of any nuclear device within those territories, subject to the safeguards of Article 8 (discussed below). Protocols 2 and 3 are open for signature by the five nuclear-weapon states. Sutherland reports that:

> Under Protocol 2 they would undertake (1) not to contribute to any act which constitutes a violation of the Treaty or its Protocols by parties to them; and (2) not to use or threaten to use any nuclear exploding device against parties to the Treaty, or any territory within the Treaty Zone for which State Parties to Protocol 1 are internationally responsible.[77]

Protocol 2 is therefore very similar in effect to Protocol II of the Tlatelolco Treaty.[78] In addition, however, in view of the sensitivity in the region of the issue of nuclear testing, which is specifically prohibited by the SPNFZT, the signatories of Protocol 3 will undertake not to test any nuclear explosive device within the Treaty Zone. It is still uncertain what sort of support these Protocols will receive. Although the Tlatelolco experience was perhaps surprisingly successful in this respect, the South Pacific region is considerably different, with established military interests of France and the US.[79] Although the issue of nuclear testing is realistically included as a separate Protocol, thus possibly (depending on the text) permitting France to become a party to Protocol 2 and yet still to continue nuclear tests, it seems unlikely that France will wish to become a party to Protocols 1 and 3 until it decides (probably for other reasons) to discontinue testing. Again the political impact of the SPNFZT on such a decision remains uncertain, but without the support of the states with a nuclear presence in the region the Zone will lack the objective character which it clearly seeks.

The fact that the Treaty comes into force after only eight ratifications (as opposed to the universal requirement of the Tlatelolco Treaty) suggests that the drafters were aware that the Treaty itself would be unlikely to command universal support but that they nonetheless attributed considerable political significance to the coordinated actions of the Contracting States. A limited recognition that the regime of the Treaty is not opposable to states from outside the region is to be found in Article 2(2) which expressly provides that:

> Nothing in this Treaty shall prejudice or in any way affect the rights, or the exercise of the rights, of any State under international law with regard to freedom of the seas.

But Article 5(2) provides that:

> Each Party in the exercise of its sovereign rights remains free to decide for itself whether to allow visits by foreign ships and aircraft to its ports and airfields, transit of its airspace by foreign aircraft, and navigation by foreign ships in its territorial sea or archipelagic waters in a manner not covered by the rights of innocent passage, archipelagic sea lane passage or transit passage of straits.

Therefore the persistent problem of whether access to international ports can be denied to foreign warships carrying nuclear weapons (which is discussed below) is left to the individual states, as is the question of whether restrictions may legitimately be imposed on such vessels purporting to exercise a right of innocent passage through territorial waters. Although these provisions have been criticised as compromising the nuclear free ideal,[80] these provisions do permit states, such as Australia and New Zealand to become parties to this convention without prejudging problems concerning regional defence treaties such as ANZUS.

The control system to verify compliance with the Treaty is established by Article 8, and has four facets. First, a system of reports and exchanges of information, under which contracting states are required to report to the Director of the South Pacific Bureau for Economic Cooperation and Development, who is the Depository of the Treaty and the Protocols, 'any significant event within its jurisdiction affecting the implementation of the Treaty'.[81] The Director is under an obligation to 'circulate such reports promptly to all the Parties' and he also must circulate any other information on matters 'arising under or in relation to' the Treaty which parties may communicate to him as part of their obligation to 'endeavour to keep each other informed'[82] on such issues. In addition, the Director is obliged to make an Annual Report to the South Pacific Forum on the status of the Treaty and matters arising under or in relation to it. The Annual Report must incorporate all reports and communications made to the Director as well as reports made under the complaints procedure (under annex 4, see below) and from the IAEA on its inspection activities in the territory of any Party (annex 2(4)).[83]

Secondly, a Consultative Committee is established by Annex 3,[84] comprised of representatives of all the Contracting States, and chaired by the representative of the state which hosted the last meeting of the Heads of Government of Members of the South Pacific Forum. This Committee may be convened by the Director, at the request of any party, for 'consultation and cooperation on any matter arising in relation to this Treaty or for reviewing its operation.'[85]

Thirdly, safeguards comprised in agreements negotiated and concluded with the IAEA on all source and fissionable material in all peaceful nuclear activities within the territories of the Parties.[86] The purpose of these safeguards is to prevent the diversion of nuclear material from peaceful nuclear activities to nuclear explosive devices. All parties agree to enter into such agreements within eighteen months of becoming bound by the SPNFZ Treaty, and the agreements must be, or be equivalent in scope or effect to, those required by the NPT. As indicated above, parties undertake to inform the Director and all Contracting Parties with copies of IAEA reports and conclusions on its inspection activities within their territory.[87]

Finally, Annex 4 sets up a complaints procedure. Under this procedure any party which considers that there are grounds for considering that any other party is in breach of its obligations under the SPNFZT must, in the first instance, make known its complaint to the party concerned, and only after giving that 'state a reasonable opportunity to provide an explanation and resolve the matter' may a complaint be taken to the Director, with a request that it be considered by the Consultative Committee. The Consultative Committee may, after giving the state complained of a further opportunity to provide an explanation, authorize a Special Inspection by 'three suitably qualified special inspectors' appointed by the Consultative Committee in consultation with the complainant and the complained of party.[88] None of the three may be nationals of the disputing states, although they may be accompanied by a representative of the party complained of. That state must give 'full and free access to all information and places within its territory which may be relevant to enable the special inspectors to implement the directive given to them by the Consultative Committee'.[89] The Consultative Committee must then report fully to all the parties on the finding of the Special Inspection, and if it finds that the state complained of is in violation of its obligations under the SPNFZT, or that the inspection requirement has not been complied with, then the parties must 'meet promptly at a meeting of the South Pacific Forum'. Indeed, such a meeting may also be called by either of the disputing parties at any time in the procedure.[90]

There is no explicit sanction for violation of the Treaty, however under Article 13:

> in the event of a violation by any Party of a provision of this Treaty essential to the achievement of the objectives of the Treaty or of the spirit of the Treaty, every other Party shall have the right to withdraw from the Treaty.

This provision reflects the general international law rule that only a material breach of a treaty justifies termination of the obligations between contracting states,[91] but it is unusual to include a right of withdrawal for a violation of the 'spirit of the Treaty', and it is a phrase which might well cause problems of interpretation, given that there is no provision in the Treaty for judicial settlement of disputes, even on a consensual basis.

Concern has also been expressed at the absence of watertight guarantees that uranium produced in Australia (for it is the only producer in the region) will not, because of the pledge of 'mutual aid' in the ANZUS Treaty, find its way into nuclear weapons produced in the US. However, it should be noted that if Australia were to ratify the SPNFZ Treaty (to which no reservations are permitted), it is already a party to the NPT regime, and has a standing agreement with the IAEA.[92]

The South Pacific Nuclear Free-Zone Treaty is not only the most recent of the multilateral treaties of its kind, it is also the most far-reaching, prohibiting as it does all forms of involvement in nuclear explosions as well as disposal and dumping of nuclear and radioactive waste. Like the Tlatelolco Treaty it seeks to establish a regime based on the adherence of all the interested states in the region as well as the nuclear weapon states, but it remains to be seen whether it will command this degree of support. If it does not, the geographical zone set out in the Treaty will remain little more than an aspiration, but the Treaty will still have a significant effect as a coordinated multilateral ban on a broad spectrum of nuclear activities within the territories of the Contracting States.

Unilateral Action

It is a basic aspect of state sovereignty that a state has exclusive control over what goes on within its own territory, including its territorial waters. Although this control may be subject to limitations imposed by international treaty and customary law, it is therefore *prima facie* legitimate for a state to take action unilaterally to restrict, in one way or another, the presence of nuclear weapons within its territory. The legality of any such unilateral action will depend in each case upon that state's preceding treaty obligations,[93] and whether or not the implementation of its policy infringes other rules of customary law,[94] but it seems likely that the establishment of national nuclear-free zones will be an important aspect of the future development of 'denuclearization'. In view of the growing strength of the anti-nuclear movement, and the political interest which is being shown in the multilateral declarations of nuclear-free zones in the areas discussed above, a growing number of states may well choose to take unilateral action to declare their territory such a zone. As indicated above, a unilateral declaration by a sovereign state of a national nuclear free zone is a quite legal means of establishing a ban on nuclear weapons within its territory, provided always that this does not result in a conflict with that state's pre-existing treaty obligations (perhaps relating to foreign military bases or strategic defence). Such a ban could apply to all land territory, internal waters and air space. However, some controversy surrounds the question of restrictions on foreign nuclear powered vessels or foreign vessels carrying nuclear weapons passing through territorial waters.

Under international law, ships of all states have the right of freedom of navigation on the high seas, and the right of innocent passage through the territorial waters of other states. The question of whether this right extended to both civil vessels and warships was debated at length at both the 1930 Hague Codification Conference and the 1958 First United Nations Conference on the Law of the Sea. In reply to a questionnaire sent out in preparation for the 1930 Conference, 16 states expressed the view that warships had the same rights of innocent passage as merchant vessels, while five considered that access to territorial waters by foreign warships required the prior permission of the coastal state.[95] The importance of this distinction has been summarized by O'Connell:

> If passage is a right, it is clear that the coastal state cannot act arbitrarily; if it is mere comity, then the coastal state may decide for itself when the right may be withdrawn, at the cost of merely being regarded as unfriendly.[96]

A supporter of the latter view at the 1930 Conference (somewhat surprisingly in retrospect) was the US, who proposed that the coastal state 'in the interests of comity' should ordinarily permit passage of warships through territorial waters.[97] A similar division of opinion was apparent in 1958, but after some tactical voting on the text,[98] Article 14 of the 1958 Convention made no reference to this, simply stating that:

> 1) Subject to the provisions of these articles, ships of all states, whether coastal or not, shall enjoy the right of innocent passage through the territorial sea.

O'Connell takes the view that this relegated the question of innocent passage of warships to customary law, and that as 'there is no evidence of state practice before very recent times other than of free and uncontested passage of warships', he regards attempts to annul this practice retrospectively as being of a 'tendentious character'.[99]

Article 16 of the 1958 Convention does permit states to suspend temporarily the right of innocent passage in certain waters 'if such suspension is essential for the protection of its security', but such restrictions must be 'without discrimination among foreign ships'. While this clearly precludes discrimination against ships of a certain nationality, it seems to leave open the question of whether the suspension could be of particular classes of vessel. The issue is not clarified by the 1982 Convention.[100] In any event it should be remembered that this provision only permits the *temporary* suspension of the right of innocent passage.

The 1982 Convention does however recognize that '[f]oreign nuclear-powered ships or ships carrying nuclear or other inherently dangerous or noxious substances' are a special case, and it requires them, when exercising a right of innocent passage, to 'carry documents and observe special precautionary measures established for such ships by international agreements'.[101] This form of words indicates that the drafters intended that such measures may not be unilateral or arbitrary, but would only be permissible when they reflected international law rules. If these international agreements establish generally accepted rules, such as those of Chapter VIII of SOLAS 1960 and 1974,[102] presumably these precautionary measures would be enforceable even if the coastal state or the flag state of the ship were not a party to the particular agreement. However, it must be contrary to the general intention of the 1982 Convention to argue that such precautionary measures would extend to total exclusion under the terms of a regional nuclear free zone treaty, if only because Article 24 prohibits the coastal state from imposing requirements 'on foreign ships which have the practical effect of denying or impairing the right of innocent passage'.

Nevertheless, there is some state practice to support the view that the passage of nuclear-powered vessels through territorial waters is an exception to the right of innocent passage, requiring specific permission and subject to conditions and guarantees. The best known examples are the Spanish legislation of 1964,[103] and the treaties concluded at that time by the US with a large number of states (including Spain) to facilitate the passage of the US nuclear ship *Savannah* through their waters.[104]

These provisions requiring compliance with such 'precautionary measures' do not however extend to warships, which under the state immunity doctrine are exempt from any form of coastal state inspection, nevertheless such a vessel may be required to leave the territorial sea if it 'does not comply with the laws and regulations of the coastal state concerning passage through the territorial sea and disregards any request for compliance therewith which is made to it' (Article 30, LOSC).[105] However, such laws and regulations must conform to the 'Convention and other rules of international law' (Article 21(1), LOSC), of which the most important is the general overriding right of innocent passage. Hence an attempt to exclude foreign warships of a particular type from exercising a right of innocent passage may be seen as a violation of the Law of the Sea, as codified in both the 1958 and 1982 Conventions.

However, it should be remembered that the right is known as *innocent* passage, and some controversy surrounds the question of whether the concept of innocence means simply compliance with the local laws of the coastal state, or whether it is capable of an objective definition. This clearly has considerable bearing on whether a coastal state may legally deny a right of innocent passage through its territorial waters to nuclear powered, or armed, vessels *per se*. Churchill and Lowe point out that Anglo-American practice over the last 200 years appears to support the latter 'objective' view which was also taken by a number of leading jurists including Schücking, whose reports 'prepared the ground for the 1930 Hague Conference'.[106] For the supporters of the 'objective' position:

> . . . it was not necessary that any coastal law should have been violated in order that innocence be lost; it was enough that vital coastal interest, such as security, be prejudiced. Conversely, it would seem to follow that not all infractions of coastal laws would deprive passage of its innocent character, but only those which did have a prejudicial effect. Furthermore, if prejudice to coastal interests were the criterion, it would not be necessary to point to any particular act of the foreign ship as being incompatible with innocence, and the mere presence of the ship could be enough to threaten the coastal state.[107]

The Hague Conference itself took a compromise position, and the adopted text required a vessel to make use of the territorial sea 'for the purpose of *doing any* act prejudicial to the security, to the public policy or to the fiscal interests' of the coastal state, in order to compromise its innocence.[108] Despite support for the 'objective' view in the ruling of the International Court of Justice in the *Corfu Channel* Case (1949),[109] it was the Hague approach which was taken by the 1958 Convention. This defined passage as innocent 'so long as it is not prejudicial to the peace, good order or security of the coastal state', and required that '[s]uch passage shall take place in conformity with these articles and other rules of international law' (Article 14(4)). However, the drafters of that Convention were unable to agree on objective criteria for determining in what circumstances a coastal state may decide that the passage of a particular ship is so prejudicial. This omission is partially remedied by Article 19 of the 1982 Convention which reproduces the formula of the 1958 Convention and in paragraph 2 lists *activities* which may be regarded as prejudicial. These include such things as:

a) any threat or use of force against the sovereignty, territorial integrity or political independence of the coastal state, or in any other manner in violation of the principles of international law embodied in the Charter of the United Nations;
b) any exercise or practice with weapons of any kind;

and there is a residual clause

1) any other activity not having a direct bearing on passage.

It does seem clear from this that the drafters intended that the exclusion of specific vessels from territorial waters should be based upon some prejudicial *activity,* rather than upon the particular characteristics of a class of vessels. In this context it seems difficult to argue that the possession of certain weaponry by a warship constitutes in itself a threat to the coastal state. Even accepting, as Churchill and Lowe comment, that the wording of the paragraph is wide enough to cover threats to states other than the coastal state,[110] it does seem that the stress on the term *activity* suggests that under the 1982 Convention at least, considerably more is necessary than the mere possession of weapons which could be utilized as a threat, or indeed form part of a system of defence strategy which involves threat and/or counter-threat. It must be said however, that in the continued absence of objective criteria for assessing the validity of a coastal state's decision on what is or is not prejudicial to its 'peace, good order and security', and at a time when the 1982 Convention has not yet entered into force, some doubt does still surround the issue. The Japanese government, amongst others, has argued that the passage of vessels armed with nuclear weapons is not a recognized exercise of the right of innocent passage.[111] The Japanese position dates from 1968 and is based on an interpretation of the 1958 Convention and customary law. The relevant Articles of the 1982 Treaty, discussed above, do purport to codify and clarify existing law rather than progressively develop it, but the Japanese position seems likely to be espoused by a growing number of states in the future.[112] It is for example, significant that the South Pacific Nuclear -Free Zone Treaty specifically leaves 'each party ... free to decide for itself whether to allow ... navigation by foreign ships in its territorial sea ... in a manner not covered by the rights of innocent passage...'(Article 5(2)). This seems to be deliberately inviting parties to consider for themselves what is and is not innocent passage, and while the general point is made in Article 2 that 'nothing in the present Treaty shall prejudice or in any way affect the rights, or the exercise of the rights, of any state *under international law* with regard to freedom of the seas',[113] it is an area of international law in which some doubts do still remain. For those states that choose not to ratify the 1982 Convention, it may be possible to maintain what might be called the Japanese interpretation of customary law. However, for those that become a party to the 1982 Convention, this issue, as a matter relating to freedom and rights of navigation, regarding 'the exercise by a coastal State of its sovereign rights of jurisdiction' (Article 297), comes within the compulsory dispute settlement procedures set out in Part XV of the 1982 Convention, [114] and any judicial rulings on this issue will clearly have a profound affect on the position under customary international law.

There is less uncertainty surrounding the position in relation to ports and internal waters. These are areas which fall within the territorial sovereignty of the state, and despite the much criticized ruling in the *Aramco* case,[115] there seems agreement that there is no general right of access to ports even for merchant vessels. For warships the position is even clearer, for as Woodliffe has pointed out:

> Both state practice and juristic opinion are unequivocal in affirming the absence in customary law of a right of entry to foreign ports for warships in time of peace, except perhaps in cases of distress.[116]

Such entry is therefore entirely dependent upon permission, and the port state is therefore free to impose such conditions, and require such guarantees as it sees fit. Indeed many states have enacted rules of law or practice regulating conditions for access of foreign naval vessels to their ports.[117] O'Connell takes the view that 'port authorities may also deny access to ships of a particular type on a non-discriminatory basis, especially nuclear-powered ships'.[118] It seems consequently quite acceptable under customary international law to ban nuclear powered vessels and by analogy those carrying nuclear arms, from ports and internal waters, provided the ban is non-discriminatory and promulgated in advance. As we shall see below, however, such action may conflict with treaty obligations, but this will be a matter of interpretation of the treaty involved.

Japan

Since World War II and the first use by the US of nuclear weapons against Japan at Hiroshima and Nagasaki, the Japanese have had an understandable aversion to nuclear weapons. Under the Constitution of 1947, Japan renounced war as a sovereign right and 'the threat or use of force as a means of settling international disputes' (Article 9). Following the 1960 US – Japanese Security Treaty and the Vietnam war of the 1960s there was a great deal of internal opposition to the possible storage of nuclear weapons on Japanese soil.[119] In 1967 both Houses of the Japanese Diet passed resolutions that Japan should not possess, produce or import nuclear weapons, and in January of the following year the Prime Minister, Eisaku Sato, announced Japan's nuclear policy, which would be to develop nuclear energy for peaceful means, to promote nuclear disarmament while relying on the US nuclear umbrella for deterrence against nuclear attack, and also to refrain from producing, possessing or bringing nuclear weapons into Japan.[120] This last principle, which it has been suggested originates from a political strategy of the Prime Minister to weaken left wing opposition to the government by adopting its most popular cause, has been called the non-nuclear principle, or the three non-nuclear principles *(Hikaku Sangensoku).* [121] The principles do not have the force of law, but having been described as 'guidelines of national policy', they have been promulgated and notified to Japan's allies – including the US.

Later in 1968, following visits by nuclear-powered ships there was further controversy about the whole question of visits of nuclear armed, as well as powered, ships and the Japanese Government announced that nuclear armed ships would not be permitted the right of 'innocent passage' in Japanese waters. It also revealed the English text of a verbal understanding reached in 1960 that prior consultations would be held under the US-Japan Security Treaty in three situations including:

> . . . b) major changes in [US] equipment: introduction to Japan of nuclear warheads and intermediate and long-range missiles and the construction of bases for such weapons.

The Japanese Foreign Ministry has also indicated that they interpret 'introduction' to include the carrying of nuclear weapons in any form or on any occasion even aboard US naval vessels, an interpretation to which the US had not objected. The US adopts the policy of refusing to confirm or deny the presence of nuclear weapons aboard its warships,[121] and the Japanese authorities in turn have refused to confirm or deny that consultation under the 1960 verbal understanding has taken place, but declare themselves able to presume that a friendly state would not violate established 'principles', hence *ex hypothesi,* for Japanese political purposes, US vessels entering Japanese waters do not carry nuclear weapons.

Despite the lack of municipal legal force of the 'non-nuclear principles' the explicit position of the Japanese government, that the passage of foreign vessels armed with nuclear weapons through its territorial waters is not recognized as a right of 'innocent passage', constitutes as discussed above important evidence of state practice.

New Zealand

Following David Lange's election as Prime Minister of New Zealand in July 1984, he announced an immediate ban on 'nuclear weapons on New Zealand soil and in our harbours'.[123] This brought him into immediate conflict with the US government with whom New Zealand has, with Australia, a defensive alliance, the 1951 ANZUS Pact.[124] As Woodliffe has pointed out,[125] the ANZUS Pact differs significantly from the NATO Alliance[126] in that there is no integrated military command and its organizational structure consists solely of a Council of Foreign Ministers who (under Article VII) may meet at any time to consider matters relating to the implementation of the Treaty. Nevertheless, the parties to the ANZUS Pact do declare their desire to 'coordinate their efforts for collective defence' and to 'declare publicly and formally their sense of unity', and they specifically undertake 'separately and jointly by means of continuous and effective self-help and mutual aid' to 'maintain and develop their individual and collective capacity to resist armed attack'.[127]

Lange took the view, however, that unlike NATO, ANZUS had always been a non-nuclear alliance, and in January 1985 rejected a formal request for a routine visit by *USS Buchanan* on the grounds that New Zealand ports were 'only open to ships which do not carry nuclear weapons'.[128] As with Japan the US followed its practice of refusing to confirm or deny that the vessel was carrying nuclear weapons, and took the view that New Zealand was in breach of the ANZUS Treaty. New Zealand-US military exercises were called off by the US, and New Zealand was excluded from the Council of Ministers and from receiving US intelligence reports.[129]

Although the initial legal justification for the New Zealand action was never made explicit, the Prime Minister has introduced a Bill into the New Zealand Parliament,[130] ostensibly giving internal effect to the South Pacific Nuclear-Free Zone Treaty which New Zealand signed at Rarotonga, Cook Islands, in June 1985. The US has declared that if the Bill is passed it will no longer regard New Zealand as a party to the ANZUS Pact.[131] The Bill (which specifically binds the government, clause 3) establishes a New Zealand Nuclear-Free Zone covering land, internal and territorial waters, as well as the air space above each (clause 4). It declares it to be a criminal offence for a New Zealand citizen or resident either in New Zealand or (if a government servant or agent) anywhere outside New Zealand, to 'manufacture, acquire, or possess, or have control over, any nuclear explosive device', or to aid, assist, or abet any other person to do the same.(clause 5).

Clause 9 specifically prohibits the Prime Minister from approving entry into New Zealand internal waters of foreign warships unless satisfied that the warships will not be carrying 'any nuclear explosive device'. The same conditions apply to foreign military aircraft (clause 10). However, the Bill does specifically provide that nothing in it shall be construed as limiting the freedom of any ship or aircraft to exercise the right of innocent passage through territorial waters and international straits, *in accordance with international law* (Clause 12). This reflects the wording of the South Pacific NFZ Treaty, but does leave open perhaps for the future, the question of whether the New Zealand Government regards itself as having the right under international law to exclude nuclear powered or armed vessels from its territorial waters.

Conclusion

Despite the number of treaties which seek to establish nuclear weapon-free zones, the whole idea is fraught with problems at both a legal and a political level. The distinction between peaceful and non-peaceful uses of nuclear material, the extent of state jurisdiction over the passage of nuclear armed ships through territorial waters, the compatibility of defence and security treaties (which are often underpinned by concepts of nuclear deterrence) with such zones, the opposability of NWFZ treaties to non-party states; these are all problems which are often left unanswered by the treaty drafters, because they are issues on which there is an absence of political agreement either among the contracting states, or between them and the nuclear weapon states with whom 'negative security assurances' are sought.

Nevertheless, an examination of the development and the structure of these treaties, particularly the Tlatelolco Treaty and the South Pacific NFZ Treaty indicates that working within these political constraints the drafters have still been able to secure a wide area of common ground. Although commentators writing from a security perspective have expressed considerable reservations about the ultimate effectiveness of NWFZs, what is perhaps most important about the Latin American Treaty is not whether it is watertight, but the degree of support it has been able to achieve. This point can be seen even more clearly in the SPNFZ Treaty, which has yet to come into force, but which indicates a much broader opposition to the problems of the nuclear age than simply nuclear weapons. The proscriptions on disposal of radioactive waste indicate an environmental as much as a security concern, however, at the same time the opposition to nuclear weapons displayed in the text of the Treaty appears almost ideological. This aspect of the motivation behind the Treaty can be seen even more clearly in the New Zealand implementing Bill: when passed this will make it a criminal offence for a government servant even to abet any person to have control over a nuclear explosive device anywhere in the world. These developments seem to be rooted in a broader anti-nuclear movement, reflected in the fact that the Treaty seeks to create a nuclear-free zone not simply a nuclear weapon-free zone. The ultimate effectiveness of nuclear weapon-free zones must depend not upon the control and verification procedures they exercise over participating states (however important these may be for other purposes), but on the compliance of the nuclear weapon states at a time of national emergency. It may well be therefore, that in contemporary political terms the most important aspect for future development lies in the impetus that the creation of nuclear weapon-free zones might give to the broader anti-nuclear movement.

Notes

1   See Felix Calderon, 'Nuclear weapon-free zones: the Latin American Experiment', in David Carlton and Carlo Schaerf, (eds), *The Arms Race in the 1980s*, Macmillan, London, 1982, pp.252-72.

2   Lauterpacht's *Oppenheim* defines demilitarization thus;

> ...the agreement of two or more States by treaty not to fortify, or station troops upon, a particular zone of territory; the purpose being to prevent war by removing the opportunities of conflict...

L. Oppenheim, *International Law: A Treatise. Vol.II:Disputes, War and Neutrality*, H.Lauterpacht (ed), Longmans, London, 7th edn, 1955, p.244, note 1. It is arguable that treaties establishing demilitarized zones create an objective regime binding upon third states and are therefore an exception to the principle *pacta tertiis nec nocent nec prosunt*. See the *Aaland Islands Dispute*, League of

Nations Official Journal, 1920, Special Supplement, No.3,3. See also D.W. Greig, *International Law,* Butterworths, London, 2nd edn, 1976, p.15.

3   Athanassios Platias and R.J. Rydell, 'International Security Regimes: the Case of a Balkan Nuclear-free Zone', in Carlton and Schaerf, op. cit., pp. 273-98 at p. 281.

4   Negative security assurances are guarantees given by extra-NWFZ NWSs that they will not use nuclear weapons against states constituting an NWFZ. For a definition of this term and its corollary, positive security assurances see Platias and Rydell, op. cit., p.292. The only state to have issued negative security assurances is China. The USSR, the UK, the US and France have issued a variety of conditional negative security assurances. Ibid.

5   Op. cit., note 3, p.279.

6   Ibid. The texts of the Gromyko proposal and the Rapacki Plan can be found in Trevor Dupuy and Gay Hammerman, *A Documentary History of Arms Control and Disarmament,* T.N. Dupuy Associates, Dunn Loring, Virginia in association with R.R. Bowker, New York, 1973, pp. 409-12 (Gromyko proposal) and pp. 436-8 (Rapacki Plan). On these proposals see also G.Delcoigne, 'An overview of nuclear-weapon-free-zones', in *International Atomic Energy Agency Bulletin,* vol.24, no. 2, June 1982, pp. 50-5 at pp. 50-1; Alastair Buchan and Philip Windsor, *Arms and Stability in Europe,* Chatto and Windus, London, 1963, pp. 46-9; Georges Fischer, *The Non-Proliferation of Nuclear Weapons,* European Publications, London, 1971, p. 198.

7   See note 53 below and the accompanying text.

8   Platias and Rydell, op. cit., p. 279.

9   Ibid., p. 280.

10   Ernest Haas, 'Why Collaborate? Issue Linkage and International Regimes', *World Politics* vol. XXXII, 1979-80, pp.357-405.

11   Platias and Rydell, op. cit., p. 279.

12   Calderon, op. cit., p.255.

13   For a definition of the terms 'horizontal' and 'vertical' proliferation, see William Epstein, 'Nuclear-Free Zones', *Scientific American,* vol. 233, no.5, November 1975 pp. 25-35 at p. 27.

14   Calderon, op.cit., p. 255.

15   Treaty on the Non-proliferation of Nuclear Weapons 1968, 729 *UNTS* 161; *UKTS* 88 (1970); 7 *ILM* 809.

16   United Nations Conference of the Committee on Disarmament, *Comprehensive Study of the Question of Nuclear Weapons free Zones in all its Aspects,* UN, New York 1976. See also *Yearbook of the United Nations*, vol. 29, 1975, pp. 8-13.

17   Op. cit., note 3, p. 294.

18   Op. cit., note 4, p. 292.

19   *SIPRI Yearbook 1976,* MIT Press, Cambridge, Mass, and London, and Almquist and Wiksell, Stockholm, 1976, p. 306.

20   See note 6 above.

21   Ibid.

22   Ibid.

23   For a discussion of these various proposals see *SIPRI Yearbook 1975* pp. 438-44. For more recent calls for the creation of NWFZs in these areas, see *Yearbook of the United Nations,* Vol. 35, 1981, pp. 44-56.

24   See note 16 above.

25   *Yearbook of the United Nations,* vol. 29, 1975, pp. 8-13 at p. 8.

26   Ibid.

27   Ibid.

28   Ibid.

29   Ibid., p. 9.
30   Ibid. For a critique of the issues of territorial application and safety zones see *SIPRI Yearbook 1976*, pp. 299-300.
31   *Yearbook of the United Nations*, p. 9.
32   Ibid., p. 10.
33   Ibid.
34   Ibid.
35   Ibid.
36   Ibid.
37   Ibid.
38   Calderon, op. cit., p. 254.
39   Ibid.
40   See O.Y. Asamoah, *The Legal Significance of the Declarations of the General Assembly of the United Nations,* Martinus Nijhoff, The Hague, 1966.
41   See note 4.
42   See Bin Cheng, 'United Nations Resolutions on Outer Space: "Instant" International Customary Law?', *Indian Journal of International Law (IJIL)* vol. 5, 1965 p. 23.
43   See note 15.
44   For a discussion of this point see *SIPRI Yearbook 1976*, pp. 299-301.
45   *Yearbook of the United Nations,* vol. 21, 1967, pp. 13-18.
46   Ibid., p.15.
47   Ibid. For an extensive discussion of the territorial application of the Treaty of Tlatelolco see below.
48   See further notes 68-92 below and the accompanying text.
49   402 *UNTS* 71; *UKTS* 97 (1961).
50   The Treaty has a limited duration of 30 years (Article XII) and therefore does not fulfil one of the principles elaborated by the CCD in its 1975 report as a necessary constituent of an NWFZ, that is, the statute of prohibition ought to subsist for an unlimited duration. See above. On the question of the creation of a dispositive regime by treaty see note 2.
51   *United Kingdom Treaty Series (UKTS)* 10 (1968), Cmnd,3519; *United Nations Treaty Series (UNTS),* Vol.610, p.205. The Treaty entered into force 10 October 1967.
52   J.E.S. Fawcett, *International Law and the Uses of Outer Space* (1968), at p. 185. On the status of UN General Assembly Resolutions see Asamoah, *The Legal Significance of the Declarations of the General Assembly of the United Nations* (1966); Cheng, op.cit., Johnson, 'The Effect of Resolutions of the General Assembly of the United Nations', *British Yearbook of International Law,* Vol. 32, 1955-56, p. 97.
53   On the Tlatelolco Treaty, see H.Gros Espiell, 'The Non-Proliferation of Nuclear Weapons in Latin America', *International Atomic Energy Agency (IAEA) Bulletin,* Vol. 22, 1980, no. 3/4, pp.81-6; J.R.Martinez Cobo, 'The Nuclear-Weapon-Free Zone in Latin America', *IAEA Bulletin* Vol.24, 1982, no.2, pp. 56-8; G. Descoigne, 'An Overview of Nuclear-Weapon-Free Zones', *IAEA Bulletin,* Vol.24, 1982, no.2, pp. 50-5; J.R. Martinez Cobo, 'The Tlatelolco Treaty: An Update', *IAEA Bulletin,* Vol.26, 1984, no.3, pp. 25-30; Calderon, op.cit.,
54   Members of this group included the Mexican diplomat Ambassador Alfonso Garcia Robles (who played a leading role in promoting the Treaty), José Sette Cámara, later the Brazilian Judge at the International Court of Justice, Carlos María Velázquez, the Uruguayan Ambassador, and Licentiate Leopoldo Benites Vinueza of Ecuador, who became the first General Secretary of OPNANOL, per

Cobo, op.cit., p.56. For the text of the Treaty see: 634 *United Nations Treaty Series (UNTS)* 326; *United Kingdom Treaty Series (UKTS)* 54 (1970), Cmnd.4409; 22 *United States Treaty Series (UST)* 762; 1967 *UN Juridical Yearbook* 272; *International Legal Materials* Vol. 6, p. 521.

55 For a list of signature and ratification dates, see Martinez Cobo, op.cit., (1984), p. 28. Note that all but Brazil, Chile and Surinam made an Article 28(2) declaration.

56 Article 25 (2) reads:

> The General Conference shall not take any decision regarding the admission of a political entity part or all of whose territory is the subject, prior to the date when this Treaty is opened for signature, of a dispute or claim between an extra-colonial country and one or more Latin American States, so long as the dispute has not been settled by peaceful means.

See also, Martinez Cobo, *IAEA Bulletin* 1984, at p. 26.

57 For text of Protocol I, see *UKTS* 54 (1970), Cmnd.4409; *TIAS* 1047; 6 *ILM* 533. Parties: UK (signature: 20 December 1967; ratification: 11 December 1969); Netherlands (signature: 15 March 1977; ratification: 20 July 1981); US (signature: 26 May 1977; ratification: 23 November 1981). In force 11 December 1969. France signed 2 March 1979, but has yet to ratify.

58 Martinez Cobo, op. cit., p.27.

59 *American Journal of International Law (AJIL)*, Vol. 72, 1978, p. 225.

60 For text of Protocol II, see 634 *UNTS* 364; *UKTS* 54 (1970), Cmnd.4409; 22 *USTS* 754; *TIAS* 7137; 6 *ILM* 534, in force 11 December 1969. Parties: China (signature 21 August 1973; ratification 12 June 1974); US (signature 1 April 1968; ratification: 12 May 1971); France (signature: 18 July 1973; ratification: 22 March 1974); UK (signature: 20 December 1967; ratification: 11 December 1969); USSR (signature: 18 May 1978; ratification: 8 January 1979).

61 'Transit' is defined as the passage of nuclear weapons aboard ships and aircraft of states outside the Zone, as opposed to 'transport' which is carriage by ships or aircraft of states within the Zone. Only Mexico and Panama have specifically forbidden the transit of nuclear weapons through their territory. Brazil has expressly legalized the passage of nuclear powered ships through its territorial waters. Of the nuclear weapon States, the UK, US and France claim the right of transit of nuclear weapons through the zone, whereas China and the USSR have declared such transit incompatible with the principles of the NWFZ. See Calderon, op.cit., p. 263.

62 Notably the UK and US.

63 Article 3, 1982 Law of the Sea Convention (LOSC).

64 Article 33, LOSC.

65 Article 57, LOSC.

66 For an extremely useful review of the evolution of South American Practice in the Law of the Sea, see F. Parkinson in W.E. Butler (ed.), *The Law of the Sea and International Shipping, Anglo-Soviet Post UNCLOS Perspectives,* Oceana, Dobbs Ferry, 1985, p.139.

67 Martinez Cobo, op.cit., 1984 p. 27. Also of interest is the US State Department Memorandum, The Right of the US to Transport Nuclear Weapons in and through Territories within the zone of application of the Tlatelolco Treaty'. *Digest of US Practice in International Law,* 1979, p.1614.

68 For text of Treaty see *International Journal of Estuarine and Coastal Law (IJECL),* Vol.1, 1986, pp. 223-31; *ILM,* Vol. 24, 1985, p.1440. For detailed comment on the background to, and content of, the Treaty, as well as its initial reception see W.M. Sutherland, 'The South Pacific Nuclear Free Zone Treaty',

IJECL, Vol.1, 1986, pp. 218-23 and G. Fry, 'Towards a South Pacific Nuclear Free Zone', *Bulletin of the Atomic Scientists,* June/July 1985, pp. 16-20.

69   See *Nuclear Test Cases* (Australia *v* France; New Zealand *v* France) *ICJ Rep.*

70   See Sutherland, op.cit., p. 218. He notes e.g. the recent fishery access agreement between Kiribati and the USSR. Note also that the *Rainbow Warrior* affair, in which members of the French Secret Service sank the Greenpeace ship in Auckland Harbour in an apparent attempt to forestall its protests at French nuclear tests in the Pacific, occurred after the Treaty was signed, but indicates the strength of feelings on both sides. France has now apologized to New Zealand and paid compensation, in return for an undertaking that the service personnel involved could serve a reduced sentence in an island prison in French Polynesia.

71   Fry, op.cit., p. 16.

72   Sutherland, op.cit., p.219.

73   Stationing is prohibited by Article 5, testing by Article 6.

74   Article 6(b).

75   Sutherland, op.cit., p.220.

76   Significantly the scope of the zone excludes the US Micronesian territories where the US has important nuclear installations, see Fry, op.cit., p. 20.

77   Sutherland, op.cit., p. 222.

78   See above.

79   See above notes 70 and 76. Fry points out the 'Kwajalein Atoll in the Marshall Islands provides a permanent missile-testing facility for the US; Guam provides a strategic bomber base at Andersen Airfield and a stockpiling site for nuclear weapons; and Kwajalein and Guam have weapons-related communication and surveillance facilities. There are also contingency plans to open bases for nuclear-armed ships and planes on Babelthuap in Palau, and on Tinian and Saipan in the Northern Marianna Islands'. op.cit., p. 20.

80   Sutherland, op.cit., p. 220. Notable criticism has come from Mr. Walter Lini, Prime Minister of Vanuatu.

81   Article 9(1).

82   Article 9(2).

83   Article 9(3) and Annex 2(4).

84   The Consultative Committee procedure is specifically without prejudice to the right of parties to consult among themselves by any other means, Article 10.

85   Article 10.

86   Annex 2(1).

87   Annex 2(2-4).

88   Annex 4(4).

89   Annex 4(6).

90   Annex 4(8-9).

91   Support for this position under customary international law can be found in the *Tacna-Arica Arbitration* (Chile *v* Peru), *Reports of International Arbitral Awards (RIAA),* Vol.2, 1925, p.921 (Arbitrator: President Coolidge, USA). See now Vienna Convention on the Law of Treaties, Article 60.

92   Sutherland, op.cit., p. 221: the Australian agreement with the IAEA under Article 3(1) of the NPT came into effect 10 July 1974, a similar agreement by New Zealand came into effect 29 February 1972. Other Forum Members party to the NPT are Fiji, Nauru, Papua New Guinea, Samoa, Tonga and Tuvalu.

93   See for example the ANZUS Treaty discussed below.

94   See discussion of the right of innocent passage, below.

95   Discussed in D.P. O'Connell, *The International Law of the Sea,* 2 Vols. Oxford University Press, Oxford, 1982, in Vol I, p.282.

96   Ibid., p.274.

97 Ibid., p.282.
98 Ibid., p.289.
99 Ibid., p.291. A number of states (including Czechoslovakia, Hungary, Romania and the USSR) entered declarations accompanying their ratification of the 1958 Convention, claiming the right to require prior authorization for the passage of foreign warships, see further R.R. Churchill and A.V. Lowe, *The Law of the Sea*, Manchester University Press, 1983 at p. 70, who report that low-level contacts between naval attachés and local naval officers on an informal basis are used in order to satisfy prior notice requirements without accepting the legal obligation to do so. Not only the Soviet bloc countries take this line, see e.g. statement by Malaysian government in 1969: 'It is an aspect of international practice that all naval vessels entering the territorial waters of another country would initially request the latter's permission.' O'Connell, op.cit., Vol. I, p.297.
100 Article 25(3) LOSC uses essentially the same terminology, although it forbids discrimination 'in form or in fact among foreign ships'.
101 Article 23 LOSC. Also note that Article 22(2) permits coastal states to require 'tankers, nuclear-powered ships and ships carrying nuclear or other inherently dangerous or noxious substances or materials' to confine their innocent passage to designated sea lanes and traffic regulation schemes.
102 1974, International Convention on Safety of Life at Sea, *UKTS* 46 (1980). 1978 Protocol, *UKTS* 40 (1981).
103 UN Legislative Series ST/LEG/B/16, p.45. This allows nuclear ships 'exceptionally' to enter ports and territorial waters subject to conditions and guarantees. According to R.W. Smith, *Exclusive Economic Zone Claims*, Martinus Nijhoff, Dordrecht, 1986, p. 10, the laws of two states (Egypt and North Korea) specifically require nuclear powered ships or ships carrying nuclear weapons to obtain permission before entering territorial waters, while the laws of three states (Djibouti, Pakistan and Yemen (Aden))specifically require such vessels to give prior notification of their intention to enter territorial waters.
104 For a list of treaties regulating the use of territorial and internal waters and providing indemnities, etc., see *New Directions in the Law of the Sea* (ed. R.R. Churchill, *et al*), Vol. II pp. 792-3. Treaties listed include those with: Greece, FRG, Netherlands, Norway, Belgium, Ireland, UK (also re Hong Kong), Denmark, Sweden, Spain, Portugal, Italy, Yugoslavia and China.
105 Article 23, 1958 Territorial Sea and Contiguous Zone Convention uses virtually the same terminology.
106 Churchill and Lowe, op.cit., p. 64.
107 Ibid.
108 Churchill and Lowe suggest that since 1930 state practice and that of international tribunals has followed the Hague compromise formula, for details, see ibid., p.65.
109 (Great Britain *v* Albania) *ICJ Reports* 1949, p.1.
110 Churchill and Lowe, op.cit., p.67.
111 Government Announcement of April, 1968. See further below.
112 See W.M. Sutherland, op.cit., p.220, who cites the opposition of Vanuatu *inter alia* to Article 2(2) of the SPNFZT. See also Smith, op.cit., No.103.
113 Article 2(2), SPNFZT.
114 For a useful discussion of the dispute settlement procedures of the LOSC see Churchill and Lowe, op.cit., pp.291-301, and J. Merrills, *International Dispute Settlement*, Sweet and Maxwell, London, 1985.
115 *Aramco* v *Saudi Arabia* (1958) 27 *International Law Reports* 117, where the Arbitrator said 'According to a great principle of public international law, the ports of every State must be open to foreign merchant vessels and can only be

closed when the vital interests of the State so require'. Churchill and Lowe point out that this issue was never argued before the tribunal, and that the conclusion is not supported by the authorities cited, op.cit., p.47. O'Connell takes the same view, op.cit., Vol I, p.848. See also A.V. Lowe, 'The right of entry into maritime ports in international law'. *San Diego Law Review,* Vol.14, 1977, pp.597-622.

116   J.C. Woodliffe, 'Port Visits by Nuclear Armed Naval Vessels: Recent State Practice', *International and Comparative Law Quarterly,* Vol. 35, 1986, pp. 730-736. He cites UN Legislative Series ST/LEG/B/15, 16, 18 and 19, as well as Oppenheim, *International Law* 5th edn.1955) p.853; H.A. Smith, *Law and Custom of the Sea* (3rd edn.1959) p. 37; McDougal and Burke, *The Public Order of the Oceans,* 1962, pp. 100, 114; Rousseau, *Droit International Public* IV 1980, para.279.

117   Ibid.

118   O'Connell, op.cit., Vol.I.p.848.

119   Article IV permits the use by US forces of facilities and areas in Japan.

120   See I. Baruma, 'We won't tell you about our nuclear weapons if you don't ask', *Far Eastern Economic Review,* 11 July 1985, p.51.

121   Ibid.

122   In 1974 US Rear Admiral Gene R.La Roque told a Congressonal subcommittee that in his experience vessels capable of carrying nuclear weapons usually did so, even when visiting ports in countries such as Japan. In response to a request from Japan for clarification, the US government explained this was the admiral's private opinion, not representative of the Administration's views. A similar incident occurred in 1981, when Edwin O. Reishauer, the former US Ambassador to Japan, said that US vessels carrying nuclear weapons regularly visited Japan without prior consultation, because of a verbal agreement that consultation was only necessary if nuclear weapons were to be unloaded and stored on Japanese soil. This too was denied by the US government. See further, I Baruma, ibid. Admiral La Roque has used these arguments to support current New Zealand Policy, see the *Guardian,* 8 November 1985.

123   From a speech given in Los Angeles, California, February 26, 1985, quoted Fry, op.cit., p.17.

124   *AJIL* Suppl., Vol.46, 1952, p.93. See also Starke, *The ANZUS Treaty Alliance,* 1965.

125   Woodliffe, op.cit.,

126   *AJIL* Suppl., Vol.43, 1949, p.1.

127   Article II, ANZUS Treaty.

128   Quoted Woodliffe, op.cit.,

129   See *Guardian,* 8 November 1985, and Woodliffe, op.cit.

130   We are grateful to the New Zealand High Commission in London for supplying us with a copy of this Bill, which at the time of writing is at the Committee stage in its progress through the New Zealand Parliament.

131   *Guardian,* 30 April 1986.

9   Nuclear Tests and International Law

Nicholas Grief

By 3l December 1985, according to available information, nearly 1570 nuclear tests had been carried out since the first test explosion at Los Alamos, New Mexico, on 16 July 1945. Over half of these had been conducted by the United States, the remainder by the Soviet Union, France, the United Kingdom, China and India. Of the 31 tests conducted in 1985, all underground, the Soviet Union was responsible for 7, the United States for 15, France for 8, and the United Kingdom for 1.[1] In spite of international pressure to halt tests,[2] the number conducted has remained high.

Some positive steps to curtail nuclear testing have been taken during the last 25 years. Most significantly, of course, the Nuclear Test Ban Treaty entered into force on 10 October 1963.[3] Known as the 'Partial Test Ban Treaty' because it does not completely prohibit the testing of nuclear weapons,[4] it was described by Soviet Premier Kruschev as 'a document of great significance' and 'a major success for all people of goodwill who for many years have been actively fighting for the discontinuance of nuclear tests, for disarmament, for peace, and international friendship.'[5] Lord Home, then United Kingdom Foreign Secretary, regarded the test ban as 'a good thing in itself not only first, because it reduces the danger of pollution in the atmosphere, but secondly because it makes the first agreement of substance which we have been able to make with the Russians for a very long time.'[6] In the Preamble to the Treaty, the three Signatories – the United Kingdom, the United States and the Soviet Union – declared their determination to continue negotiations in order to achieve the discontinuance of all test explosions of nuclear weapons for all time.[7] Negotiations have indeed been conducted, and discussions have also continued within the Conference on Disarmament[8] with a view to concluding a Comprehensive Test Ban Treaty prohibiting all nuclear test explosions. However, no such agreement has yet emerged. Verification is regarded as a major stumbling-block by the US and the UK. For the foreseeable future, therefore, it seems that the Partial Test Ban Treaty will remain the only multilateral agreement which expressly prohibits nuclear tests.[9]

The history of American and British nuclear tests

The first atomic weapons tests carried out by the United States beyond its own territorial limits took place in July 1946 on Bikini Atoll in the Marshall Islands, in the Pacific Ocean, before the Pacific Islands became a Trust territory.[10] After they had been placed under United Nations Trusteeship with the United States as the Administering Authority, the US insisted that the entire territory be declared 'strategic' under Article 82 of the UN Charter, and in December 1947 informed the UN Security Council that an area of the territory had been closed 'for security reasons' in pursuance of Article 13 of the Trusteeship Agreement.[11] Eniwetok Atoll and its territorial waters were established as a danger area for a period of one year and a zone of 30 000 square miles was declared to be dangerous to all ships, aircraft and personnel. At times of actual danger, the area was patrolled to ensure that no ships or aircraft entered it inadvertently.[12] The zone's validity was subsequently extended 'until further notice'[13] and in 1953, because of the limited size of Eniwetok, the testing area itself was extended to include Bikini Atoll, 'to accommodate the rapidly expanding program of developing and testing new and improved nuclear weapons'. The danger zone now covered an area of 50 000 square miles but was increased to 400 000 square miles in March 1954 when it became apparent that the existing zone was inadequate.[14] In May 1954, all the zones were cancelled, but Bikini and Eniwetok Atolls and their territorial waters remained closed areas.[15] In 1957, the United Kingdom established a danger area at least as extensive as the Bikini–Eniwetok area around Christmas Island, also in the Pacific Ocean.[16]

The establishment of these danger areas and the carrying out of the tests themselves provoked considerable controversy as to their compatibility with the freedom of the high seas.[17] Protests were made, particularly by the Japanese government, and questions were asked in the House of Commons in London.[18] Margolis was firmly of the opinion that the establishment by the United States of a danger zone of 400 000 square miles could not be reconciled with the freedom of the high seas, including the freedom of aviation in the air space above the high seas.[19]

He considered that such 'quarantining' of the high seas and the super-jacent air space could only be based upon a treaty provision, and since the Trusteeship Agreement did not permit the US to close the sea and air space beyond the territorial limits of the Islands in the Trust Territory, he concluded that the danger zone first established in 1947 and then progressively extended was unlawful. The fact that the purpose of the zone was entirely humanitarian was no justification for its establishment: '[t]he completely humanitarian purpose behind the establishment of such an area – that of warning ships and planes of a very real hazard to their safety – loses its force as a logical and legal justification when it is recalled that the hazard is artificially introduced'.[20] He also considered that the tests conducted by the United States constituted unlawful interference with the interests of other states in fishing the high seas; a breach of the *Trail Smelter* rule; and a violation of the UN Charter and the Trusteeship Agreement.[21]

McDougal and Schlei disagreed with Margolis, however. They argued that the US tests and the establishment of the danger zones constituted lawful measures for security:

> [t]he claim of the United States is in substance a claim to prepare for self-defense. It is not, as commonly in self-defense, a claim to respond with force to an attack....It is, however, a claim to take certain preparatory measures under conditions comparable to those traditionally held to justify measures in self-defense. It is a claim to take certain actions in contiguous zones and upon the high seas, with the minimum possible interference with others, under conditions of high necessity....The contemporary development of instruments of destruction makes it possible for a war-bent nation-state utterly to destroy an opponent and perhaps much of the world.[22]

They therefore concluded that the US claim to conduct hydrogen bomb tests, and to establish danger zones of considerable size, was 'under contemporary conditions, a reasonable assertion which contravenes no prescription or policy of the international law of the sea'.[23]

The political reality prevailing at the time of the tests certainly influenced the United Kingdom government. Following Japanese protests concerning the tests conducted in the vicinity of Christmas Island, the government stated that, 'it is impossible to consider the question of stopping nuclear tests without having regard to the wider problem of preventing war in general, including of course nuclear war'.[24] The statement continued:

> It has to be borne in mind that the mere banning of nuclear tests in

isolation would not prevent those countries who have already tested nuclear weapons from continuing to produce them. The cessation of nuclear tests must therefore be linked with the cessation of the manufacture of these weapons within a framework of a comprehensive disarmament agreement which would cover nuclear and conventional disarmament.[25]

The Japanese protests were perfectly understandable. In 1954, radiation from tests conducted by the United States within the danger zone of 50 000 square miles had caused the death of one Japanese fisherman, injury to others and the contamination of substantial quantities of fish caught by a Japanese fishing vessel. Japanese nationals on Rongelap Atoll were also injured. Neither the fishing vessel nor Rongelap Atoll had been within the danger zone declared by the United States, but because of a sudden change of wind and the miscalculation of the explosions' force, radiation from the tests had been experienced outside the zone. The government of the United States gave medical and other assistance, and also paid compensation. In respect of the Japanese nationals, the compensation for personal injuries and economic loss was expressly stated to be *ex gratia*.[26]

The British government was sympathetic towards the Japanese Fishermen's Organization which objected to its plans to conduct nuclear tests in the Pacific in 1957, but expressed the conviction that there would be no danger. The tests were to be high air bursts not involving heavy fall-out. Furthermore, extensive safety precautions had been taken: a danger area had been declared for the period 1 March until 1 August, and all shipping and aircraft had been warned to remain clear of the area during this time. The warning had been issued well in advance, and no permanently inhabited island lay within the area. In addition, weather stations, weather ships and reconnaissance aircraft would provide continuous meteorological information.[27]

The government also declared that the

temporary use of areas outside territorial waters for gunnery or bombing practice has never been considered a violation of the principles of the freedom of navigation on the high seas. The present site has been chosen because it lies far from inhabited islands and avoids as far as possible shipping and air routes. It is incidentally some four thousand miles from Japan.[28]

Owing to their distance from Japan, moreover, the waters were not considered to be traditional Japanese fishing grounds. However, the government did state that if any claim were received for damage or loss said to have been incurred as a result of the tests, it would be carefully examined, and the response would be dependent upon the facts of each case.[29] From the point of view of air traffic, leaving aside the consequences of the nuclear tests themselves, the damage caused to aviation by the establishment of danger areas above the Pacific does appear to have been slight. There were no scheduled airlines operating in the immediate vicinity of the Christmas Island area. With regard to the Bikini–Eniwetok area, an aircraft operated by an American airline flying between Guam and Wake Island three times weekly had to be rerouted to the north of the danger zone, adding some 50 miles to each flight throughout the duration of the 1954 tests.[30]

The view that international law did not prohibit the use of the high seas for the purpose of conducting nuclear tests was also expressed by the government of the United States in 1958. It declared that the high seas had long been used by the nations of the world for naval manoeuvres, weapons tests and other similar purposes, and continued: '[s]uch measures no doubt result in some inconvenience to other users of the high seas, but they are not proscribed by international law'.[31] However, it also stated that it would be prepared to consider the question of compensating Japan or Japanese nationals for substantial economic losses if evidence of such losses were officially presented.[32]

Besides the tests in the Pacific islands, between 1952 and 1957 twelve British atmospheric tests were conducted in Australia, on the Montebello Islands, off the north-west of Australia, and at Maralinga and Emu Plains in South Australia.[33] In July 1984, the Australian government recommended the establishment of a Royal Commission under Mr. Justice McClelland, to conduct an inquiry into those tests.[34] The Commission examined the measures that had been taken for protection against the effects of radiation, fall-out and waste, as well as those of the 'minor trials' simulating the accidental detonation of plutonium weapons, which caused plutonium to be spread over a considerable expanse of land.[35] During the course of the Inquiry, it emerged that scientists had failed to predict the path of radioactive fall-out, so that clouds of fall-out swept over the water supply of the most densely populated areas of Australia.[36] The Commission was critical of the way in which the tests had been conducted and stated that cancers had probably been caused among the Australian people. It was also critical of the fact that, despite attempts to clean up the test sites, Maralinga was still heavily contaminated and its Aboriginal owners were denied access.[37]

The Commission's main recommendations were, *inter alia*, that the British government should bear the total cost of decontaminating the Maralinga site in order to render it 'fit for unrestricted habitation by the tradional Aboriginal owners as soon as possible', and also the Emu and Montebello sites; that servicemen and civilians should be compensated by the Australian government for any damage to their health, the onus of proof being on the government in all cases; that Aboriginal land-owners should be compensated by the Australian government for loss of the use of their lands and for consequent deprivation and social disruption; and that a national register be compiled of test veterans and others possibly exposed to radiation.[38]

Without officially endorsing the findings of the Commission, the Australian government sought at least partial British funding for the decontamination still required. However, the British government denied moral or legal responsibility, principally on the grounds that the tests had been carried out with the permission of the Australian Prime Minister, and that two previous Australian governments had absolved the United Kingdom from any further liability in agreements concluded after decontamination work undertaken in 1967 and 1979.[39]

The legality of nuclear tests on and above the high seas: discussion at the Geneva Conference on the Law of the Sea, 1958

The final draft articles on the law of the sea submitted to the Geneva Conference by the International Law Commission contained no reference to the use of the high seas or the superjacent airspace for the purpose of conducting nuclear tests. Draft Article 27 merely provided that the high seas were not subject to the sovereignty of any state, and gave an inexhaustive list of freedoms comprised by the freedom of the high seas.[40] In its commentary to the draft article, the Commission acknowledged the absence of any express pronouncement concerning freedom to conduct nuclear tests, but drew attention to the general principle that, on the high seas, '[s]tates are bound to refrain from any acts which might adversely affect the use of the high seas by nationals of other States'.[41] The Commission also referred to Draft Article 48, paragraphs 2 and 3 of which provided for every state to draw up regulations to prevent pollution of the seas from the dumping of radioactive waste, and to cooperate in the drawing-up of regulations designed to prevent pollution of the seas or superjacent airspace through experiments with radioactive materials or other harmful agents.[42] The Commission concluded by stating that it did not want to prejudge the findings of the Scientific Committee set up under a General Assembly resolution to study the effects of atomic radiation.[43]

At the Geneva Conference itself, the question of nuclear testing was discussed more thoroughly, first within the Second Committee and subsequently at the Plenary Meetings of the Conference. Within the Second Committee, which was concerned with the general regime of the high seas, there were initially three draft measures relating to nuclear tests. These included a draft resolution submitted by India and amended by Ceylon, which was subsequently adopted by a substantial majority.[44] The essence of the draft resolution was a decision to refer the question of nuclear tests on the high seas to the United Nations General Assembly 'for appropriate action'. However, it also recognized a serious and genuine apprehension on the part of many States that nuclear explosions constituted an infringement of the freedom of the high seas.[45]

Besides adopting the draft resolution, the Second Committee introduced changes to Draft Article 48. As a result of these changes, draft paragraphs 2 and 3 were replaced by a draft resolution,[46] and an additional Draft Article was inserted, providing, *inter alia,* for all states to cooperate with the competent international organizations in taking measures for the prevention of pollution of the high seas or airspace above, resulting from any activities with radioactive materials or other harmful agents.[47]

Further, more illuminating discussion was to follow at the Plenary Meetings of the Conference, at which a strong tendency to condemn nuclear testing was apparent. In particular, attention was focused upon a proposal submitted jointly by Czechoslovakia, Poland, Yugoslavia and the Soviet Union to add a new Article prohibiting all nuclear testing on the high seas.[48] This naturally provoked considerable debate. For the United States, Mr Dean argued that to adopt an article on nuclear tests might materially jeopardize the delicate disarmament negotiations, and declared that his country was not opposed to the prohibition of nuclear tests provided that there was effective international control. He appealed for the proposal to be withdrawn, arguing that to proceed with it would endanger the work of other UN bodies, an implicit reference to the General Assembly and the Disarmament Commission, in particular.[49]

The Soviet Union's representative at the Conference, Mr Tunkin, stated his country's belief that the prohibition of nuclear testing on the high seas was a logical consequence of the freedom of the high seas. He said that the Soviet Union was quite prepared to refrain from conducting nuclear tests on the high seas. The Conference was bound to include in the Convention a provision concerning nuclear tests, he argued, and it was fallacious to argue that the question should be left aside because it formed part of the wider problem of disarmament.[50]

Following this predictably uncompromising exchange between the representatives of the United States and the Soviet Union, Sir Reginald Manningham-Butler, for the United Kingdom, stated that the proper forum for discussing the question of nuclear testing was the General Assembly and its Disarmament Commission, not the Geneva Conference on the Law of the Sea. It was artificial to isolate the issue of nuclear tests on the high seas from the wider problem of disarmament in general. The British government, he said, had conducted its tests with a scrupulous regard for the interests of the users of the high seas, and scientific research had established that they had had no harmful effects on human, animal or marine life. He therefore appealed for the proposal's withdrawal. It seemed inappropriate, at a time when Heads of State were engaged in seeking to overcome problems which undermined international peace and security, for the Conference to encroach upon the work and competence of the General Assembly.[51]

The Czechoslovakian representative, Mr Zourek, supported the proposal because he considered that nuclear tests were the most dangerous threat to the freedom of the high seas since that principle had been generally recognized. He had no doubt that such tests constituted a flagrant violation of the freedom of the seas, since they closed vast areas to navigation and fishing and would endanger people and marine resources alike. Nuclear tests on the high seas were therefore already contrary to existing international law.[52]

The Indian representative agreed with the substance of the proposal being discussed. His government's view was that all nuclear tests, whether on land or at sea, were contrary to humanitarian principles and international law. Moreover, nuclear tests at sea were also a serious infringement of the freedom of the high seas. However, he believed that the introduction of the proposal at this stage would complicate the discussion of other serious issues and he therefore asked that the Indian draft resolution be voted upon first.[53]

According to the Polish representative, nuclear tests on the high seas, and the establishment of prohibited zones, were a violation of the freedom of the seas and a threat to human and marine life. He commended the proposal as a positive contribution to the codification of international law.[54] The Yugoslavian representative said that his government was opposed to all nuclear tests, whether on land or at sea. He did not consider that adopting the proposal would be incompatible with the work of the Disarmament Commission.[55] The representative of the United Arab Republic expressed his government's view that nuclear tests on the high seas were already contrary to international law,[56] and the Romanian representative urged that a prohibition of nuclear testing on the high seas was essential if States really were to enjoy the freedoms of navigation and fishing.[57] However, the Ceylonese representative said that the proposal should not be voted upon in case its rejection were interpreted as an indication that the Conference had refused to ask states to refrain from conducting nuclear tests on the high seas, which were obviously a violation of international law.[58]

After the views of various governments had been expressed, the President of the Conference first put to the vote the draft resolution relating to nuclear tests, in accordance with the rules of procedure. As this was adopted without any negative votes,[59] the joint proposal to insert a new article prohibiting nuclear tests on the high seas was pursued no further.

It is significant that no one voted against the resolution. Even for those who had wanted a clear prohibition, the resolution was a definite achievement, more desirable than a rejection of the proposed prohibition, which world opinion might have misunderstood, or at least chosen to misunderstand. The fact remains, however, that the 1958 Geneva Convention on the High Seas does not clearly prohibit the testing of nuclear devices on or above the high seas. Besides declaring that the high seas are not subject to the territorial sovereignty of any State, Article 2 of the Convention merely provides that the four freedoms enumerated, 'and others which are recognized by the general principles of international law, shall be exercised by all States with reasonable regard to the interests of other States in their exercise of the freedom of the high seas'.[60] This raises the question whether nuclear testing on or above the high seas is a recognized freedom, or contrary to the freedoms of other States.[61] Significantly, however, the resolution adopted in connection with Article 2 records the serious and genuine apprehension among many states that nuclear testing infringes the freedom of the high seas. In addition, Article 25(2) of the Convention requires all states to cooperate with the competent international organizations in taking measures for the prevention of pollution of the seas or airspace above, resulting from any activities with radioactive materials.

Given the absence of a clear prohibition in the Geneva Convention, it is not surprising that after its entry into force the question of the legality of nuclear tests on and above the high seas continued to be controversial. Further Japanese protests followed in 1962, when the US Defense Department and the US Atomic Energy Commission issued a joint announcement designating as a test region an area measuring some 480 000 square miles around Christmas Island. Another joint announcement established a new testing area centred on Johnston Island, and enlarged the existing Christmas Island zone. The Johnston Island zone had a radius of 470 nautical miles at sea level and 700 nautical miles at 30 000 feet, later enlarged to 600 nautical miles at sea level and 810 nautical miles at 40 000 feet. The zone affected flights between Hawaii and Australia, and also between Hawaii and Japan. Nevertheless, the US government denied any violation of international law, asserting that the use of the high seas and the superjacent air space for military exercises of all kinds was traditional and not unreasonable.[62]

The Nuclear Test Ban Treaty, 1963[63]

The conclusion of the Partial Nuclear Test Ban Treaty represented the first step taken by the world's leading powers to restrict the testing of nuclear weapons. Article 1(1) of the Treaty requires the parties

> to prohibit, to prevent, and not to carry out any nuclear weapon test explosion, or any other nuclear explosion, at any place under its jurisdiction or control: (a) in the atmosphere; beyond its limits, including outer space; or underwater, including territorial waters or high seas; or (b) in any other environment if such explosion causes radioactive debris to be present outside the territorial limits of the State under whose jurisdiction or control such explosion is conducted.

The Treaty clearly prohibits all nuclear tests in the atmosphere, therefore. It does not ban underground tests, however, as long as radioactive debris is contained within the territorial limits of the State under whose jurisdiction or control they are conducted.

In spite of the prohibition of atmospheric tests, however, there has been speculation that certain contracting parties have violated their Treaty obligations. On 25 October 1979, the US State Department announced that signals received from a US observation satellite indicated the possibility that a low-yield atmospheric nuclear explosion had taken place on 22 September somewhere in a broad zone south and east of South Africa.[64] Although the South African Foreign Minister denied any knowledge of the alleged explosion, the US announcement gave rise to speculation that South Africa had acquired a nuclear weapons capability. A statement issued on 29 October by the Soviet news agency, TASS, named South Africa as the testing state, and categorically rejected claims by the South African media that an explosion had occurred on a Soviet nuclear submarine off the South African coast.[65] Evidence presented to Congressional committees by the CIA substantiated the allegations that a nuclear explosion had occurred,[66] and on 21 February 1980 the Canadian Broadcasting Service reported that Israel had detonated a nuclear device in the South Atlantic in September 1979, with the assistance and cooperation of South Africa.[67]

South Africa and Israel are both parties to the Nuclear Test Ban Treaty and are consequently bound by its prohibition of atmospheric nuclear tests. If the above allegations are well founded, there was a violation of the Treaty, either by South Africa alone, or possibly by South Africa and Israel. If the CBS report was correct, Israel conducted a nuclear test in violation of Article 1(1) of the Treaty, and South Africa encouraged and participated in the carrying out of a prohibited test, contrary to Article 1(2).[68]

Although the Treaty clearly prohibits states parties from conducting nuclear tests in the atmosphere, it is important to consider whether the Treaty has also generated a similar prohibition binding upon all States as a rule of customary international law. This question is not just of academic interest, for the Treaty can be denounced by a state in the exercise of its national sovereignty, 'if it decides that extraordinary events, related to the subject matter of this Treaty, have jeopardized the supreme interests of its country'.[69] Also, certain states are conspicuous by their absence from the list of contracting parties, notably China and France, both of which have the capacity to conduct nuclear tests.

There can be little doubt that the Treaty did not codify pre-existing customary international law. That it was considered necessary to conclude the Treaty is evidence that customary law did not at that time prohibit atmospheric nuclear tests. The practice of states prior to the Treaty's conclusion is significant, as is the fact that, in 1963, the British and US governments urged the French government to sign the Treaty,[70] implicit recognition that French atmospheric nuclear tests, conducted initially above the Sahara desert and later above the Pacific Ocean,[71] did not violate existing customary international law. Such recognition was also implicit in the provision allowing denunciation of the Treaty.[72] However, a customary prohibition may have emerged subsequently on the basis of the Treaty.

The process whereby a Treaty can generate a rule of customary international law was considered by the International Court of Justice in the *North Sea Continental Shelf Cases*.[73] There, the Court was asked to decide whether the 'equidistance principle' contained in Article 6(2) of the Geneva Convention on the Continental Shelf, 1958, relating to the delimitation of the continental shelf as between adjacent coastal states, had become part of customary international law. It stated that this clearly involved

> treating that Article as a norm-creating provision which has constituted the foundation of, or has generated a rule which, while only conventional or contractual in its origin, has since passed into the general corpus of international law . . . so as to have become binding even for countries which have never, and do not, become Parties to the Convention. There is no doubt that this process is a perfectly possible one [and] constitutes indeed one of the recognized methods by which new rules of customary international law may be formed. At the same time this result is not lightly to be regarded as having been attained.[74]

The Court then discussed the requirements which must be fulfilled in order to permit the conclusion that a Treaty provision has generated a rule of customary international law binding upon states independently of the Treaty itself.

First, the Treaty provision in question must be of a fundamentally norm-creating character, at least potentially. In relation to Article 6(2) of the Geneva Convention, the Court doubted whether this was so, partly because the obligation to use the equidistance method was subsidiary to the primary obligation to effect delimitation by agreement; and partly because the Convention allowed contracting parties to formulate reservations to the provision. Whilst it recognized that the faculty of making reservations did not altogether prevent the equidistance principle from being received as general law, the Court felt that it did make such a conclusion considerably more difficult to reach.[75]

Next, the Court held that regard must be had to the degree of participation in the Treaty in question: 'it might be that, even without the passage of any considerable period of time, a very widespread and representative participation in the convention might suffice of itself, provided it included that of States whose interests were specially affected'.[76] The Court then considered whether, regardless of the extent of formal participation in the Convention, state practice concerning continental shelf delimitation had, since the conclusion of the Convention, reflected the equidistance principle contained within it:

> [a]lthough the passage of only a short period of time is not necessarily, or of itself, a bar to the formation of a new rule of customary international law on the basis of what was originally a purely conventional rule, an indispensable requirement would be that within the period in question, short though it might be, State practice, including that of States whose interests are specially affected should have been both extensive and virtually uniform in the sense of the provision invoked – and should moreover have occurred in such a way as to show a general recognition that a rule of law or legal obligation is involved.[77]

The Court thus stressed the need for both a settled practice and *opinio juris*.

The above criteria must be applied to the Nuclear Test Ban Treaty. In this context it is appropriate to refer to the *Nuclear Tests Cases*[78] brought by Australia and New Zealand against France, which is not a Party to the Nuclear Test Ban Treaty. The cases concerned the legality of French nuclear tests in the atmosphere above the South Pacific Ocean.[79] France had been conducting nuclear tests on Mururoa Atoll since 1966, and with a view to excluding shipping and aircraft from the test area, the French government had designated *prohibited zones* for aircraft and *dangerous zones* for aircraft and shipping.[80] Shortly before the commencement of each series of tests, the dangerous zones were activated by *Notifications to Airmen and Mariners*. The precise extent of the dangerous zones varied considerably from one test series to another, and those relating to aircraft covered a larger area than those applicable to shipping. At their most extensive, in 1970 and 1971, the dangerous zones applicable to aircraft covered an area of approximately 1 132 000 square nautical miles.[81] Not surprisingly, therefore, one of the grounds on which the legality of the French tests was challenged by Australia and New Zealand was that they violated their freedoms of navigation and overflight on and above the high seas.[82]

The International Court of Justice thus had what appeared to be an excellent opportunity to determine the legality of such tests. However, it chose not to do so on the basis that the claims no longer had any object following statements by the French government that atmospheric testing would cease in 1974:

> [i]n announcing that the 1974 series of atmospheric tests would be the last, the French Government conveyed to the world at large..its intention effectively to terminate these tests. The objects of these statements are clear and they were addressed to the international community as a whole, and the Court holds that they constitute an undertaking possessing legal effect..[83]

The Court therefore decided that the applicants' objectives had been achieved. It concluded:' [o]nce the Court has found that a State has entered into a commitment concerning its future conduct it is not the Court's function to contemplate that it will not comply with it.'[84]

In a Separate Opinion, Judge Gros expressed the view that if the Nuclear Test Ban Treaty was not opposable to France, a non-party, there was no dispute which the applicants could submit to the Court.[85] He concluded that the Treaty was merely a bipolar statute, accepted by a large number of states but not binding upon those remaining outside it: '[n]one of the three nuclear Powers described as the "Original Parties"..has ever informed the other nuclear Powers, not Parties thereto, that this text imposed any obligation whatever upon them; on the contrary, the three Original Parties, even today, call upon the Powers not Parties to ·accede to the Treaty.'[86] Moreover, the French government had always refused to recognize the existence of a rule opposable to it.[87] Even if the existence of a customary rule could have been established, therefore, it would not have been opposable to a state which had steadfastly declined to accept it.[88]

In another Separate Opinion, Judge Pétren considered that the Application presupposed the existence of a rule of customary international law whereby states are prohibited from causing, through atmospheric nuclear tests, the deposit of radioactive fall-out on the territory of other states.[89] In order to ascertain whether such a rule existed, he felt it important to discover the attitude of states which had not yet carried out such tests:

> [i]f a State which does not possess nuclear arms refrains from carrying out the atmospheric tests which would enable it to acquire them, and if that abstention is motivated not by political or economic considerations but by a conviction that such tests are prohibited by customary international law, the attitude of that State would constitute an element in the formation of such a custom.[90]

However, the Judge considered that the necessary practice and *opinio juris* did not exist. The fact that China had recently exploded a very powerful nuclear bomb in the atmosphere was sufficient to demolish the contention that there existed at that time a rule of customary international law prohibiting such tests. The attitude and behaviour of the state with the largest population in the world could not be ignored.[91]

Judge Pétren also found it significant that the numerous states on whose territory radioactive fall-out had been deposited had not, generally speaking, protested that atmospheric nuclear tests were in violation of customary international law. The resolutions adopted by the UN General Assembly could not be regarded as equivalent to legal protests, but merely indicated a strong current of opinion in favour of proscribing such tests.[92]

In their Separate Opinions, therefore, Judges Gros and Pétren both strongly denied that the Nuclear Test Ban Treaty had, by 1973, generated a customary prohibition opposable to France. Given that it is now some fourteen years since the *Nuclear Tests Cases,* however, it is important to consider the present position. On 1 July 1986, although 115 states were parties to the Nuclear Test Ban Treaty, the list of contracting parties still excluded China and France.[93] It must therefore remain doubtful whether the degree of formal participation in the Treaty has yet reached the point when it can be regarded as sufficiently widespread and representative.[94]

Besides the extent of formal participation in the Treaty, however, it is necessary to examine the practice of states to see whether it has been 'both extensive and virtually uniform in the sense of the provision invoked' and whether it has 'occurred in such a way as to show a general recognition that a rule of law or legal obligation is involved'.[95] In accordance with the undertaking relied upon by the International Court, France has conducted no atmospheric tests since 1974. Since the spring of 1975, all French tests have been underground in French Polynesia. *Prima facie,* therefore, for the last twelve years French practice has been consistent with the Nuclear Test Ban Treaty. However, it is doubtful whether the change of practice was accompanied by the necessary *opinio juris*. The move to underground testing was explained in the following manner by the French Minister for Foreign Affairs in a speech to the UN General Assembly in September 1974: '[w]e have reached a stage in our nuclear technology that makes it possible for us to continue our programme by underground testing, and we have taken steps to do so as early as next year'.[96] In 1978, the French Foreign Ministry expanded upon that explanation: '[n]uclear or thermo-nuclear testing is therefore no longer dependent upon atmospheric conditions, and can take place throughout the year as technological requirements dictate. In the past, weather and winds had to be reckoned with, to avoid the risk of atmospheric pollution'.[97]

It seems, therefore, that the French decision to cease atmospheric testing and to continue underground was motivated, not by any sense of legal obligation, but rather by expedience and advances in technology, although the 1978 statement could suggest recognition that international law requires states to avoid causing atmospheric pollution. If Chinese practice is also considered, the conclusion that a customary prohibition has been generated on the basis of the Treaty appears to be even more doubtful. Although China has not conducted any nuclear tests in the atmosphere since 1980, the longest period without a Chinese atmospheric test,[98] it has been reported that facilities for carrying out atmospheric tests are still maintained at its test site at Lop Nor in northwest China.[99] It seems, therefore, that the virtually uniform practice and *opinio juris* required by the International Court are not yet established.

On the other hand, the first of the Court's requirements, that the provision be of a fundamentally norm-creating character, may be satisfied. The obligation to refrain from carrying out any atmospheric nuclear explosion, contained in Article I(1) of the Nuclear Test Ban Treaty, is of primary importance, and although the Treaty is silent concerning reservations, a reservation which sought to modify or exclude that obligation would not be permissible.[100] In any case, it can be argued that a provision's norm-creating character is not jeopardized by the possibility of formulating a reservation to it.[101] It is true that Article IV permits contracting parties to withdraw from the Treaty under certain conditions,[102] and some might regard this as implying that a state would always be free to conduct atmospheric nuclear tests under customary international law. However, it is submitted that Article IV does not affect the norm-creating potential of Article I(1) and cannot of itself impede the development of a customary prohibition.

The conclusion that the Nuclear Test Ban Treaty has not generated a rule of customary international law prohibiting atmospheric nuclear tests is supported by the existence of resolutions of the UN General Assembly calling upon states which are not yet parties to the Treaty to adhere to it forthwith.[103] However, at least one writer is of the opinion that the Treaty 'may itself have started, or at least acknowledged, a general rule of customary international law, dating approximately from 1963, to the effect that all atmospheric tests of nuclear weapons are illegal'.[104]

In 1967, D'Amato argued that the 'nearly universal acceptance of the Treaty indicates an international consensus of overwhelming force in favour of the principles contained therein', and suggested that the Treaty itself, and the subsequent practice under it – restraint from conducting atmospheric tests and restraint from exercising the right to withdraw from the Treaty – could be evidence of a customary rule banning atmospheric nuclear tests.[105] Whether the absence of such states as China and France from the list of contracting parties can, even now, be disregarded is doubtful, however. Furthermore, it is submitted that undue significance should not be attached to the restraint shown by states parties to the Treaty. The fact that none has exercised its right of withdrawal is probably due to the absence of any need to withdraw, given that underground testing is possible. This may well also explain why, with the possible exceptions of South Africa and Israel,[106] parties have honoured their obligations under the Treaty. In any case, the restraint shown concerning atmospheric testing could simply be due to a readiness to comply with Treaty obligations, without it implying recognition that the prohibition is also part of customary international law. Even if a customary prohibition had been generated by the Treaty, moreover, it would not be binding upon states which had consistently and unequivocally manifested a refusal to accept the rule.[107]

Although a customary prohibition does not appear to have been generated by the Nuclear Test Ban Treaty, however, it is submitted that there are other reasons why atmospheric nuclear testing, and the establishment of danger zones for that purpose on and above the high seas, are contrary to international law. It is important that a distinction be drawn between the use of the high seas and superjacent airspace for firing practice, rocket tests or naval manoeuvres on the one hand, and nuclear tests on the other. These activities are qualitatively different and the danger area for nuclear experiments is necessarily more extensive, in terms of both area and time.[108] As Margolis has argued, the humanitarian purpose behind the establishment of such a zone is no justification given that the danger, which is considerably greater than that created by the other activities mentioned, is artificially introduced.[109] Also, whereas ordinary firing practice can be stopped immediately without damage to an aircraft or vessel which enters a danger zone by mistake, this is not possible in the case of nuclear testing.[110] The claim to exercise temporary exclusive competence on or above the high seas for the purpose of conducting nuclear tests is not legitimate, therefore, and cannot be reconciled with the freedom of the high seas proclaimed by Article 2 of the Geneva Convention on the High Seas, 1958.[111]

The establishment of danger zones in the airspace of the high seas must also be considered in the light of the Chicago Convention on International Civil Aviation, 1944.[112] Although the Convention gives each Contracting State the right, for certain purposes, to prohibit or restrict air traffic over some areas of its territory, there are no provisions giving States such rights over the high seas. Annex 2, which prescribes flight rules to be observed by aircraft, contains a provision that 'aircraft shall not be flown over areas where there are flight restrictions, the particulars of which have been duly published, except in accordance with the conditions of the restriction or by permission of the appropriate authority of the State imposing the restriction'.[113] According to the definitions contained in Chapter 1 of the Annex, a prohibited or restricted area means 'a specified area within the land areas of a State or territorial waters adjacent thereto'. As Pépin has concluded, therefore, Annex 2 contains no indirect recognition of a right to establish prohibited or restricted areas over the high seas.[114]

Above the Pacific Ocean, however, the governments of the United States and the United Kingdom did not establish prohibited or restricted areas, but merely 'danger areas', the extent of which was announced in *Notices to Airmen*.[115] There is no reference to danger areas in the Chicago Convention, although the concept was introduced into International Civil Aviation Organization regulations by the Council of ICAO, which gave the following definition of the term in Chapter 1 of Annex 2: '[a] specified area within or over which there may exist activities constituting a potential danger to aircraft flying over it'. Since this definition does not specify that danger areas must be situated within the limits of a state's land or sea territory, it appears that states are entitled to establish them over the high seas. However, in accordance with the principle of the freedom of aviation in the airspace of the high seas, there is no provision in Annex 2 which makes it obligatory for foreign aircraft to respect these areas.[116]

The use of the high seas for nuclear testing would also appear to be inconsistent with Article 25(2) of the Geneva Convention on the High Seas, which requires states to cooperate with the competent international organizations in taking measures for the prevention of pollution of the seas or airspace above, resulting from any activities with radioactive materials. It is true that the freedom of scientific research is guaranteed by Article 87(1)(f) of the UN Convention on the Law of the Sea 1982,[117] but only for peaceful purposes.[118] Even if this means 'non-aggressive' rather than 'non-military' purposes,[119] and even if nuclear testing can be regarded as 'scientific research', the freedom is still subject, *inter alia*, to the requirement that 'marine scientific research shall not unjustifiably interfere with other legitimate uses of the sea compatible with this Convention'.[120] Besides presupposing that the research is itself a legitimate use of the high seas, which is doubtful as far as nuclear testing is concerned, this provision excludes any activity which constitutes an unjustifiable interference with other legitimate uses of the high seas. Because of the nature of nuclear testing and the extent of the danger zones required, it is submitted that there would indeed be unjustifiable interference with the established freedoms of navigation, overflight and fishing.

Furthermore, Part XII of the 1982 Convention is specifically concerned with the protection and preservation of the marine environment. According to Article 192, states have a general obligation to protect and preserve that environment, and it is clear that this includes minimizing to the fullest possible extent the release of harmful or noxious substances through the atmosphere.[121] Moreover, Article 194(2) provides that

> [s]tates shall take all measures necessary to ensure that activities under their jurisdiction or control are so conducted as not to cause damage by pollution to other States and their environment, and that pollution arising from incidents or activities under their jurisdiction or control does not spread beyond the areas where they exercise sovereign rights in accordance with this Convention.

This provision reflects Principle 21 of the Stockholm Declaration on the Human Environment, 1972,[122] according to which states have the responsibility to ensure that activities within their jurisdiction or control do not cause damage to the environment of other states or of areas beyond the limits of national jurisdiction.[123] The conduct of nuclear tests on or above the high seas could well violate this Principle, which is acknowledged to be a rule of customary international law.[124]

The same rule is equally applicable in respect of nuclear tests conducted in the atmosphere above national territory. Irrespective of actual damage being caused, moreover, it is submitted that the mere intrusion of intrinsically harmful radioactive particles into the territory of another state would violate the territorial integrity of that state.[125] It might also be argued that the involuntary receipt of such particles would violate the receiving state's decisional sovereignty in that its capacity to determine for itself what level of radioactivity to permit within its territory would be compromised.[126]

Most fundamentally, however, it would appear that atmospheric nuclear testing undermines the basic human right, the right to life.[127] According to a UN study published in 1981,[128] 'all past atmospheric tests could be equivalent to about 150 000 premature deaths world-wide, and approximately 90 per cent of these could be expected to occur in the Northern Hemisphere'.[129]

The threat to life must be taken seriously. A large number of US servicemen and civilians who took part in the Pacific tests did develop cancers and other illnesses which they claimed to have resulted from exposure to radiation,[130] and in 1979 the US authorities acknowledged that a cancer risk existed.[131] In May 1984, moreover, a federal district court judge in Salt Lake City ruled that ten victims of cancer had contracted the disease because of exposure to radioactive fall-out from atmospheric nuclear tests in the 1950s. This was the first time that a federal court had recognized a clear link between atmospheric nuclear testing and cancer.[132] In March 1985, a former member of the Royal Air Force who had been stationed on Christmas Island shortly after the 1957/58 test series became the first British ex-serviceman to win Ministry of Defence recognition of a radiation-induced injury, when he was awarded compensation for blindness.[133]

Furthermore, it is submitted that nuclear explosions in the atmosphere do not become legitimate because the state conducting them considers them to be essential to its security interests. States do not have the right to pursue their security needs in a manner which endangers the health and welfare of other people.[134] Indeed, according to the International Law Commission's Draft Articles on state responsibility, a serious breach of an international obligation for the safeguarding and preservation of the human environment, such as those prohibiting massive pollution of the atmosphere or of the seas, may constitute an international crime.[135]

Underground nuclear tests

It has already been shown that the Nuclear Test Ban Treaty does not prohibit underground tests as long as they do not cause radioactive debris to be present outside the territorial limits of the state under whose jurisdiction or control the explosion is conducted.[136] However, this is stated to be without prejudice to the conclusion of a treaty resulting in the permanent banning of all nuclear test explosions.[137] Steps have been taken towards that goal but so far no comprehensive test ban treaty has been forthcoming, although in July 1974 the United States and the Soviet Union did conclude a Treaty on the Limitation of Underground Nuclear Tests.[138] According to this Treaty, which has not been ratified by the US, each party undertakes to prohibit, prevent, and not to carry out any underground nuclear weapon test having a yield exceeding 150 kilotons at any place under its jurisdiction or control.[139] Furthermore, each party is required to limit the number of its underground tests to a minimum.[140] The Protocol to the Treaty provides for the exchange of certain data on the basis of reciprocity for the purpose of verifying compliance with the Treaty.[141]

The yields of the US and Soviet tests carried out since 1976 appear to have been consistent with the 1974 Treaty's limit of 150 kilotons.[142] In accordance with the Treaty, that threshold has also been observed in the British underground tests, carried out at the Nevada test site in the United States. The largest French underground test is reported to have had a yield of 150 kilotons, and the Chinese tests conducted in 1984 had yields of about 100 kilotons.[143]

The 1974 Limitation Treaty does not apply to underground nuclear explosions carried out for peaceful purposes, however. These are governed by another bilateral Treaty concluded by the US and the USSR in May 1976.[144] Like the 1974 'Threshold' Treaty, this also prohibits individual explosions having a yield exceeding 150 kilotons.[145] The Protocol to the 1976 Treaty establishes the minimum distance underground at which explosions may be conducted and also requires the party intending to carry out an explosion to provide the other party with certain information in advance.[146]

Although underground nuclear testing is less hazardous than atmospheric testing, the danger to life must not be underestimated. If an underground test takes place relatively close to the surface, the explosion might break through the surface and release radioactivity into the atmosphere. During the first years of underground testing, there were a few instances of 'venting' on such a scale that it could be detected outside the borders of the country where the test was conducted.[147] If this occurred today, it would constitute a violation of the Nuclear Test Ban Treaty by contracting parties and possibly of Principle 21 of the Stockholm Declaration, which represents customary international law.[148] The territorial integrity and decisional sovereignty of other states might also be violated.[149] It is reported that underground test explosions are now contained to a much higher degree, however, although any leak would naturally increase the total radioactive contamination of the biosphere.[150]

The French underground tests conducted in French Polynesia have attracted particular criticism from neighbouring countries and environmentalists alleging that they have caused serious damage to the environment and health of the Polynesian people. In response to this criticism, the French government invited an inspection team to visit the Mururoa test site. Following the visit in autumn 1983, the team of experts concluded, *inter alia,* that there was no geological evidence of short-term radioactive leakage from the underground tests, although leakage could occur from the detonation chambers in between 500 and 1000 years' time. However, the health statistics provided by the French government, on which the conclusions were based, have been criticized as inadequate. Also, the team was not allowed to inspect all areas of the atoll or to observe and monitor an actual test.[151]

Clearly, if the right to life is undermined as a result of an underground nuclear test, the state responsible for the test has violated international law.[152] Article 12(1) of the International Covenant on Economic, Social and Cultural Rights,1966,[153] is also significant. According to this provision, states parties to the Covenant 'recognize the right of everyone to the enjoyment of the highest attainable standard of physical and mental health'.[154] In contrast, France claims the 'right to pursue an action that it considers essential for its security (and) which neither violates international legal obligations nor harms the security or interests of the States of the region'.[155] As suggested earlier, however, no state has the right to pursue its security needs in a manner which endangers the health and welfare of other people.

The Non-Proliferation Treaty, 1968[156]

Although it contains no explicit reference to nuclear tests, the Treaty on the Non-Proliferation of Nuclear Weapons does impose constraints upon contracting states with regard to nuclear testing. According to Article I, each nuclear weapon state[157] party to the treaty undertakes, *inter alia,*not to assist, encourage or induce any non-nuclear weapon state to manufacture or otherwise acquire nuclear weapons or other nuclear explosive devices. Any assistance or encouragement to conduct a nuclear weapon test, given by a nuclear weapon state party to a non-nuclear weapon state, would violate this obligation.

Similarly, Article II requires non-nuclear weapon states parties to the Treaty, *inter alia,*not to manufacture or otherwise acquire nuclear weapons or other nuclear explosive devices, and not to seek or receive any assistance in the manufacture of such weapons or devices. Non-nuclear weapon states which are parties to the Treaty are implicitly prohibited from conducting nuclear weapon tests, therefore, from seeking or receiving assistance to do so. Subject to Articles I and II, however, the right of all parties to develop research, production and use of nuclear energy for peaceful purposes is guaranteed by Article IV.

Conclusion

Besides the obligations imposed by the Nuclear Test Ban Treaty and the Non-Proliferation Treaty, it has been argued that there are other rules of international law which may be violated by atmospheric nuclear tests and even by tests conducted underground. Many resolutions have been adopted by the UN General Assembly calling for the cessation of all nuclear tests.[158] Indeed, more than twenty years ago, in the Preamble to the Nuclear Test Ban Treaty, the three original parties expressed their determination to continue negotiations to achieve the discontinuance of all test explosions of nuclear weapons for all time.[159] Those negotiations were adjourned in 1980 without the achievement of that objective, although discussions continue within the Conference on Disarmament.[160] The United States has argued that serious verification problems and the West's need to retain a credible nuclear deterrent make the conclusion of a comprehensive test ban treaty impossible at the present time.[161] It has also rejected proposals for a moratorium on nuclear testing 'in the absence of reductions in nuclear arsenals and in the absence of sufficiently effective means of verification'.[162]

The claim that existing means of verification are inadequate has been challenged, however, not only by the Soviet Union.[163] Two US seismologists have concluded that 'the technical capabilities needed to police a comprehensive test ban down to explosions of very small size unquestionably exist; the issues to be resolved are political'.[164] Indeed, some fourteen years ago the Secretary-General of the United Nations declared that all the technical and scientific aspects of the problem had been so fully explored that only a political decision was necessary in order to achieve final agreement on a comprehensive test ban treaty.[165] It is to be hoped that all outstanding issues can soon be resolved, not only because of the health and environmental implications of such a treaty, but also because no other multilateral agreement could have a greater effect on limiting the further refinement of nuclear weapons.[166]

Notes

1   See Stockholm International Peace Research Institute *Yearbook*, 1986, p. 126, Appendix 6A.
2   See e.g. General Assembly Resolution 38/62 of 15 December 1983.
3   *United Nations Treaty Series*, vol. 480, p. 43.
4   The Nuclear Test Ban Treaty will be discussed further below.
5   *The New York Times*, 6 August 1963.
6   *Hansard*, House of Lords Debates, vol. 252, col. 914, 26 July 1963.
7   Nuclear Test Ban Treaty, preamble, paragraph 3.
8   Formerly the Committee on Disarmament. See UN General Assembly Official Records, 38th Session, Supp. No. 27, (Doc.A/38/27), para. 21.
9   The multilateral Treaty on the Non-Proliferation of Nuclear Weapons, 1968, implicitly restrains the testing of nuclear weapons, however. In July 1974, the US and the USSR concluded a bilateral Treaty on the Limitation of Underground Nuclear Tests. This was followed in May 1976 by another bilateral Treaty on Underground Nuclear Explosions for Peaceful Purposes. These Treaties will be discussed below.

10   See generally Whiteman's *Digest of International Law*, vol. 4, pp. 553-607. See also E. Margolis, 'The Hydrogen Bomb Experiments and International Law', *The Yale Law Journal*, vol. 64, 1954-55, p. 629 at p. 630; M.S. McDougal and N.A. Schlei, 'The Hydrogen Bomb Tests in Perspective: Lawful Measures for Security', ibid., p. 648 at pp. 650-1.

11   Margolis, op. cit., pp. 630-1; McDougal and Schlei, op. cit., pp. 650-1. For the text of the US communication to the President of the UN Security Council, see Whiteman's *Digest*, p. 556.

12   McDougal and Schlei, op. cit., p. 651.

13   Margolis, op. cit., p. 631.

14   Ibid., pp. 631-2; McDougal and Schlei, op. cit., p. 651.

15   Ibid., pp. 651-2.

16   UN Conference on the Law of the Sea, 1958, Official Records, vol. 1, p. 64. Doc.A/CONF.13/4, E. Pépin, 'The law of the air and the draft articles concerning the law of the sea adopted by the International Law Commission at its eighth session', para. 41.

17   Ibid. See e.g. the contrasting argument of Margolis, op. cit., and McDougal and Schlei, op. cit.

18   *Hansard*, H.C. Debates, vol. 550, col. 29, 12 March 1956. For the substance of the Japanese protest and the US reply, see Whiteman's *Digest*, supra., pp. 585-7.

19   Margolis, op. cit., p. 635.

20   Ibid.

21   Ibid., pp. 640-5. According to the *Trail Smelter* rule, 'no State has the right to use or permit the use of its territory in such a manner as to cause injury by fumes in or to the territory of another or the properties or persons therein, when the case is of serious consequence and the injury is established by clear and convincing evidence.' See *Trail Smelter Arbitration, U.S.* v. *Canada*, 1938 and 1941, 3 *UN Reports of International Arbitral Awards*, p. 1905 at p. 1965.

22   McDougal and Schlei, op. cit., p. 686.

23   Ibid., p. 688.

24   *Hansard*, H.C. Debates, vol. 568, Written Answers, cols. 27-9, 2 April 1957.

25   Ibid.

26   Whiteman's *Digest*, pp. 565-72.

27   *Hansard*, see note 24 above.

28   Ibid. For a more recent government statement that naval exercises and weapons tests may be conducted as part of the freedom of the high seas, see *Hansard*, H.L. Debates, vol. 388, col. 915, 1 February 1978.

29   *Hansard*, see note 24 above.

30   Pépin, para. 45.

31   Whiteman's *Digest*, p. 595.

32   Ibid., p. 587. A similar position was adopted by the British government. See p. 596, ibid.

33   Ferm, op. cit., p. 78.

34   Ibid., pp. 78-9.

35   *Keesing's Contemporary Archives*, vol. XXXII, 1986, p. 34171.

36   Ibid.

37   Ibid.

38   Ibid.

39   Ibid. The US government has agreed to pay for the rehabilitation of Bikini atoll. See F. Blackaby and N. Ferm, *SIPRI Yearbook*, 1986, p. 125.

40   *Yearbook of the International Law Commission*, 1956, vol. II, p. 278.

41   Ibid. Para. 3 of commentary to Draft Article 27.

42   Ibid. Draft Article 48 appears on pp. 285-6.

43   Ibid., p. 278. Para. 3 of commentary to draft article 27. The General Assembly resolution referred to is resolution 913 (X) of 3 December 1955.

44   By 51 votes to 1, with 14 abstentions. See UN Conference on the Law of the Sea, 1958, *Official Records*, vol. II, Report of the Second Committee, pp. 98-9, paras. 71-3.
45   Ibid., p. 101, Annex II: Draft resolution relating to nuclear tests.
46   Ibid., draft resolution relating to article 48.
47   Ibid., p. 98, paras. 57-8. The new article became Article 25 of the Geneva Convention on the High Seas, 1958.
48   Ibid., p. 22, para. 32. Doc. A/CONF.13/L.18.
49   Ibid., para. 33, p. 23, para. 34.
50   Ibid., p. 23, paras. 35-8.
51   Ibid., paras. 39-41.
52   Ibid., paras. 42-3.
53   Ibid., para. 44 and note 45 above.
54   Ibid., pp. 23-24, para. 45.
55   Ibid., p. 24, para. 46.
56   Ibid., para. 48.
57   Ibid., para. 49.
58   Ibid., para. 47.
59   Ibid., paras. 51, 55. The resolution was adopted by 58 votes to 0 with 13 abstentions. For text, see UNCLOS, *Official Records*, p. 143, Doc. A/CONF.13/L.56, I.
60   *UNTS*, vol. 450, p. 82. The four freedoms enumerated in Article 2 are the freedom of navigation, the freedom of fishing, the freedom to lay submarine cables and pipelines, and the freedom to fly over the high seas. Cf. Article 87 of the U.N. Convention on the Law of the Sea, 1982, *International Legal Materials*, vol. 21, 1982, p. 1261.
61   See the Dissenting Opinion of Judge De Castro, *Nuclear Tests Cases, ICJ Reports*, 1974, p. 253 at p. 390.
62   See Luke T. Lee, *The Legality of Nuclear Tests and Weapons*, World Rule of Law Booklet Series, No. 45 (1968), pp. 315-16, note 31.
63   *UNTS*, vol. 480, p. 43. The Treaty entered into force on 10 October 1963. As at 1 July 1986, there were 115 contracting parties, including the UK, the USA and the USSR but excluding China and France.
64   *Keesing's Contemporary Archives*, vol. XXVI, 1980, p. 30196.
65   Ibid.
66   Ibid.
67   Ibid. This report was denied by the South African and Israeli governments, however.
68   Article I(2) of the Nuclear Test Ban Treaty prohibits parties to the Treaty from causing, encouraging, or in any way participating in the carrying out of a prohibited nuclear explosion.
69   See Article IV of the Nuclear Test Ban Treaty. A state wishing to withdraw must give notice of withdrawal to all other states parties three months in advance.
70   *Hansard*, H.C. Debates, vol. 859, cols. 58-9, 2 July 1973.
71   See *French Nuclear Testing in the Pacific*, Ministry of Foreign Affairs, Wellington, New Zealand, 1973, p. 9, paras. 2-3.
72   Article IV.
73   *Federal Republic of Germany* v. *Denmark*; *Federal Republic of Germany* v. *The Netherlands, ICJ Reports*, 1969, p. 3.
74   Ibid., para. 71 of Judgment.
75   Ibid., para. 72. But cf. the Dissenting Opinions of Judge Morelli, p. 198; Judge Lachs, pp. 223-225; and Judge *Ad Hoc* Sørensen, at p. 248.
76   Judgment of the ICJ, ibid., para. 73.

77 Ibid., para. 74.

78 *Australia* v. *France; New Zealand* v. *France, ICJ Reports*, 1974, pp. 253, 457.

79 Both applicants sought declarations that the carrying out of further nuclear tests in the atmosphere would violate international law. Australia also sought an injunction to prevent France conducting any further atmospheric tests. Ibid., pp. 256, 460.

80 *French Nuclear Testing in the Pacific*, p. 12, para. 18.

81 Ibid., pp. 12-13, para. 20.

82 See *Nuclear Tests Cases, Request for the Indication of Iterim Measures of Protection, ICJ Reports*, 1973, p. 103, para. 22 and and p. 139, para. 23.

83 *ICJ Reports*, 1974, p. 269, para. 51 and p. 474, para. 53.

84 Ibid., p. 272, para. 60 and p. 477, para. 63.

85 Ibid., p. 286, para. 16.

86 Ibid., pp. 286-7, para. 17.

87 Ibid., p. 287, para. 18.

88 On 'persistent' and 'subsequent' objectors, see I. Brownlie, *Principles of Public International Law*, 3rd edition, 1979, pp. 10-11.

89 *ICJ Reports*, 1974, pp. 304, 488.

90 Ibid., pp. 305-6, 490.

91 Ibid.

92 Ibid.

93 Other contracting parties include India, Iran, Iraq and Libya. Besides China and France, states which are not parties to the Treaty include Argentina, Cuba, North Korea, North Vietnam and Pakistan. See M.J. Bowman and D.J. Harris, *Multilateral Treaties, Index and Current Status*, 1984, and *Cumulative Supplements*, Treaty No. 454.

94 *North Sea Continental Shelf Cases*, para. 73.

95 Ibid., para. 74.

96 *Nuclear Tests Cases*, p. 266, para. 39.

97 See *The Times*, 24 July 1978, p. 4, col. c.

98 *SIPRI Yearbook*, 1986, Appendix 6A.

99 Ferm, op. cit., p. 79.

100 Such a reservation would be incompatible with the Treaty's object and purpose. See Article 19(c) of the Vienna Convention on the Law of Treaties, 1969. Cf. the *North Sea Continental Shelf Cases*, note 73, para. 72.

101 See the Dissenting Opinions of Judges Morelli, Lachs and Sørensen in the *North Sea Continental Shelf Cases*, supra., note 75.

102 See above, note 69 and accompanying text.

103 See e.g. resolution 38/62 of 15 December 1983, operative paragraph 5. *UN General Assembly Official Records*, 38th Session, p. 55. The resolution was adopted by 119 votes to 2, with 26 abstentions.

104 A. D'Amato, 'Legal Aspects of the French Nuclear Tests', *American Journal of International Law*, vol. 61, 1967, p. 66 at pp. 76-7.

105 Ibid., p. 77.

106 See above notes 64-8 and accompanying text.

107 See Brownlie, op. cit.

108 Lee, op. cit., p. 315, note 31.

109 Margolis, op. cit., p. 635.

110 Lee, op. cit., p. 315, note 31.

111 See *French Nuclear Testing in the Pacific*, p. 63, paras. 44-5. Cf. M.S. McDougal and W.T. Burke, *The Public Order of the Oceans*, 1962, pp. 771-3. If access to a state's ports were hindered, the freedom of communications and of maritime commerce could also be violated. Cf the Judgement of the ICJ on the merits in the

Case Concerning Military and Paramilitary Activities in and Against Nicaragua, *ICJ Reports*, 1986, p. 14. at pp. 111, 128-9.

112   *UNTS*, vol. 15, p. 295.
113   Pépin, para. 42.
114   Ibid.
115   Ibid., para. 43.
116   Ibid.
117   *ILM*, vol. 21, 1982, p. 1261.
118   See Articles 88 and 240(a) of the UN Convention on the Law of the Sea, 1982.
119   For the view of the UK government that 'rocket and other weapons tests' would not violate Article 88 of the UN Convention, see *Hansard*, H.L. Debates, vol. 388, col. 842, 1 February 1978.
120   See Article 240(c) of the UN Convention on the Law of the Sea, 1982.
121   Ibid., Article 194(3)(a). It is submitted that the obligation to protect and preserve the marine environment is also a principle of customary international law. See e.g. Principle 7 of the Stockholm Declaration on the Human Environment, 1972, *ILM*, vol. 11, 1972, p. 1416. This requires states to take 'all possible steps to prevent pollution of the seas by substances that are liable to create hazards to human health, to harm living resources and marine life, to damage amenities or to interfere with other legitimate uses of the sea.' The Declaration was adopted by acclamation by the 113 states which participated in the UN Conference on the Human Environment. The USSR and other communist states did not attend, however.
122   See above.
123   Cf. the *Trail Smelter* rule. Principle 21 of the Stockholm Declaration also recognizes that states have the sovereign right to exploit their own resources pursuant to their own environmental policies, in accordance with the UN Charter and the principles of international law.
124   See e.g. D.J. Harris, *Cases and Materials on International Law*, 3rd edition, 1983, p. 204, note 1.
125   This was argued by the Applicants in the *Nuclear Tests Cases*. See the Dissenting Opinion of Judge *Ad Hoc* Barwick, p. 391 at pp. 431-4.
126   Ibid.
127   See Article 3 of the Universal Declaration of Human Rights, 1948, UN Doc. A/811. See also Article 6(1) of the International Covenant on Civil and Political Rights, reproduced in *AJIL*, vol. 61, 1967, p. 870. The Universal Declaration is considered by many to have the status of customary international law. See e.g. J.P. Humphrey, 'The Universal Declaration of Human Rights: Its History, Impact and Judicial Character' in *Human Rights Thirty Years After The Universal Declaration*, ed. B.G. Ramcharan, 1979, p. 21 at p. 28.
128   *Comprehensive Study on Nuclear Weapons*, UN, New York, 1981.
129   Ibid., p. 86, para. 260.
130   *Keesing's Contemporary Archives*, vol. XXXII, 1986, p. 34170.
131   Ibid.
132   R. Ferm, 'Nuclear Explosions', *SIPRI Yearbook,* 1985, p. 75.
133   Ibid. The UK government claimed that no harm had been caused to anyone involved in the Pacific test programme, however.
134   Cf. Margolis, op. cit., p. 647. See also para. 24 of the New Zealand application to the ICJ instituting proceedings against France, *French Nuclear Testing in the Pacific*, p. 14.
135   Draft Article 19(2)(d). *Yearbook of the International Law Commission*, 1979, vol. II (Part Two), p. 87 at p. 92.
136   See above.

137 Article I(1)(b) of the Nuclear Test Ban Treaty.
138 *ILM*, vol. 13, 1974, p. 906.
139 Article I(1) of the Treaty on the Limitation of Underground Nuclear Tests.
140 Ibid., Article I(2).
141 Article I of the Protocol, *ILM,* p. 908. As the Treaty has not been ratified, however, the exchange of information has not taken place.
142 Blackaby and Ferm, op. cit., pp. 116-18
143 Ibid, p. 123 Ferm, op. cit., p. 75.
144 Treaty on Underground Nuclear Explosions for Peaceful Purposes, *ILM*, vol. 15, 1976, p. 891. The Treaty has not been ratified. According to Article VIII(1), neither Party is allowed to terminate this Treaty while the Treaty on the Limitation of Underground Nuclear Tests remains in force.
145 Treaty on Underground Nuclear Explosions for Peaceful Purposes, Article III(2)(a).
146 See Articles I and II of the Protocol, *ILM*, p. 893.
147 *Comprehensive Study on Nuclear Weapons*, p. 87, para. 262.
148 See above.
149 See above.
150 *Comprehensive Study on Nuclear Weapons*, note 147 above.
151 Ferm, op. cit., pp. 76-7.
152 See note 127.
153 Reproduced in *AJIL*, vol. 61, 1967, p. 861. contracting parties include France, India, the UK and the USSR.
154 According to Article 12(2)(b), moreover, states parties to the Covenant must take the steps necessary for the improvement of all aspects of environmental hygiene.
155 From a statement made by the French representative at the Conference on Disarmament with regard to the South Pacific Nuclear Free Zone Treaty, 1985, discussed in Chapter 8, above. UN Doc. CD/PV.296, pp. 46-7, 296th Plenary Meeting, 5 March 1985.
156 *UNTS*, vol. 729, p. 169. The Treaty entered into force on 5 March 1970. As at 1 July 1986, there were 134 Contracting Parties, including the UK, the US and the USSR but excluding China, France and India. For fuller discussion of the Treaty, see Chapter 5, above.
157 For the purposes of the Non-Proliferation Treaty, a nuclear weapon state is one which has manufactured and exploded a nuclear weapon or other nuclear explosive device prior to 1 January 1967. The only states which satisfy this definition are China, France, the UK, the US and the USSR.
158 Nearly 50 such resolutions have been adopted by the General Assembly. See e.g. resolution 38/62 of 15th December 1985, adopted by 119 votes to 2, with 26 abstentions. The U.S. and the U.K. voted against the resolution. See also Resolution 3(I) adopted by the UN Conference on the Human Environment, Stockholm, 1972, UN Doc.A/CONF.48/14 and Corr. 1, Section IV.
159 Nuclear Test Ban Treaty, 1963, third preambular paragraph. As parties to the Non-Proliferation Treaty of 1968, moreover, the UK, the US, and the USSR are required to pursue negotiations in good faith on effective measures relating to cessation of the nuclear arms race at an early date and to nuclear disarmament, and on a treaty on general and complete disarmament under strict and effective international control. See Article VI of the Non-Proliferation Treaty, above. Cf. General Assembly resolution 39/52 of 12 December 1984, operative paragraph 5.
160 Sweden has submitted a draft treaty which would ban all nuclear test explosions. See UN Doc. CD/381 of 14 June 1983.

161   See UN Doc. CD/PV. 296, p. 18. See also 'The Testing of Nuclear Weapons', *Defence and Disarmament Issues 7*, Foreign and Commonwealth Office, London, Arms Control and Disarmament Unit, March 1984.

162   UN Doc. CD/PV.296, above. The USSR began a unilateral moratorium on nuclear testing on 6 August 1985. See *The Times*, 30 July 1985, p. 1, col. b. Originally intended to last five months, the moratorium was later extended and observed despite further US underground tests in the Nevada desert. See *New York Times*, 11 April 1986, I, p. 1, col. 4. See also *The Times*, 19 August 1986, p. 1, col. a. In December 1986, however, the Soviet government announced that it would abandon its moratorium after the first test carried out by the US in 1987. See *The Times*, 19 December 1986, p.1, col. f.

163   See e.g. UN Doc. CD/PV.295, p. 23. The issues relating to verification have been defined and discussed by the *Ad Hoc* Working Group on a Nuclear Test Ban. See e.g. *General Assembly Official Records*, 38th Session, Supp. No. 27, Doc. A/38/27, Report of the Committee on Disarmament, pp. 18-21.

164   See L.R. Sykes and J.F. Evernden, 'The Verification of a Comprehensive Nuclear Test Ban', *Scientific American*, October 1982, p. 29. The US and the UK have repeatedly argued that the adequacy of means of verification can only be determined by each State on the basis of its national requirements.

165   See General Assembly resolution 39/52 of 12 December 1984, preamble.

166   The view expressed by the UN Secretary-General in a message to the 1985 Session of the Conference on Disarmament. See UN Doc. CD/PV.296, p. 37. Cf. the Delhi Declaration of 28 January 1985 by the Heads of State or Government of Argentina, Greece, India, Mexico, Sweden and Tanzania, *Keesing's Contemporary Archives*, vol. XXXI, 1985, p. 33379.

Index